The COMPLETE

IDIOT'S

GUIDE TO

PCs

3rd Edition

by Joe Kraynak

Contributing Author
Jennifer Fulton

que

A Division of Macmillan Computer Publishing
A Prentice Hall Macmillan Company
201 W. 103rd Street, Indianapolis, IN 46290 USA

To Bob Dylan, for keeping me sane.

©1995 by Que® Corporation

International Standard Book Number: 1-56761-584-8

Library of Congress Catalog Card Number: 94-079736

98 97 96 95   8 7 6 5 4 3 2

Interpretation of the printing code: the rightmost double-digit number is the year of the book's first printing; the rightmost single-digit number is the number of the book's printing. For example, a printing code of 95-1 shows that this copy of the book was printed during the first printing of the book in 1995.

Screen reproductions in this book were created by means of the program Collage Plus from Inner Media, Inc., Hollis, NH.

Printed in the United States of America

Top Ten DOS Commands

DOS, pronounced "*dawss*," has its own language. Here are 10 commands that will help you survive. To enter the command, type it and then press the **Enter** key.

DOS Command	What It Does
c:	Changes to drive C, your computer's hard drive.
cd\	Changes to the root (1st) directory on the active drive.
dir /a:d	Displays a list of directories on the active drive.
cd *directory*	(In place of *directory* type the directory's name.) Changes to the specified directory on the current drive.
dir *.* /p	Displays a list of all the files in the current directory and pauses the list if it is too long for the screen.
ver	Displays the DOS version number.
help	If you have DOS version 5.0 or greater, displays help for working with DOS.
copy /?	If you have DOS version 5.0 or greater, displays help for using the COPY command, the command you use to copy files.
dosshell	If you have a version of DOS that includes the shell, this displays a screen that makes it easier to work with files.
win	If your computer has Microsoft Windows, this runs Windows—so you can avoid DOS altogether.

Top Ten Windows Shortcuts

➤ Enter **win :** to start Windows and bypass the advertising screen.

➤ To run the Windows tutorial, open the Program Manager's **Help** menu and select **Windows Tutorial**.

➤ Press **Ctrl+S** to save a file.

➤ Press **Ctrl+P** to print a document.

➤ Press **Ctrl+Esc** to view a list of applications that are running.

➤ Press **Alt+F4** to quit an application or leave Windows.

➤ Hold down the **Alt** key while pressing **Tab** repeatedly to cycle through the running applications.

➤ When running a DOS application from Windows, press **Alt+Enter** to run it in a window (instead of full-screen).

➤ To have Windows run an application on startup, drag the application's icon into the StartUp window.

➤ To save the arrangement of your screen, open the **Options** menu and make sure there is a check mark next to **Save Settings on Exit**.

The Complete Idiot's Reference Card

Ten "Get Out of Trouble Free" Cards

When you start using a computer, you should get 10 "Get Out of Trouble Free" cards. Since you don't, I'll give you a set:

➤ Press the **Esc** (Escape) key. This will usually back you out of any trouble or display a menu.

➤ Press the **F1** key to get help.

➤ Blank screen? Make sure the screen's brightness control is turned up.

➤ Look at the bottom of the screen. Many programs display important information where you would never think to look for it.

➤ If your computer freezes, wait 10 seconds. If it's still frozen, press **Ctrl+Alt+Del** to reboot it. If that doesn't work, turn it off, wait a couple of minutes, and then turn it back on.

➤ Lose a window in Windows? Open the **Window** menu. A list of open windows appears at the bottom of the menu.

➤ Never assume that the computer is broken. Most problems are caused by software (the programs).

➤ If you have a problem with a piece of equipment, turn everything off and check the connections. You may have a loose cable.

➤ If you can't get your printer to print, make sure the printer has paper, is turned on, and is online. You may have to press an online button on the printer.

➤ If you can't get your printer to stop printing, turn off its power, wait a couple of minutes, and then turn it on again.

Ten Things You Should Never Do to Your Computer

Although your computer is fairly sturdy, there are some things you should never do to it:

➤ Don't spill anything on the keyboard.

➤ Don't put your computer where the sun can beat down on it.

➤ Don't connect (or disconnect) anything while the power is on.

➤ Don't pull a disk out of the disk drive when the drive light is on.

➤ Don't turn off your computer until you have quit the program you were working in.

➤ Don't forget to save your work.

➤ Don't keep flipping the computer's power on and off. When you turn the computer off, wait at least a minute before turning it back on.

➤ Don't type the FORMAT command without specifying a drive letter A or B. For example, type **format a:** or **format b:**, not just **format**.

➤ Don't type **del *.*** unless you are sure you want to delete all the files in the current directory.

➤ Don't overestimate the intelligence of your computer.

Publisher
Roland Elgey

Vice President and Publisher
Marie Butler-Knight

Editorial Services Director
Elizabeth Keaffaber

Publishing Manager
Barry Pruett

Managing Editor
Michael Cunningham

Development Editor
Heather Stith

Production Editor
Kelly Oliver

Technical Editor
C. Herbert Feltner

Manuscript Editor
Barry Childs-Helton

Book Designer
Barbara Kordesh

Cover Designer
Karen Ruggles

Illustrator
Judd Winick

Indexer
Brad Herriman

Production Team
*Angela Calvert, Brad Chinn, Kim Cofer, Lisa Daugherty, Jennifer Eberhardt
David Garratt, Joe Millay, Erika Millen, Beth Rago, Karen Walsh, Robert Wolf*

Contents at a Glance

Contents

Introduction: What Have You Gotten Yourself into This Time?

You fell for it, too. They said the computer would make your job easier, take over some of the busy work, give you more time to play golf and bounce little Egbert on your knee. You believed them. We all did.

Now that it's time for you to start using the computer, things don't seem all that easy. The computer is about as friendly and helpful as a dead fish, and the books that came with the computer are just as bad. Sure, they have all the information you need, assuming you can find the information and translate the instructions into something that resembles English. But who has the time? You need a book that will teach you the basics: a book that tells you plain and simple just what you need to know—no more, no less.

Welcome to The Complete Idiot's Guide to PCs

The Complete Idiot's Guide to PCs works on the premise that you don't need to be an auto mechanic in order to drive a car. In this book, I won't pack your head with high-tech fluff. I'm not going to explain how a computer chip works, how a monitor displays pretty pictures, or how a printer prints. I won't give you a hundred DOS commands—ninety of which you won't use. I promise.

Instead, you'll learn practical, hands-on stuff such as:

➤ How to kick-start your computer (and restart it when all else fails).

➤ How to use DOS to run other programs (and avoid DOS when possible).

➤ How to get around in Microsoft Windows.

➤ How to find, copy, delete, and undelete files.

➤ How to print your creations, and what to do when your printer goes on strike.

➤ How to buy a computer that's not overly obsolete.

➤ How to make your computer feel like the inferior being it is.

➤ How to get out of trouble.

You'll be surprised at how little you *need* to know in order to use a computer, and at how much you can learn to use it more effectively.

How Do You Use This Book?

You don't have to read this book from cover to cover (although you may miss something funny if you skip around). If you're going computer shopping, skip to the "Savvy Computer Shopping" chapter. If you want a quick lesson in using DOS, skip to the DOS chapter. Each chapter is a self-contained unit that includes the information you need to survive one aspect of the computer world. However, to provide some structure to this book, I divided it into the following seven Parts:

➤ Part 1 deals with the basics: the parts of a computer; how to select a computer, set it up, and get it running; how to work with disks; and how to use a keyboard and mouse.

➤ Part 2 introduces operating systems. In this Part, you'll learn how to survive DOS, how to zip along in Windows and Windows 95, and how to survive OS/2.

➤ Part 3 focuses on applications (the programs you use to perform tasks such as writing letters and creating graphs). I'll introduce the various application types, explain how to install and run applications, and tell you how to enter commands and get help.

➤ Part 4 takes a hands-on approach. You'll learn how to type in most applications, format documents (improve their appearance), save and open files, and print your creations.

➤ Part 5 teaches you everything you need to know about disks, directories, and files. Here, you'll learn how to prepare disks for storing data, copy and delete files, organize files with directories, and find misplaced files.

➤ Part 6 launches you into the world of telecommunications. In this Part, you'll learn how to select and install a modem, connect to an online service, surf the Internet, and send and receive faxes.

➤ Part 7 provides the tools you need to prevent and recover from disasters. In addition, you'll learn how to clean up your hard disk drive, back up your files, and keep your computer running at peak performance.

How We Do Things in This Part of the Country

I used several conventions in this book to make the book easier to use. For example, when you need to type something, here's how it will appear:

TYPE THIS

Just type what it says. It's as simple as that.

If you want to understand more about the command you're typing, you'll find some background information in boxes. Because it's in boxes, you can quickly skip over the information if you want to avoid the gory details.

There are two special icons used in this book that help you learn just what you need:

Techno Nerd Teaches

Skip this background fodder (technical twaddle) unless you're truly interested.

By the Way...
In these boxes, you'll find a hodgepodge of information including easy-to-understand definitions, time-saving tips, hints for staying out of trouble, and amusing anecdotes from yours truly.

Acknowledgments

Unlike most new editions, this book has undergone a major overhaul. We took a wrecking ball to chapters that described specific programs, and we built new chapters that teach you how to perform practical tasks such as making floppy disks useful, installing new applications, and using a modem.

Several people had to don hard hats and get their hands dirty to build a better book. I owe special thanks to Heather Stith (development editor) for guiding the content of this book and keeping it focused on new users. Thanks to San Dee Phillips (copy editor) for tightening my language and making me define the scary terms. And thanks to Herb Feltner (technical editor) for making sure the information in this book is accurate and timely. Kelly Oliver (production editor) deserves a free trip to the Bahamas for shepherding the manuscript (and art) through production, and our production team merits a round of applause for transforming a collection of electronic files into such an attractive bound book.

Trademarks

All terms mentioned in this book that are known to be or are suspected of being trademarks or service marks are appropriately capitalized. Que Corporation cannot attest to the accuracy of this information. Use of a term in this book should not be regarded as affecting the validity of any trademark or service mark.

Part 1
Getting Started

This is war! From the time you flip the power switch on your computer to the time you beat it into submission, your computer is trying to defeat you. Its tactics are irrational and overwhelming. You enter a command, and your computer displays "Bad command or filename." You click on a button, and the manuscript you've been working on for hours disappears in a flash of light. You try to open a file you created and saved, and you find that it has apparently gone AWOL. With this constant barrage of illogical assaults, the computer hopes to wear you down, to force you into unconditional surrender.

To win the war (or at least put up a good fight), you need to learn about the enemy: what it's made up of, how it thinks, and how you can tell it what to do. In this Part, you'll get the basic training you need to survive.

Chapter 1

The Least You Need to Know

Most people like to play around with a machine until they're absolutely sure they don't know what they're doing. As a last resort, they pull out the manual and start reading. There's nothing wrong with that approach. In fact, I encourage it—the more you play, the more you learn. However, if you run into trouble when you're poking around, scan the questions in this chapter. Chances are, you'll find the answer you need.

1. How Do I Turn On a Computer?

Once all the parts of a computer are connected, turning it on is as easy as turning on your TV. Just flip the power switch on the system unit, the monitor, the printer, and any other devices that look like they might be connected to your computer. Wait till all the grinding and beeping stops, and then you should be ready to go.

2. What Will I See When the Computer Starts?

As the computer starts, it runs a series of commands, which you may see on the screen. What happens after that depends on how your computer is set up. Here are the four most common things you may see:

> ➤ **Microsoft Windows** Many newer computers are set up to run Microsoft Windows automatically. When you start your computer, you'll see a screen that looks something like the one shown on the next page. If that's what you get, skip ahead to Chapter 8, "Ditching DOS: Running Microsoft Windows," to see what to do next.

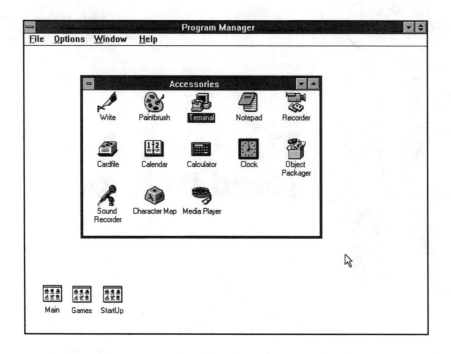

One kind of opening screen for a computer with Windows.

➤ **The DOS prompt** In the old days, all computers were set up to display the infamous DOS prompt. If you see something like this:

　　C:\>

or this:

　　A:\>

or this:

　　A>

on your screen, skip ahead to Chapter 7, "DOS (If You Must)." There, you'll learn how to deal with the DOS prompt (and how to get rid of it).

➤ **Navigator screen** Many computer manufacturers set up the computer to display a screen that's designed to make your computer easier to use. For example, Packard Bell computers display the Navigator, which provides buttons for running applications, playing games, or learning how to use your computer.

➤ **A menu** Some computers come with a menu of all the applications that are on the computer. If you see such a menu, don't panic. Just read everything on the screen (especially the stuff at the bottom). The screen will often include messages that tell you what to do next or how to get help.

3. Will I Hurt Anything If I Press This Button?

You won't break your computer by pressing buttons. The only way you can hurt the hardware (the machine itself) is to drop it, spill something on it, or connect something when the power is on. Of course, there are a few more creative ways to destroy a computer, but I'll leave those to David Letterman.

4. How Do I Stick This Disk in the Computer?

You can shove a disk into a disk drive (the slot on the front of the system unit) in any number of ways: upside down, sideways, or folded in half (ouch!), but the disk is designed to fit only one way. Grab the disk by its labeled edge, so your thumb is on the top of the label. Pull it out of its paper or plastic sleeve, and insert it into the drive as shown below. If the drive has a lever on it, flip the lever down so it crosses the slot.

Insert the disk with label facing up (or to the left if your computer is standing on end).

When you remove a disk, first make sure the drive light near the disk drive slot is NOT lit. (If the light is lit, the drive is reading from or writing to the disk.) When the light is off, press the eject button or flip the drive lever up so it no longer crosses the drive slot. Gently pull the disk out of the drive, and insert it back into its sleeve.

5. What Do You Mean, Drive A, Drive B, Drive C?

Many computers have three disk drives: A, B, and C, as shown on the following page. Whenever you want to work with a file that is on a disk in one of the drives, you have to "change to" or *access* that drive. You usually change drives by selecting the drive from a list on-screen, or by typing the drive letter followed by a colon and pressing Enter. For example, if you are at the DOS prompt and you want to switch to the disk in drive A, you type **a:** and press **Enter**.

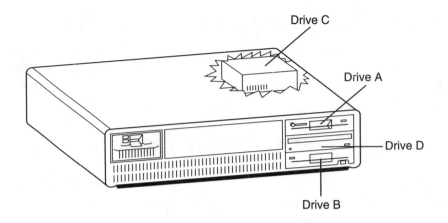

Your computer knows its disk drives as A, B, C, and D.

To complicate things a bit, some computers have only one floppy disk drive, so they have a floppy drive A and a hard drive C, but no drive B. Other computers divide the hard disk into C, D, E, and numerous other letters; and still other computers have a CD-ROM drive, which is usually drive D.

6. I Have a Mouse, But How Do I Use It?

If you have a mouse attached to your computer, you can use it to enter commands in most programs. First, however, you have to master the following four basic mouse moves:

➤ **Point** To point, you roll the mouse around on your desk until the tip of the mouse pointer is over the item you want to point to. Nothing really happens, however, until you click.

➤ **Click** Move the mouse pointer over the desired object or menu, and then press and release the mouse button without moving the mouse.

➤ **Double-click** Move the mouse pointer over the desired object or command, hold the mouse steady, and press and release the mouse button twice pretty fast.

➤ **Drag** Move the mouse pointer over the item (point to it), and hold down the mouse button while sliding the mouse over the desk or mouse pad.

For more on using a mouse, see Chapter 2, "Parts Is Parts: Computer Anatomy 101."

7. How Do I Do Windows?

If you are not sure whether your computer has Windows, display the DOS prompt (it looks something like C:\>), type **c:**, and press **Enter**. Then type **win** and press **Enter**. If Windows is there, that command ought to run it. To get around in Windows, use this picture as your guide:

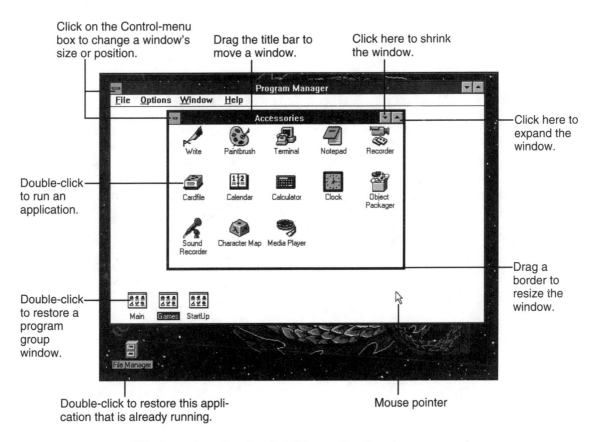

Windows allows you to select things rather than type commands.

8. I Just Bought a New Application. Now What?

Applications typically come on one or more floppy disks. In the old days, you could stick the floppy disk into the disk drive and run the application immediately from the floppy drive. Nowadays, you have to *install* the application first. (Installing consists of copying

7

the files from several floppy disks to a directory on the computer's hard disk, and then decompressing the files so your computer can use them.) For all the gory details, see Chapter 12, "Installing New Applications."

9. I Installed the Application, Now Where Is It?!

Whenever you install an application in Windows, the installation program usually creates a program group window and an icon for the application. If the icon is visible, double-click on it. If you can't see the icon, or if you're trying to run a DOS application, skip ahead to Chapter 13, "Firing Up Your Applications," to learn what to do.

10. When I'm Done, Can I Just Turn It Off?

No, not until you close down the applications you've been working with. Otherwise, you may lose the work you created, and you may scramble your computer's brains. Most applications have an Exit or Quit command that you should use to leave the application. This command does two things: 1) if you haven't saved your work, it warns you, and 2) it removes the applications, in an orderly fashion, from your computer's memory. If you just turn off the computer, you bypass this important safety net.

To exit most applications, open the **File** menu and select **Exit** or **Quit**. With Windows applications, hold down the **Alt** key and press the **F4** key. Even when you are using Windows, you should get back to the DOS prompt before turning off the power.

Chapter 2

Parts Is Parts: Computer Anatomy 101

By the End of This Chapter, You'll Be Able To:

➤ Name the parts (hardware) that make up a computer

➤ Tell your friends where a computer keeps its brain

➤ Identify a CD-ROM drive in a police lineup

➤ Tell the difference between a monitor and a TV set

➤ Explain the concept of software to a foreign exchange student

PC Stands For... personal computer and was used specifically for IBM personal computers (as opposed to Apples, Macintoshes, and Commodores). In this book, I use the term specifically for IBM and compatible computers (Compaqs, Packard Bells, and so on).

As long as you're sitting at the computer, you really don't need to know the names of all the parts. You can point and say, "That thing there started grinding, so I pressed this button, and now I can't find anything." Or, "I stuck one of these flat things in this here hole, and now I can't get it out." However, when people start talking computers at a cocktail party, you better know your part names.

What Makes a Computer a Computer?

Before I start dissecting the computer and describing what each part does, look at the figure shown below to get the big picture of what a typical PC is made up of.

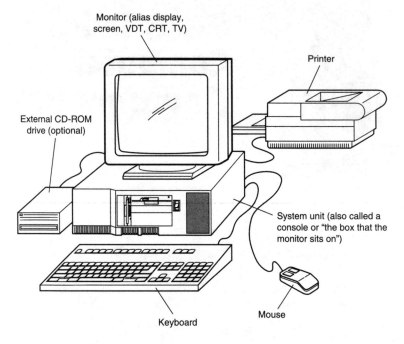

A personal computer consists of a few basic parts.

Bring in the Clones

IBM introduced its first personal computer (the IBM PC) in 1981. As PC sales started to soar, other companies began making and selling computers that looked and worked like the PC. These clever copies were (and are) called **IBM-compatibles**, **PC-compatibles**, or **clones**.

The System Unit: Brains in a Box

Although the system unit doesn't look any more impressive than a big shoe box, it contains the following elements that enable your computer to carry out the most complex operations:

Memory chips   Crunchier than taco chips, these chips act as your computer's brain cells. They store instructions and data temporarily while your computer is using them. Whenever you run a program, the program's instructions are kept in memory. Whatever you type into the computer is also stored in memory so your computer can work with it.

Central processing unit   The central processing unit (CPU, pronounced "sea-pea-you") is the brain of the computer. Whenever your computer has to perform a calculation, "the brain" does the work and spits out the right answer… well, most of the time.

Peripherals
The system unit is the central part of the computer. Any devices that are attached to the system unit are considered **peripherals**. Peripheral devices include the monitor, printer, keyboard, mouse, modem, and joystick. Some manufacturers consider the keyboard and monitor to be essential parts of the computer rather than peripherals.

Input and output ports   Located at the back of the system unit are several outlets into which you can plug your keyboard, mouse, monitor, printer, modem, and other devices.

Floppy disk drives   Appearing as slots on the front of the system unit, these devices read from and write to diskettes (those square plastic things you stick in the slots). Most computers come with one floppy disk drive for using 3.5" diskettes.

Hard disk drives   A hard disk drive is usually inside the system unit, so you can't see it or stick anything in it. The hard disk itself acts as a giant floppy disk, storing hundreds of times more information than a regular floppy disk.

CD-ROM drive   Most new computers come with a CD-ROM drive that acts a lot like a CD player. You can buy compact discs that contain programs, encyclopedias (with sound and motion pictures), and fancy games, and play them in the CD-ROM drive. You can even plug in headphones and listen to your favorite music CD as you work.

Power switch or button   Usually located on the front of the system unit, this switch or button lets you turn on your computer. Most power buttons are placed right next to a floppy disk drive's eject button, making it easy to accidentally turn off your computer when you're trying to eject a diskette. Chapter 5, "Turning On the Juice," gives more details about powering up your system.

Pecking Away at the Keyboard

A keyboard is a typewriter without the mess. You don't have to change ribbons, feed it paper, or pull the little letter arms apart when they get jammed. (That stuff is reserved for the printer.) The keyboard is simply a board that has a lot of keys and a wire that snakes over to the system unit. You peck away at the keys to enter data and commands.

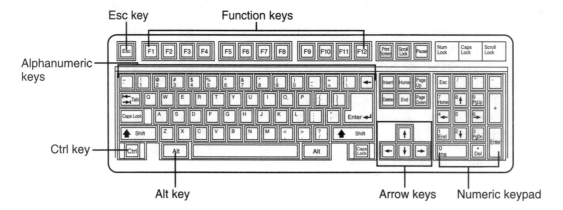

The keyboard has lots and lots of keys.

The keyboard has more keys than a high school custodian (another product of the human penchant to overcomplicate). Although the locations of keys on your keyboard may vary, all PC keyboards contain some standard keys:

Alphanumeric keys *Alphanumeric* is a fancy term for "letters and numbers." This area of the keyboard also includes a Shift key (for uppercase letters), an Enter (or Return) key, a Spacebar, a Tab key, and a Backspace key.

The F Key, the 3 Key, and the F3 Key

A sure way of being identified as a beginning user is to press the F key and the 3 key when told to press F3. You'll hear roaring laughter from the gray-skinned computer geeks; I guess we are all supposed to know from birth that F3 is a single, solitary key.

Function keys The function keys are the 10 or 12 F keys ("eff" keys) at the top or left side of the keyboard. These keys are numbered F1, F2, F3, and so on. You'll use them for entering commands. Which commands? That depends on the program.

Arrow keys Also known as cursor-movement keys, the arrow keys move the cursor (the blinking line or box) around on-screen.

Numeric keypad The numeric keypad consists of a group of number keys positioned like the keys on an adding machine. This keypad includes a Num Lock key. With Num Lock turned on, you use the keypad to type

12

numbers. With Num Lock turned off, you use the numeric keypad to move around on-screen (as indicated by the arrows and abbreviations).

Ctrl and Alt keys The Ctrl (Control) and Alt (Alternative) keys make the other keys on the keyboard act differently from the way they normally act. For example, if you press the F1 key by itself, the computer may display a help screen; but if you hold down the Ctrl key and press F1 (Ctrl+F1, in computer lingo), the computer will carry out an entirely different command.

Esc key You can use the Esc (Escape) key in most programs to back out of or quit whatever you are currently doing.

Poking Around with a Mouse

The mouse, also called a "Mexican hairless," is a critter that sits next to the keyboard. You slide the mouse over your desktop or mouse pad to move a pointer around on the monitor. The buttons on the mouse let you select commands and other objects that appear on the monitor.

A typical mouse.

The neat thing about a mouse is that you really don't have to know what you're doing in a program in order to use the program. You just poke around with the mouse until you find something useful. However, you do have to know how to poke around. Here are the four basic mouse moves you need to know:

13

Point   To point to something on-screen, you roll the mouse on your desktop or table until the tip of the mouse pointer is touching the desired area or command. (Pointing really doesn't do anything.)

Click   To select a command or move to an area on-screen, point to the command or area, hold the mouse still, and press and release the mouse button. (You'll hear the mouse button click; it sounds like an elf clipping his nails.) Unless you're told otherwise, you should use the left mouse button. Programs reserve the right mouse button for deselecting or for other special actions.

Double-click   Double-clicking (click-click) consists of pressing and releasing the left mouse button twice quickly without moving the mouse. You usually double-click to give a command.

Drag   Dragging consists of holding down the mouse button while moving the mouse. You usually drag to select letters or words, move something on-screen, or draw a line or shape. (It has nothing to do with cross-dressing.)

Mice are moody little varmints, and you have to get used to their moods. If this is your first date with a mouse, keep the following tips in mind:

➤ **Hold still when clicking.** If you move when you're clicking, you may move the mouse pointer off the item you want to select. For example, you may choose Delete instead of Copy.

➤ **Click to select; double-click to enter.** If you click on something, it is selected, but nothing will happen. If you want something to happen, click-click.

➤ **Quick with the double-click.** Two clicks is not a double-click. If you click twice slowly, you will select an item twice.

The Monitor: Your Computer's Windshield

The monitor is your computer's windshield. As you drive your computer, the monitor lets you see where you're going. It even collects about as much dirt as your car's windshield—everything from tiny bits of dust to globs of unidentifiable gunk. Whenever you run a program, the program displays a window, menu, or *prompt* that allows you to enter a command or type text.

You'll run into all sorts of monitors: CGA, EGA, VGA, SVGA. For now, just keep in mind that CGA=Bad Picture, EGA=Mediocre Picture, VGA=Very Good Picture, SVGA=Super Very Good Picture. Chapter 3, "Savvy Computer Shopping," talks more about the types of monitors you can buy.

The Printer: Getting It on Paper

The printer has all the messy parts that used to be on the typewriter: the roller, print ribbon, and the little metal arms with the letters on them (or their equivalents). The printer's job is to transform the electric burps and beeps in your computer into something that normal people can read.

Printers range from inexpensive dot-matrix types, which print each character as a series of dots, to expensive laser printers, which operate like copy machines. In between are inkjet printers, which spray ink on the page (sounds messy, but it's not). For more information about the various types of printers, see Chapter 3, "Savvy Computer Shopping."

Prompt
In this case, means "blank stare." The computer basically looks at you and says, "Tell me something." In other words, the computer is prompting you (or prodding you) to enter information or a command. A prompt can look as simple as the **C:>** DOS prompt, or it can appear as a message in a box on-screen, such as **Type your name and company name.**

Software: Sending Your Computer to School

Before your computer can do anything useful, it needs an education—some instructions that tell it what to do. In the computer world, these instructions are called *software*.

To illustrate how software works, imagine this. You stick a wafer in your mouth, and you automatically know how to perform brain surgery. Spit the wafer out and stick another one in your mouth. You forget all you knew about brain surgery and you are now a Certified Public Accountant.

In the case of a computer, the software comes on bite-sized disks that you can feed to the computer (using the floppy disk drive I talked about earlier). This software gives the computer all the knowledge it needs to do something useful such as calculate a budget. However, the computer's limited brain can't know everything. So when you quit the program, your computer forgets everything it learned. When you load another program, the computer learns how to do something else.

Your computer uses two basic types of software: operating system software and application software. I'll explain these next.

Operating System Software: Giving Your Computer the Basics

The operating system software provides the instructions your computer needs to live and breathe. It tells the system how to get and store information on disks, how to display information on-screen, and how to use the computer's memory and processing unit. In addition, it sets the rules by which all other programs have to play.

Three operating systems are commonly used on PCs: DOS, Windows, and OS/2 (a.k.a. Warp). These operating systems come with the tools you need to manage disks, directories, and files, and to run applications (the programs you use to perform specific tasks). You'll learn more than you want to know about these operating systems in Part 2 of this book.

Application Software: Applying the Knowledge to Useful Tasks

With an operating system, your computer has the basics, but it can't apply itself to any practical task such as helping you write business letters or figure out whether it would pay to refinance your home.

What your computer needs is *application software*. This software consists of a set of specialized instructions your computer uses to apply itself to a useful task. This is the software (or programs) you buy to do your work: write letters, find a phone number, or play Tetris. In Part 3 of this book, you'll learn about the various types of applications and what they're good for.

The Least You Need to Know

In this chapter, you learned about the basic parts that make up a computer and the function of each part. If you don't want to pack your memory full of details, at least remember the following:

➤ The system unit contains the memory and brain power of your computer.

➤ The floppy disk drives, which are on the front of a computer, allow you to feed instructions and information on-disk into the system unit.

➤ A keyboard connected to the system unit enables you to type information and enter commands that tell the system unit what to do.

➤ A mouse is a device that allows you to point to and select commands and objects rather than typing commands with the keyboard.

➤ The monitor connects to the system unit and provides a way for you to interact with your computer and see the effects of what you are doing.

➤ A printer transforms your work from its electronic form inside the computer to a printout on paper.

➤ Software provides your computer with the instructions it needs to operate and perform useful tasks.

Chapter 3

Savvy Computer Shopping

By the End of This Chapter, You'll Be Able To:

➤ Buy a computer that won't be obsolete in a year

➤ Pick the fastest and the most affordable chip

➤ Get a hard disk drive that's big enough... and fast enough

➤ Avoid getting stuck with a slow modem

➤ Pick out the perfect monitor

➤ List five important things to look for in a notebook computer

If you already bought your dream computer, reading this chapter may be hazardous to your mental health. You may find out that the computer you have is already obsolete (I know mine is). Maybe you should have gotten 8 megabytes of RAM instead of 4. Maybe the slimline (space-saving) case wasn't the best choice, and you really should have considered buying a graphics accelerator card. All these doubts and second-guesses can only make you bitter, so skip ahead to the next chapter and retain your blissful ignorance.

For the rest of you, you chronic procrastinators who have put off buying a computer, read on. These pages will show you that although you really can't afford the ideal computer, you can make the right trade-offs to get the best computer for your budget.

Deciphering Computer Ads

Before you start any serious shopping, get the Sunday newspaper and flip through the advertisements to get some idea of what's out there. While you're at it, go to the magazine stand (or wherever it is you get your magazines) and pick up a copy of *PC Computing*. Don't worry if you can't understand the ads yet. As you work through this chapter, you'll learn most of the technical jargon you need to know to decipher these ads.

Finding a Brainy Computer (Chip)

One of the first things you'll encounter in any ad is the name of the computer's microprocessor (the computer's brain). This may appear as 486DX2 (or something similar), Pentium (or P5), or PowerPC. The chip label, which is printed on the chip and usually on the front of the system unit, tells you three things:

Chip number   The chip number (for example, 486) tells you the chip's IQ. A 286 is a dropout; 386 is a slow learner; 486 is above average; and the Pentium (586) is a genius (even though it has gotten some bad press).

Chip speed   Chip speed is measured in megahertz (pronounced "MEG-a-hurts"). The higher the number, the faster the chip works. But be careful: a 60MHz Pentium processes data faster than a 75MHz 486 because the Pentium is more advanced. Compare speeds only between chips that have the same number.

Chip type   The chip name may be followed by an abbreviation, such as SX or DX or DX2. The SX chip is a scaled-down version of the DX; for example, the 486SX is a 486DX without a math coprocessor. The 2 after the DX (DX2) indicates that the chip has a *clock doubler* which makes the chip process at twice the speed; for example, a DX2 66MHz chip is a 33MHz chip with a clock doubler. For portable computers, SL is commonly added to the chip type, indicating that the chip is specially designed for portable computing.

If you want some free advice, here goes. Don't even think about buying a 386. You can get a 486DX2 for a real bargain because manufacturers are trying to dump them. Your best option at this point is to go with the Pentium; new computers have the updated (fixed) Pentium chip.

All Chips Are Not Created Equal

Several factors contribute to making one chip better than another: data bus structure, clock speed, and built-in cache size. The *data bus structure* determines how much information the processor can handle at one time: 16 bits (286), 32 bits (386 and 486), or 64 bits (Pentium). The *clock speed* determines how fast the chip cycles (think of it in terms of RPMs). A *built-in cache* is memory that's on the chip; this provides the processor with quick access to data, so the chip doesn't have to fetch data from RAM. 486 chips have an 8K cache, and Pentiums have a 16K cache.

The latest great chip is the PowerPC, a chip that's fast, dependable, and inexpensive (half the cost of a Pentium). Although Macintosh computers quickly incorporated the PowerPC chip, PC compatibles have lagged far behind. It may be awhile before PowerPCs make their mark in the PC market.

Thanks for the Memory (RAM)

Whenever the microprocessor is deep in thought, it's shuffling instructions and information into and out of RAM (random-access memory). When it runs out of RAM, it has to use the hard disk drive, which is much slower. So get the most RAM you can afford, and don't settle for less than 8 megabytes.

Also, make sure the computer comes with RAM *cache* (pronounced "cash"). This is a set of fast memory chips that stand between the normal (slower) RAM and the microprocessor. The RAM cache stores frequently used instructions and data, so the microprocessor can get the instructions and data more quickly. Most computers offer a 128K or 256K RAM cache.

You Don't Hear Much About the BIOS

Every computer has a built-in set of instructions called the BIOS (pronounced "BUY-ose," short for Basic Input-Output System). Think of the BIOS as the little black box inside new cars that keeps everything working in sync. The three most common BIOSs are AMI (pronounced "AM-ee"), Phoenix, and Award. Of those three, AMI has the best reputation.

In addition to the BIOS manufacturer, check the BIOS date. Some computer manufacturers cut corners by using an old version of the BIOS. The BIOS date is usually displayed when you first turn on the computer, but it's easier to just ask the salesperson.

A Hard Disk: How Big? How Fast?

Consider two things when you're looking at hard drives: size and speed. Size is measured in megabytes, and it ranges from 200 megabytes to over a gigabyte (1,000 megabytes). My recommendation is to look for a drive in the 300 to 800 megabyte range. If that sounds massive to you, consider the fact that Math Blaster Plus consumes over 10 megabytes, Windows gobbles up another 10, and Microsoft Works lays claim to over 20 megabytes.

Speed is advertised as access times, which are expressed in milliseconds (ms)—the lower the number, the faster the drive. Good access times are between 10 and 15 ms. Stay away from anything over 17 ms.

Floppy Disk Drive Size and Capacity

A computer should have at least one floppy disk drive so you can transfer programs and data files from floppy disks to your hard disk. When considering floppy drives, look at size and capacity:

Disk size   Most new computers come with a single 3.5" floppy disk drive. This should suffice unless you share files with people who use 5.25" disks or you have old programs on 5.25" disks.

Capacity   New computers come with high-capacity drives. You won't find a low-capacity drive unless you buy the computer at a garage sale. For more details about disk capacities, see Chapter 6, "Feeding Your Computer: Disks, Files, and Other Munchies."

Monitors: Get the Picture?

When you shop for a monitor, pretend you are shopping for a TV. You want a big clear picture. In addition, look for the following:

SuperVGA (SVGA)   Super VGA displays clear pictures with lots of colors. If you get a lower display standard (such as VGA), photos and movie clips will look blocky and fuzzy.

Size   Most computers come with a 14" or 15" monitor. The bigger 17" to 21" monitors are excellent for desktop publishing and graphics, but expect to pay dearly for the increased size.

Dot pitch   Dot pitch is the space between the dots that make up the display. In general, the closer the dots, the clearer the picture: .28mm is good, .39mm is fair, .52mm is bad.

Non-interlaced   Look for a non-interlaced monitor. Interlaced monitors have an imperceptible flash that can be hard on your eyes. Non-interlaced monitors don't flash.

Tilt/swivel base   You'll want to adjust your monitor for comfort, so be sure the base can be adjusted easily.

Flat screen   Most monitor tubes are curved, making them more susceptible to glare. Look for a flat screen.

(Monitor Not Included)
Many computer stores advertise low prices by not including the monitor in the price of the computer. Make sure you figure in this cost when comparing prices.

Antiglare   Some monitors are built to prevent glare. With other monitors, you have to purchase a special anti-glare screen that fits over the monitor; these can be cumbersome.

Swedish MPR II low-emissions standard   If you're worried that the low-level emissions coming out of your PC may cause health problems, make sure the monitor meets the Swedish MPR II low-emissions standards.

When you're looking at monitors, you may encounter the terms video memory and local bus video. Don't let these terms scare you. Video memory is a separate storage area that the computer uses to display pictures on the screen. Giving the monitor its own memory helps it display pictures faster. You should try to get a computer that offers at least 1 megabyte (preferably 2 megabytes) of video memory. Local bus just means that the monitor communicates directly with the computer, increasing the display speed.

CD-ROM: Information and Great Games

CD-ROM stands for Compact-Disc Read-Only Memory and is pronounced "see-dee-ROM." It is a storage technology that uses the same kind of discs you play in an audio CD player. A single disc can store over 600 megabytes of information, which is equivalent to a complete set of encyclopedias. CDs are best known for their multimedia capabilities. For example, in National Geographic's *Mammals* CD, you can read about a cheetah, view a movie clip of cheetahs running and playing, and even listen to the cheetah's eerie purr.

The most important consideration when shopping for a CD-ROM drive is speed. Although the current standard is the 2X or double-speed drive, the 4X quadruple-speed drives are quickly becoming more popular and more affordable. Personally, I wouldn't waste my money on a 2X CD-ROM drive.

Sound FX with Sound Boards and Speakers

Many computers come with a CD-ROM drive but without a sound board. I guess the manufacturer expects you to plug a set of earphones into the CD-ROM drive and pretend you're wired to a Walkman. If no sound board is included, have it added on; in most cases, you can add a sound board for $150 to $200. Also make sure the sound board is 16- or 32-bit. Older, 8-bit sound cards cannot take full advantage of the sound enhancements in newer games and CDs. Don't get hung up on terms like "16-bit"—just understand that 16-bit sounds better than 8-bit.

Modems: Fast and Feature-Rich

Most computers come with a modem that allows you to connect with other computers and services over the phone line. As a general rule, look for a 14,400 bps (14.4 bps) data/fax modem. If you want to use your computer for voice mail, make sure the modem offers voice support. If you want to know more about modems, see Chapter 23, "Buying, Installing, and Using a Modem."

The All-Important Ports

The back of every system unit has receptacles for plugging in other equipment. Most system units come with the following standard ports:

Printer port   To connect a printer.

Communications port   To connect a mouse, printer, or modem.

Monitor port   To plug your monitor into the system unit.

Keyboard port   To plug the keyboard into the system unit.

Mouse port   To connect a mouse to your computer. You can connect the mouse to the mouse port or the communications port.

Game port   This really isn't a standard port, but it's nice to have if you plan on playing many computer games. You can plug a joystick (sort of like a stick shift lever) into the port for controlling the game, rather than having to use the awkward mouse or keyboard.

Planning for Expansion

After you shell out two thousand bucks for a computer, the last thing you want to think about is spending more money to make it better. Therefore, when you purchase a computer, you should think ahead. The following sections list some of the things you should consider.

Adding Internally with Expansion Boards

Every part of a computer plugs into a big circuit board (inside the system unit) called the *motherboard*. The motherboard contains several *expansion slots* that enable you to increase the capabilities of your system by plugging in *expansion boards* (or *cards*). For example, you can plug a sound board into the slot so you can connect speakers and a microphone, or add an internal modem to your computer by plugging it into one of the slots. Make sure you get a computer that has at least four open expansion slots.

To further complicate matters, all expansion slots (and boards) are not created equal. There are four expansion standards you may encounter:

➤ **ISA** (Industry Standard Architecture) is for older expansion boards; you'll want two or three of these to handle some of the expansion boards that are currently on the market.

➤ **PCI** (Peripheral Component Interconnect) is the newest popular standard, and you'll want two or three PCI slots to handle any current and future technology.

➤ **VESA** (Video Electronics Standard Association) is similar to PCI, but less popular at this time.

➤ **MCA** (Micro Channel Architecture) is IBM's standard, which never caught on. You may want to avoid MCA expansion slots, because very few manufacturers support this standard.

Cases Big and Small
An easy way to tell whether a system is expandable is to look at the case. Space-saving cases (usually called *slimlines*) usually have few expansion slots and unoccupied drive bays. Tower cases usually have eight drive bays and six or more expansion slots. Standard cases fall in the middle, but provide sufficient expandability for most users.

Again, don't feel as though you have to understand all the standards; just keep in mind that you want some ISA slots and some PCI or VESA slots.

Drive Bays: For Floppy Drives or CD-ROM

Some computers come with only one floppy drive, but they contain additional *drive bays* so you can add drives later (for example, a CD-ROM drive, another floppy drive, or a tape backup unit). Look for a computer with at least three bays: one for a 3.5" drive, one for a 5.25" drive, and one for an optional drive.

Adding Memory to Your System

Find out how much memory you can add to the computer. Most computers come with eight megabytes of RAM and are expandable to 32 megabytes (or more). But knowing that you can add memory to your computer later is not enough; adding memory to some types of computers can be costly and difficult. Watch for the following traps:

➤ **Memory chip swapping required.** With some computers, you have to remove and discard the old chips to add chips that have a greater storage capacity. You should get a computer that lets you upgrade to at least 32 megabytes *without* swapping chips.

➤ **Proprietary memory chips only.** Some computers require that you use only brand name chips that usually cost twice as much as the generic brand.

➤ **Memory board required.** You shouldn't have to install a memory board in order to add memory. You should be able to add memory in one- or two-megabyte units by plugging chips (or *SIMMs*, single in-line memory modules) into the motherboard.

All Keyboards Are Not Created Equal

Keyboards look different because they have different arrangements and numbers of keys, but there's not much difference between them; they all perform the same tasks. The important thing is how the keys feel to you. Some keys click when you press them, some offer little resistance, and some just feel funny. Buy a keyboard that feels comfortable.

Printers: Quality, Speed, and Price

The price of a computer rarely includes the price of a printer, so you usually purchase that separately. For low-cost printing, look for a dot-matrix printer. For affordable quality, check out inkjet printers. For high quality and speed, lasers are the best choice. When comparing printer prices, consider the price of the printer and its *consumables*. Consumables are office supplies (ink ribbons, toner cartridges, paper, and so on) that you use up during printing.

Printer Type	Price Range	Consumables	Output Quality	Speed
Dot Matrix	$150–$500	1/2–2 cents per page	180–360 dpi*	1–4 ppm 80–450 cps
Inkjet or Bubblejet	$200–$600	2–10 cents per page	300–360 dpi	2–4 ppm
Laser	$400–$3000	3–7 cents per page	300–1,000 dpi	4–10 ppm

* dpi stands for dots per inch
  cps stands for characters per second
  ppm stands for pages per minute

Getting More for Your Buck with IBM-Compatibles or Clones

IBM-compatible computers (sometimes called *clones*) work exactly like IBMs, except that many compatibles are faster, cost less, and use higher quality parts than their IBM counterparts. You may have heard of some of the better known IBM-compatible computers, including Compaq, Gateway 2000, Packard Bell, and ZEOS.

Software Included?

Some dealers include the cost of the operating system in the price they quote you; others don't. (Most systems come with DOS and Microsoft Windows, which are described in Chapters 7 and 8.) If the computer does not come with an operating system, you won't be able to use it, so complain loudly and make sure the dealer installs it for you. And another thing—make sure you get the documentation you need to learn the system.

Many dealers also offer free applications with a computer. For example, computers often come with Microsoft Works installed. When you're comparing prices, consider this too.

It's Not Easy Being Green

As you shop for a computer, you may encounter dealers offering "green PCs," and you may wonder why they don't look green. The "green" label marks the PC as meeting the

U.S. Environmental Protection Agency's criteria for its Energy Star program. To meet these criteria, the computer must consume no more than 90 watts (30 for the system unit, 30 for the monitor, and 30 for the printer) when not in sleep mode (not in use). Some computer manufacturers go even further, making their computers out of recycled plastic and being careful about the waste materials produced during manufacturing.

On the Road with Notebooks

More and more users are opting for the portability of laptops (small), notebooks (smaller), and subnotebooks (smallest). Notebook computers enable you to work anywhere and keep your information with you at all times. What makes one notebook better than another? Here is a list of things to look for:

Bad Reps
The word **clone** is a derogatory term describing a compatible computer assembled by a local computer dealer. Clone computers have the same status as generic food—they cost less, but may not offer the same quality as the name-brand compatibles.
I say *may not* because some clones are actually superior to their name-brand counterparts.

Weight   Keep in mind that you'll be carrying this notebook around with you. Get the lightest notebook you can afford (3–8 pounds). In the notebook arena, the lightweights win.

Display   Notebooks generally offer four types of displays: gas plasma, liquid crystal (LCD), passive matrix, and active matrix. Gas plasma screens can crack if they freeze. Liquid crystal screens are becoming less popular. Active matrix screens produce the clearest picture, but they are more expensive. Passive matrix screens offer affordable quality.

Hard drive   Hard drives on notebook computers are usually smaller than those on desktops. A 200 megabyte hard drive is considered large.

Don't Buy Just for Freebies
Don't purchase a computer solely because it comes with a lot of freebies. Often, dealers will bundle a bunch of soft-ware with a computer to sucker the buyer into purchasing an obsolete computer

Battery   Look for a notebook with a nickel metal hydride battery or nickel-cadmium battery. Find out how long it takes to charge the battery, how many hours you can operate the notebook between charges, and how many times you can charge the battery. Also, make sure you get the AC adapter you need to recharge.

Keyboard   The last thing you'll think about when shopping for a notebook is the keyboard. However, the keyboard and display are the two things you'll use most, so give them a good test. Make sure the keys aren't too close together for your hands, and that they feel "right" when you type.

Trackball If you want to run Windows applications on your notebook, make sure it comes with a trackball or other pointing device.

Floppy drive If you have to swap files between your notebook and desktop or if you exchange files with a colleague, make sure the notebook has one floppy drive.

PCMCIA expansion slot The newest feature in portable computing is the PCMCIA expansion slot. This slot enables you to insert credit-card-sized expansion boards into the system to add devices such as a fax modem, CD-ROM drive connection, tape backup system, network card, or even a hard disk drive. You simply pop one card out and another one in, depending on what you want to do.

The Least You Need to Know

Okay, I admit it, this is way too much information to remember when you go to the local computer store. To help, here's a list of what you should look for in a computer:

➤ A Pentium processor chip

➤ Eight megabytes RAM, expandable to 32 megabytes on the motherboard

➤ MS-DOS and Microsoft Windows

➤ Minimum 300 megabyte hard drive

➤ 3.5" (1.44 megabyte) floppy drive

➤ Mouse

➤ SVGA monitor and one megabyte of video memory

➤ Printer included?

➤ 14,400 bps data/fax modem

➤ Double-speed CD-ROM drive

➤ 16-bit sound card

➤ Three drive bays, at least two unoccupied

➤ Five open expansion slots: three ISA and two PCI or VESA

Docking Stations
For the best of both notebook and desktop computing, consider purchasing a notebook computer with a *docking station*. You slide the notebook computer into the docking station to connect it to a Super VGA monitor, a set of speakers, a CD-ROM drive, a printer, or any other peripheral devices you may have. However, currently this option is almost as costly as having both a notebook and a desktop computer.

Chapter 4

Some Assembly Required

> ## By the End of This Chapter, You'll Be Able To:
>
> ➤ Find a good place for your computer
>
> ➤ Rattle off a list of 10 safety tips to protect you and your computer during setup
>
> ➤ Connect the keyboard, mouse, monitor, and printer to the system unit without destroying anything
>
> ➤ Figure out what to do with all the papers that came with your computer

Your computer may already be set up. Maybe the guy at the computer store came over and hooked everything up, or maybe you bribed a friend, neighbor, or your kid to set it up for you. Whatever the case, if your computer is set up and everything seems to be working, skip this chapter. However, if you just brought your computer home and the parts are still sitting in boxes, you may want to read this chapter to figure out what to do.

Making Your Computer Feel at Home

When I bought my first computer, I stuck it in the basement, along with the rest of our major purchases: a set of encyclopedias, a Solo Flex, and a game table that combines air hockey, table tennis, and pool. The good thing was that the computer was out of the way.

The bad thing was that nobody used it. First lesson: Make your computer as accessible as your TV set and microwave oven. This place should also offer the following benefits:

Near a phone jack. If you plan on using a modem, make sure the computer is near a phone jack.

Clean, cool, and dry. The kitchen and laundry room are too dirty. The basement may be too damp; the attic may be too hot.

Near a stable power source. Don't plug the computer into an outlet that's on the same circuit as an appliance that draws a lot of current, such as a photocopier, space heater, or a clothes dryer. Power fluctuations can damage your data as well as your computer.

Before You Start: Safety First

Read these important safety tips before you start. Note that most tips keep your computer safe. You'll be okay as long as you don't stick a finger into a wall socket or jab a screwdriver through your hand.

Surge Protectors
Instead of plugging everything into a wall outlet, get a **surge protector power strip**. It contains five or six outlets, protects your system from damaging power surges, and enables you to turn everything on at once. Go to an electronics store and ask for it by name.

Clean your work area. You don't want to set your brand new computer in a dust bowl. Clean up before you start.

No drinks in the work area. Drinks spill, and if a drink spills on a computer part, it may ruin the part. Have that soft drink or beer when you're done. It'll taste better in an hour, anyway.

Don't turn anything on until you connect everything. If you plug something in while the power is on, you may ruin the part. (I know a lady who toasted her keyboard doing this.)

Be careful with knives. If everything is still packed in boxes, try to open the boxes without cutting them. If you cut into a box, you may scratch a part or hack through a cable.

Don't force anything. If a plug doesn't slide smoothly into an outlet, you probably have the wrong pins in the wrong holes (it's okay, it happens). Take a look at the outlet and plug again and try to match the pins to the holes.

Work close to the ground, if possible. If you drop your monitor from six inches off the ground, it has a fighting chance. Drop it off a table, and it's history.

Exile pets, young kids, and nagging spouses from the work area. Kids love tools and small parts. Get the kids their own tools and send them over to the neighbors' for an hour or so. (The neighbors will call in about five minutes; don't answer.) While you're at it, send your better half to the neighbors', too; it just may save your marriage.

Unpacking the Parts

Okay, enough preliminaries. You want to see all the stuff you just shelled out two thousand bucks for, right? Dig in. Pull each part out of its box and set it on a stable surface—the floor or the desk. Take receipts, packing slips, and other important items, shove them into an envelope or bag, and stick the envelope or bag in a safe place. You can look at the paperwork later. If books came with the computer, keep them handy—you may need them if you run into trouble. When unpacking, remember three things: unpack everything, save everything (including the boxes), and don't drop anything.

Figuring Out Where You Want Everything to Go

Don't plug in anything until you know where you want all the parts to go. If you connect everything and then start moving stuff around, the cables get all twisted and tangled.

Set the system unit down first. Make sure the system unit can breathe; don't block the fan at the back of the unit or any of the holes on the sides or front. While you're looking at the system unit, remove any flat cardboard pieces from the slots (the floppy disk drives) on the front of the system unit. These cardboard pieces keep the parts in the disk drives from rattling around during shipping.

Set the monitor in front of where you'll sit, screen facing you. You'll want the top of the monitor at about eye-level when you sit down (that's why many users set the monitor on the system unit). You can raise the monitor to eye level by sticking some books under it. Just make sure the monitor doesn't wobble; you don't want it to come crashing down on your desk.

If you have a mouse, set it to the left or right of where you'll sit, depending on whether you are a lefty or righty. If your printer came with the rest of your computer, set it in a convenient location where you can get paper to it in a hurry.

31

Now, take a seat in front of your desk (or whatever you are using for a desk). Feel comfortable? Can you reach everything you'll need? Think of the computer as a dashboard in a car you are test-driving. Move things around until they feel just right.

Connecting All the Parts

Now that you know where you want everything, you are ready to start connecting the parts. To figure out where to plug things in, look for words or pictures on the back (and front) of the system unit; most receptacles are marked. If you don't see any pictures, try to match the plugs with their outlets. Look at the overall shape of the outlet and look to see if it has pins or holes. Count the pins and holes and make sure there are at least as many holes as there are pins. As a last resort, look for the documentation that came with the computer.

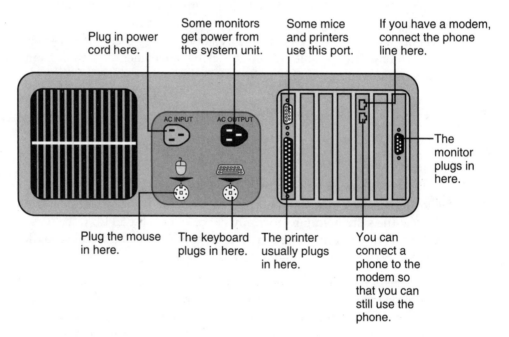

The back of the system unit usually shows where the plugs go.

Connecting the Monitor

The monitor has two cords: one that connects it to the system unit and one that connects it to a power supply. Connect the monitor to the system unit first so you won't toast the monitor if the power is on. The plug that connects the monitor to the system unit has 15 pins or fewer (mine has 11). Plug it into the 15-hole socket, and then tighten the screws (if there are screws to tighten).

What about the other cord? Look at the back of the computer for a power receptacle (it will look a lot like an outlet on the wall). If you find one of these outlets *and if it matches the monitor plug*, plug the monitor into it. If not, unplug the power strip (if you got anxious and plugged it in), and then plug the power cord into the power strip.

Port O' Plug
The receptacles at the back of the computer are called **ports** (like the ports where ships pick up and deliver cargo). In this case, the ports allow information to enter and leave the system unit.

Connecting the Keyboard

The keyboard is easy to connect, once you figure out where to connect it. Some of the newer computers come with a keyboard port on the front. Other computers hide all the ports together at the back. Search for a socket that looks like the one shown on the next page (the socket on your computer may have only five holes).

Once you find the socket, align the pins on the plug with the holes in the socket, and slide the plug in. Most cord/socket combinations have a groove or some other marking to help you align the plug with the socket. Don't look for a power cord; the keyboard has only one cable.

To Tighten or Not to Tighten?
Some folks will tell you, "Don't tighten the screws; you may need to unplug the monitor later." Like when? I once had my monitor plug come loose (not completely out, but loose), and my screen turned mauve. I spent half the day figuring out the cause. Moral of the story: Tighten the screws.

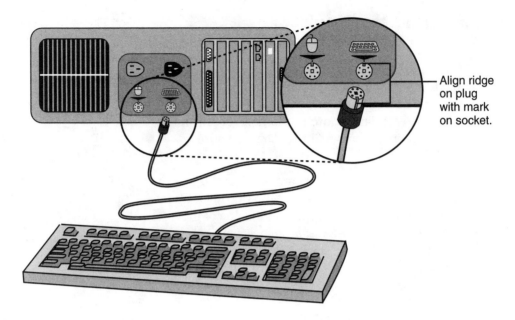

Align ridge
on plug
with mark
on socket.

The keyboard has a port of its own.

Plugging In the Mouse

The connector at the end of the mouse tail looks a lot like the connector on the keyboard cord *or* like the connector on the monitor. (In other words, depending on the mouse, the connector may look like anything.) Find a socket that matches the pins on the mouse connector; it may be labeled with a picture of a mouse or with the word "Mouse" or "COM." (*COM* stands for COMmunications port, a port commonly used for mice, printers, and modems.) Find the socket and plug the mouse in. If the mouse tail is really long, wrap it around your system unit.

Hooking Up the Printer

Most printers come with a sheet of paper that says "Read Me First," which tells you how to remove all the retainers and protective gear they use to protect the printer during shipping. Read it, because some of the packing gizmos look as though they belong there. Remove all the brackets and little plastic braces and pitch them; they won't do you any good.

Now that you have disarmed your printer, the next challenge is to find a cable that connects it to the system unit. There's a 50/50 chance that the dealer included this all-important cable. To figure out which cable you need, look at the printer port at the back of the computer. Most printers are *parallel* printers that require a 25-pin parallel printer cable. The other, slower printers (*serial* printers) use a serial cable that connects to a 25-pin or 9-pin serial port. Make sure the cable is long enough to reach your printer, but no longer than 20 feet. At 20 feet, your printer can't hear what your system unit has to say.

Plug the cable into the printer port in the back of the computer and plug the other end into the printer. Tighten any screws to secure the cable in place. Many printers have little wire clips (instead of screws) to secure the plug in the port. Snap the clips in place. After connecting the printer cable, plug the power cord into the power strip.

Parallel and Serial Printers

There are two types of printers: **parallel** and **serial**. Parallel printers allow the computer to send several pieces of data at the same time, using a clock to make sure the pieces arrive in the proper sequence. With serial printers, the computer must send data one piece at a time in the proper sequence, making serial printers slower than parallel printers. If you're given the choice of a parallel or serial printer, choose a parallel printer—unless the printer has to be more than 15 feet from your computer.

What About the Software?

Most new computers come with DOS and Windows installed on the hard disk drive, so you don't have to worry about the complexities of installing an operating system. If the manufacturer *bundled* additional software with the system, that software is usually installed on the hard disk drive, as well. If that software is not installed, or if you have other programs you want to install, skip ahead to Chapter 12, "Installing New Applications."

Preinstalled Software

Many computers do not come with the original software applications on floppy disks. The only copy is the one on the hard drive. In such cases, you should create backup copies of the files on your hard drive. See Chapter 28, "Backing Up Your Work."

Taking Care of Warranties and Registration Cards

Remember all the paperwork you shoved into the envelope or bag? Get it out and look for any cards or paper that have "Warranty" or "Registration" or "Read Me First" printed on them. Fill out any cards and mail them in. That way, if your system dies in its first year or so of life, you can get it fixed for free.

If your computer came with any software in boxes, open the boxes, look for the registration cards, fill them out, and mail them in. Why fill out all this garbage? For several reasons:

➤ You'll be able to get technical support of some sort if your software is registered.

➤ If a company decides to upgrade its equipment or programs (or recall it), the company will notify registered users and usually let them buy the upgrade at a reduced price.

➤ You'll have a secure feeling, knowing that if the pirate police raid your house or business, you'll have only bona fide, registered, paid-for versions of your software.

The Least You Need to Know

In this chapter, you learned the details of connecting the various parts that make up your computer. Here are the bare essentials:

➤ Before you start, make sure all equipment is unplugged and turned off.

➤ Pictures or words on the back of the computer usually tell you where to connect each device.

➤ The connector for the monitor has up to 15 pins. First, plug the monitor into the 15-hole outlet; then plug the monitor into a power source.

➤ The keyboard connector has 5 or 6 pins. Plug it into the keyboard port at the back or front of the computer.

➤ If you have a mouse, plug it into the mouse port or one of the COM ports (usually COM1).

➤ If you have a parallel printer, connect it to the 25-hole female port at the back of the computer. This port should be labeled Parallel, Printer, or LPT1. Then plug the printer into a power source.

➤ If you have a serial printer, connect it to the 25-pin or 9-pin male COM port; then plug the printer into a power source.

Chapter 5

Turning On the Juice

By the End of This Chapter, You'll Be Able To:

➤ Turn on the parts of your computer in the proper order (as if it really matters)

➤ Impress your friends by turning on everything at once with a power strip

➤ "Boot" your computer without kicking it

➤ Reboot your computer (when it needs an attitude adjustment)

➤ Turn off your computer (when you find something more interesting to do)

In order for your computer to become a living, thinking being, you have to turn it on. In this chapter, I will tell you which switches you need to flip and in what order (even though it really doesn't matter). I'll tell you how most computers respond to the rude awakening known as "the boot" (or "das boot" in German), and you'll learn how to turn the computer off. Don't worry—nothing you do in this chapter will hurt your computer.

Step 1: Fire Up the Power Strip

If you have everything plugged into a power strip, you have to turn on the power strip first to get electricity to the other plugs. Otherwise, when you turn on your monitor and system unit, nothing will happen.

First, make sure the power strip is plugged in; then flip the switch on the power strip. Some power strips have a small light that winks to let you know the strip is turned on.

Step 2: Monitor First

Although you can turn on a monitor at any time, waiting till later is like driving your car before you scrape the snow off the windshield. As long as the monitor is off, you won't be able to see what's going on. Do this to turn on the monitor:

1. Find the power switch. Try the back of the monitor, the side, behind a hidden panel, or the last place you'd ever look—smack dab on the front of the monitor.

2. Flip the switch or press the power button. If there is a I and an O on the switch (these labels are cowinners of the 1995 User Unfriendly award), just remember that I means "on," and O means "off." You'll hear a high-pitched tone like the one you hear when you turn on your TV.

3. Don't worry if the screen is still blank. It remains blank until you turn on the system unit.

Step 3: Turn On the Printer

If you want to use the printer, go ahead and turn it on. If you're not going to use it right now, you can leave it off. The printer doesn't need to be on for you to use the rest of the computer, and you have bigger fish to fry. When you need the printer, do this:

1. Find the power switch or button.

2. Flip the switch or press the button.

3. Look for a button labeled "Online" or "On Line." If you find it, make sure the light next to it is lit (not flashing). If it's flashing or off, you probably need to load paper into the printer. If you're not out of paper, pressing the button will probably turn the light on.

Step 4: Booting... Finally

Your computer sleeps like a log. Call its name, jostle it, pull the covers off, and it will remain in a deep coma. To wake it, you have to "boot" it. That is, you have to turn it on with the operating system instructions (DOS) in place. If you have a computer that has

DOS installed on the hard disk, booting is a simple procedure:

1. Remove any disks from the floppy disk drives (the slots on the front of the computer). You may have to flip a lever, lift a door, or press an eject button below the disk drive. Then pull the disk out.

2. Find the power switch (or button). It's there somewhere. Try the back of the system unit, the side, behind a hidden panel, or the front of the system unit.

3. Flip the switch or press the power button. You may see the hieroglyphics again. Ahhh, this is where the fun starts. Stuff appears on-screen. Lights flash; disk drives grind. You'll hear beeps, burps, gurgles, and grunts.

Insert System Disk in Drive A

If you hear some rude grinding and you see a message on-screen telling you to insert a system disk in drive A, don't worry. You (or some-one else) may have left a disk in drive A when you turned off the computer. The computer can't find the system information it needs to wake up. No biggy; remove the disk from drive A and press **Enter**.

The Computer Starts to Wake Up

Once you've turned on the system unit, listen and watch the screen. You'll see some stuff appear on-screen as the computer goes through its internal checks and carries out its startup commands.

What's Going On in There?

Every computer comes with a built-in set of instructions that tell it how to get started and where to look for DOS. One of the first things the startup instructions do is perform a Power-On Self-Test (POST for short). If the test reveals that any component is not working properly, the computer displays an error message on-screen giving a general indication of which component is causing problems. In most cases, everything checks out okay.

DOS, Are You There?

In the old days, all computers displayed the same thing at startup, the notorious `c:\>` DOS prompt. The C represents the letter of the active disk drive; C is usually the hard disk drive. The prompt indicates that you can now type commands to run applications or perform tasks. For details about how to proceed, see Chapter 7, "DOS (If You Must)." If you don't see the DOS prompt, don't panic. Several things may be going on:

➤ If your screen is still blank, make sure the monitor is on. If it's on, the brightness knob may be turned way down. Try turning the brightness up.

➤ If you see a pretty screen with lots of pictures, the dealer probably set up Microsoft Windows to run automatically on your computer. (DOS is ugly; you'll know it when you see it.) Skip ahead to Chapter 8, "Ditching DOS: Running Microsoft Windows," to figure out what to do.

➤ If you see a list of choices, the dealer probably set up something else on your computer to confuse you. Read the screen; it usually tells you what to do.

➤ If you see your kid's Christmas list, she knows a lot more about computers than she's letting on.

Packard Bell computers start with the Navigator.

Turning Everything On at the Power Strip

You've seen it before. Some nerd walks up to his computer, flips a single switch, and all the lights come on—monitor, system unit, printer, the works. How'd he do that? The answer is the power strip. The secret is that once everything is on, you turn it off and on from the power strip. This saves wear-and-tear on switches and buttons and gets everything up and running in a hurry.

Cold Boots, Warm Boots, and the Reset Button

When you turn on your computer, electricity flows through the system like blood through veins, warming your computer's innards. Then the computer reads its startup instructions and starts thinking. This is called a *cold boot*, because your computer has to warm its chips before it can start doing anything else.

Cold Boot Once a Day

Ideally, you should cold boot your computer only once each day—when you first turn it on. If you keep warming and cooling its chips all day, they'll get soggy or stale. (If you had to wake up more than once a day, you'd start to feel soggy or stale, too.)

Warm Booting: Rebooting Your Computer

During the day, your computer may lock up, refusing to do any more work. You press Esc, click the mouse everywhere, press the F1 key, and press all the other keys, and it gives you the same blank stare.

When this happens, you will be tempted to turn the computer off and then on. Resist the temptation. Try to *warm boot* the computer first. To warm boot the computer, hold down the **Ctrl** key and the **Alt** key while pressing the **Del** key. This key combination, Ctrl+Alt+Del, is commonly referred to as the "three-key salute." Warm booting is preferred to cold booting because it doesn't jolt your computer with another startup surge.

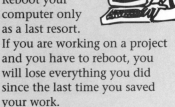

Avoid Rebooting
Reboot your computer only as a last resort. If you are working on a project and you have to reboot, you will lose everything you did since the last time you saved your work.

If you try to warm boot from Windows, you get a warning screen that explains the potential risks and your options. Read the entire screen before proceeding. In most cases, your computer is busy performing some task, or one of the applications you're running is conflicting with Windows. You can probably regain control without rebooting.

The Reset Button

Sometimes the Ctrl+Alt+Del key combination doesn't work. You press the combination, and nothing happens. What next? If your computer has a Reset button, try pressing the **Reset** button to reboot your computer. Like Ctrl+Alt+Del, the Reset button reboots your computer without turning the power off and on.

The Cold Boot Reboot: The Last Resort

If a warm boot doesn't work and your computer doesn't have a Reset button, you will have to cold boot your computer. To cold boot your computer, start by flipping the system unit power switch to the Off position.

Wait 15 to 30 seconds for the system to come to a complete rest and to allow the system to clear everything from memory. Listen to your computer carefully, and you'll be able to hear it "power down" for a few seconds. After the sound of powering down ends, flip the system unit power switch to the On position.

Turning Everything Off

Although your computer may look like nothing more than a fancy TV, you can't just turn it off when you're done watching it. Doing so could destroy data and foul up your programs. Here's the right way to turn off your computer:

1. **Save anything you've been doing on a disk.** Your work is stored on brain cells that require electricity. If you turn off the juice without saving your work on a disk, your computer forgets your work, and you probably won't remember it either. See Chapter 18, "Saving, Closing, and Opening Files," for details.

2. **Quit any programs you are currently using.** When you close a program, it makes sure you've saved all your work to disk, and then it shuts itself down properly. If you turn off the power without quitting your programs, you may lose your work and scramble your computer's brain.

3. **Put your floppy disks away.** Floppy disks can become damaged if you leave them in the disk drives. Remove the floppy disks from the disk drives and put them away. Make sure that the floppy drive light goes off before you pull out the disk that's in it.

4. **Turn off your computer.** Flip the power button on the power strip, or flip each switch or button on the individual computer parts.

5. **Pour libations to the computer gods.** Without divine intervention, no computer task is possible.

The Least You Need to Know

In this chapter, you learned everything you need to know about turning a computer on and off. You also learned a lot of things you don't need to know. So, here's what you absolutely need to know:

➤ Before you turn anything on, make sure everything is plugged in and the power strip (if you have one) is turned on.

➤ Turn on the monitor and printer first; then turn on the system unit.

➤ If DOS is installed on your computer's hard disk, the computer will automatically boot and be ready to run other programs.

➤ If you turn on your computer and it displays the message **Non-system disk or disk error**, you probably left a disk in the floppy disk drive by mistake. Remove the disk and press any key on the keyboard.

➤ If you have a computer without system software installed (or without a hard disk drive), you must boot from a floppy disk.

➤ If your computer locks up, try to warm boot it by pressing **Ctrl+Alt+Del**.

➤ Before you turn off your computer, save any work you've done and quit any programs you were using.

Chapter 6

Feeding Your Computer: Disks, Files, and Other Munchies

By the End of This Chapter, You'll Be Able To:

➤ Stick your finger in a floppy disk drive

➤ Figure out which drive is drive A and whether your computer has a drive B, C, or D

➤ Touch a floppy disk without violating its integrity

➤ Insert a disk into a disk drive (and coax one out)

➤ Find the disk on a diskless workstation

Computers eat bite-sized, cracker-shaped things called *disks*. Well, they don't actually eat the disks. They just read information off the disks and write information on the disks. Your job is to stick the disks in the computers' mouths—the disk drives—without getting bitten.

So, if it's that simple, why have an entire chapter devoted to it? Because it's not that simple. Computers complicate everything.

What's a Disk?

A disk is a circular piece of plastic that's covered with microscopic magnetic particles. A disk drive inside the computer can "read" the charges of the magnetic particles and convert them to electrical charges that are stored in the computer's memory. The drive can also write information from memory (RAM) to the disk by jolting the magnetic particles and changing their charges.

Disk Drives: Easy As A-B-C

Most computers have three disk drives, as shown below. DOS refers to the drives as A, B, and C. Newer computers also have a CD-ROM drive, usually called drive D.

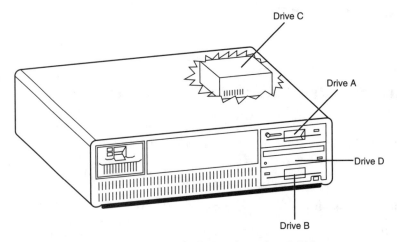

DOS refers to disk drives using letters from the alphabet.

The Floppy Disk Drives: A and B

The two drives on the front of the computer are the *floppy disk drives* (the drive's not floppy, the disk is—but even the disk isn't very floppy). The top drive is usually drive A. The bottom drive is usually drive B. If your computer has only one floppy disk drive, it is drive A, and there is no drive B.

When feeding your computer, make sure you feed it only *floppy disks*. Use the disk identification guide that is shown here:

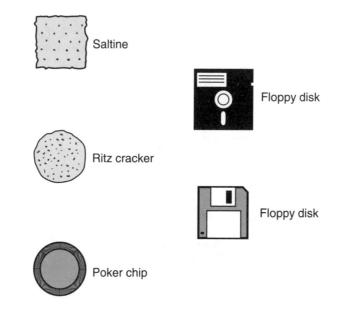

Disk identification guide.

The Hard Disk Drive: C

The drive shown inside the computer is the *internal hard disk drive*, usually called drive C. Some computers have an *external* hard drive, which sits outside of the computer and connects to the system unit by a cable (it's still drive C). With hard drives, you don't handle the disk; it's hermetically sealed inside the drive.

The CD-ROM Drive: D?

If you're lucky, your computer has a CD-ROM drive. If it's an internal CD-ROM drive, it will be near the floppy drives. If it's an external drive, it will stand alone, connected with a cable to your system unit. Either way, the CD-ROM drive is usually drive D.

Some CD-ROM drives come with a removable carriage. You place a CD into the carriage and then insert the carriage into the drive. Other drives have a built-in carriage that's sort of like a dresser drawer. You press a button to open the carriage, and then you place the CD in the carriage and push it closed (or press the Load/Eject button, which automatically closes the carriage).

Serving Information to the Computer on Floppy Disks

Think of a floppy disk as a serving tray. Whenever you want to get information into the computer, you must deliver the information on a floppy disk. Likewise, if there is something in your computer that you want to store for safekeeping or share with another user, you can copy the information from the computer to a floppy disk.

Two characteristics describe floppy disks: *size* and *capacity*. Size you can measure with a ruler. The size tells you which floppy drive the disk will fit in. You can get 3.5" disks or 5.25" disks, as shown here.

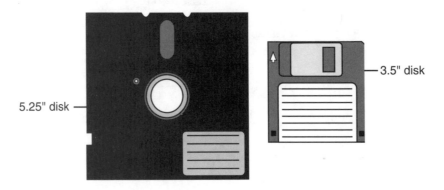

5.25" disk

3.5" disk

Floppy disks come in two sizes.

Capacity refers to the amount of information the disk can hold; it's sort of like pints, quarts, and gallons. Capacity is measured in *kilobytes (K)* and *megabytes (MB)*. Each *byte* consists of 8 *bits* and is used to store a single character—A, B, C, 1, 2, 3, and so on. (For example, 01000001 is a byte that represents an uppercase A; each 1 or 0 is a bit.) A kilobyte is 1,024 bytes—1,024 characters. A megabyte is a little over a million bytes. Grababyte means to go get lunch.

Two Disks in One
A hard disk drive can be **partitioned** (or divided) into one or more drives, which DOS refers to as drive C, drive D, drive E, and so on. (Don't be fooled; it's still one disk drive.) The actual hard disk drive is called the *physical* drive; each partition is called a *logical* drive.

A disk's capacity depends on whether it stores information on one side of the disk (single-sided) or both sides (double-sided) and on how much information it lets you cram into a given amount of space (the disk's *density*).

To understand density, think of a disk covered with magnetic dust. Each particle of dust stores one piece of data. No matter how large or small the particle, it still stores only one piece of data. With low-density disks, the

48

particles are large, so the disk can hold fewer particles (less data). With high-density disks, the particles are small, so more particles can be packed into less space and the disk can store more data.

Table 6.1 shows the four basic types of floppy disks and how much information each type can hold.

Table 6.1 Four Basic Types of Floppy Disks

Disk Size	Disk Type	Disk Capacity
5.25"	Double-sided Double-density (DS/DD)	360K
5.25"	Double-sided High-density (DS/HD)	1.2MB
3.5"	Double-sided Double-density (DS/DD)	720K
3.5"	Double-sided High-density (DS/HD)	1.44MB

Can My Drive Read This Disk?

In general, a disk drive can read disks that are equal to or less than its own capacity. A high-capacity disk drive can read low-capacity disks, but the reverse will not work; a low-capacity disk drive cannot read high-capacity disks.

Floppy Disk Handling DOs and DON'Ts

Every beginning computer book contains a list of precautions telling you what *not* to do to a disk. Don't touch it here, don't touch it there, don't get it near any magnets, blah blah blah…. Although these are good warnings, by the time you get done reading them, you're too afraid to even pick up a disk.

My recommendation is to chill out when it comes to disks. They're pretty sturdy, especially the 3.5" variety. Throw a disk across the room; it'll survive. Touch the exposed part (God forbid), and your data will probably remain intact. The best advice I can give you is to treat a disk as if it is your favorite CD or cassette tape. However, if you really want to screw up a disk, perform the following acts of destruction:

➤ Chew on it like a pen cap.

➤ Use a disk as a coaster to keep those ugly rings off your desk.

➤ Walk on the disk with spike heels.

Sticking It In, Pulling It Out

A disk will fit into a floppy drive in any number of ways: upside-down, sideways, even backwards. But a disk drive is like one of those dollar changer machines; if you don't insert the disk the right way, the drive won't be able to read it. To insert the disk properly:

1. Hold the disk by its label, with the label facing up.

2. Insert the disk into the drive, as shown in the following figure.

3. If the floppy drive has a lever or a door, close the door or flip the lever so it covers the slot.

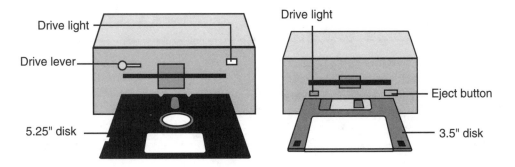

A disk drive cannot read a disk unless the disk is inserted properly.

Now that you have the disk in the drive, how do you get it out? Here's what you do:

1. Make sure the drive light is off.

2. If the drive has an eject button, press the button, and the disk will pop out like a piece of toast. If the drive has a lever or door, flip the lever or open the door, and the disk will partially pop out.

3. Gently pull the disk from the drive. Insert the disk into its pouch so the label faces out.

Making a Floppy Disk Useful

You get a brand new box of disks. Can you use them to store information? Maybe. If the disks came preformatted, you can use them right out of the box. If they are not *formatted*, you'll have to format them yourself, with the help of DOS or Windows (see Chapter 20, "Formatting and Copying Floppy Disks").

Formatting divides a disk into small storage areas and creates a *file allocation table* (FAT) on the disk. Whenever you save a file to disk, the parts of the file are saved in one or more of these storage areas. The FAT functions as a classroom seating chart, telling your computer the location of information in all of its storage areas.

Inside the Belly of Your Computer: The Hard Disk

Like I said earlier, floppy disks are bite-sized morsels—mere finger-food for a computer. Any computer worth its salt can gobble up a handful of floppy disks in a matter of seconds and still be grumbling for more. To prevent the computer from always asking for more disks, computer engineers have given modern computers stomachs. The stomachs are called *hard disk drives*, and hard disks can store lots of information.

The hard disk drive is like a big floppy disk drive complete with disk (you don't take the disk out, it stays in the drive forever). To get information to the hard disk, you copy information to it from floppy disks, or you save the files you create directly to the hard disk. The information stays on the hard disk until you choose to erase the information. When the computer needs information, it goes directly to the hard disk, reads the information into memory, and continues working. You don't have to spoon-feed it floppies.

Wait Till the Drive Light's Off

Pulling a disk out of its drive when the drive light is on is like pulling a record off the record player when the needle is on it. If the drive light is on, the drive is reading or writing to the disk. If you pull the disk out, you may scramble the information on the disk, damage the disk, and/or damage the read-write mechanism in the disk drive.

51

Don't Feed the Animals: Diskless Workstations

If your computer is part of a network, it may not have any floppy disk drives or a hard disk drive. If that's the case, forget all this babble about floppy disks and hard disks. Your network probably has a *server* with a disk drive as big as an elephant that stores all the information and programs everyone in the company needs. A person called the *network administrator* acts as the zookeeper: feeding the server, making sure all the information you need is on hand, and keeping the server happy.

The Food on the Disks: Files

Information doesn't just slosh around on a disk like slop in a bucket. Each packet of information is stored as a separate file that has its own name.

Your computer uses two types of files: *data files* and *program files*. Data files are the files you create and save—your business letters, reports, the pictures you draw, the results of any games you save. Program files are the files you get when you purchase a program. These files contain the instructions that tell your computer how to perform a task. A program may consist of a hundred or more interrelated files.

In Chapter 18, you'll learn how to save the files you create. In Chapters 21 and 22, you'll learn how to find, copy, delete, and organize files.

The Least You Need to Know

In this chapter, I've given you a lot to chew on. Make sure the following stuff sticks to your ribs:

➤ Most computers have three disk drives: A and B (the floppy drives) and C (the hard drive).

➤ There are four types of floppy disks: 5.25" double-density (360K), 5.25" high-density (1.2MB), 3.5" double-density (720K), and 3.5" high-density (1.44MB).

➤ Take good care of your floppy disks.

➤ A high-density floppy disk drive can read high-density and low-density disks, but a low-density disk drive can read only low-density disks.

➤ Do not pull a floppy disk out of a drive when the drive light is lit.

➤ Whenever you create something on the computer, you should save it in a file on disk.

Part 2
Doing DOS, Windows (Old and New), and OS/2

You can't watch a football game nowadays without seeing a commercial for an operating system. Whether it's a flock of Catholic nuns touting the miraculous OS/2, or some young executive in a shirt and tie poking around in Windows, you get the vague notion that you have to know this stuff, no matter what your calling happens to be.

In this Part, you'll learn everything you need to know to start using any of the big four operating systems: DOS, Windows 3.1, Windows 95, and OS/2 Warp. You'll type cryptic DOS commands, poke around in Windows with a mouse, take a peek into the future with Windows 95, and find out what those nuns are talking about when they mention OS/2 Warp. Plus, you'll learn how to run applications in any of those operating systems, so you can avoid the operating system altogether.

Chapter 7

DOS
(If You Must)

By the End of This Chapter, You'll Be Able To:

➤ Pronounce DOS correctly (**hint:** rhymes with "sauce")

➤ Enter five harmless DOS commands

➤ Figure out what's on a disk

➤ Ditch DOS by running an application

It's time for DOS to wander off onto an ice floe somewhere and die a peaceful death. DOS (pronounced "dawss") has simply outlived its usefulness. Its commands are cryptic, its prompt is clueless, and its error messages are downright rude. We want menus. We want tiny pictures of things. We want Microsoft Windows.

However...

As long as there are DOS applications, and as long as the best computer games demand to be run from the DOS prompt, you're going to need to know a little bit about DOS. In this chapter, you'll learn the least you need to know to survive the DOS prompt.

What Exactly Does DOS Do, Anyway?

DOS is the boss, the supervisor, of your computer. As boss, DOS performs the following job duties:

Traffic cop DOS tells your computer how to interpret input (from the keyboard and mouse), how to process data, and how to produce output (on the monitor or printer).

Application launcher You can run your other applications from the DOS prompt. DOS retreats to the background (where it belongs), silently managing any communications between the other application and your computer.

Jack-of-all-trades DOS gives you the tools to manage your disks and files: to prepare disks to store information, to copy files to a disk, to move or rename files, and to delete files.

Facing the DOS Prompt

When you boot your computer, you may see the DOS prompt (as shown in the following figure), displaying the letter of the active drive and hinting that you can enter a command. It doesn't tell you much else. To enter a command, you type the command and press the **Enter** key. But what do you type and how do you type it? You'll learn all that later in this chapter.

Here's what the nefarious DOS prompt looks like:

```
c:\>
```

If you don't get the ugly DOS prompt when you start your computer, your computer may be set up to automatically run Windows or some other application. In such a case, you may not need to rub elbows with DOS. You can probably skip the rest of this chapter. If you want to play with DOS, however, you'll have to exit the other application or Windows before you'll be able to do any of the fun stuff described in this chapter.

Harmless DOS Commands, Just for Practice

Before you get into the heavy, important DOS commands where mistakes *do* count, try a few light commands that can't hurt anything. (Oh yeah, if any of the DOS commands in this section don't work, try typing **cd\dos** and pressing **Enter**. Then enter the command again.)

What's Today's Date?

Unless you picked up your computer at a garage sale or an auction (circa 1984), it has an internal, battery-powered clock that keeps track of the date and time. To tell DOS to display the date on-screen, do this:

1. Type **date** and press **Enter**. DOS displays something like the following:

   Current date is Tue 06-01-95
   Enter new date:

2. If the date is correct, press **Enter**. If the date is incorrect, type the correct date in the form *mm-dd-yy* (for example, 07-04-95) and press **Enter**.

What Version of DOS Do You Have?

Every time Microsoft Corporation or some other maker of DOS releases an updated version of DOS, the version number increases, and the program can do more new things or can do old things better (at least theoretically). Hence, DOS 6.2 is better than DOS 4.01. To find out which version of DOS you have, do this:

1. Type **ver** and press **Enter** (VER stands for "version"). DOS displays the version number on-screen.

2. Write down the version number and keep it next to your computer. (You may need to know it later.)

Sweeping Up the Screen

Now that you have the date, time, and DOS version number displayed on-screen, your screen probably looks like an alphabetical junkyard. To clear the screen, type **cls** and press **Enter**. (CLS stands for CLear Screen.)

Internal and External Commands
A DOS command is an order that you tell DOS to carry out. There are two types of DOS commands: *internal* and *external*. Internal commands, such as DIR, are stored in memory for quick access. External commands, such as FORMAT, are small programs that are stored on disk. When you enter an external command, DOS runs the program required to perform the task.

Capitalization Doesn't Matter
Don't worry about capitalization: date, DATE, and dAte are all the same to DOS. However, if you leave out a space, add too many spaces, or use punctuation marks that I don't tell you to use, DOS won't recognize the command. For example, if you typed **date.** and pressed **Enter**, DOS would display the message **Invalid date**.

Giving DOS a Makeover

The DOS prompt normally shows only the letter of the active disk drive (for example, A:\>, B:\>, or C:\>). You can change the look of the DOS prompt by using the PROMPT command. Try typing one of these funky prompt commands:

➤ Type **prompt nq** and press **Enter**. $n tells DOS to display the current drive, and $q tells it to display the equal sign (=). The prompt should now look like **C=**.

➤ Type **prompt $v nb** and press **Enter**. $v tells DOS to display the DOS version number, and $b tells it to display a vertical line called the pipe symbol (|). The prompt should now look something like **MS-DOS Version 5.0 C|** (though why you would want a prompt like this is beyond me).

When you are done fooling around, type **prompt pg** and press **Enter**. $p tells DOS to display the directory name, and $g tells DOS to display the right angle bracket (>). The remaining commands in this chapter assume that you will be able to see the drive and directory names at the DOS prompt.

Dissecting a DOS Command

A typical DOS command, as shown here

copy c:\data\johnson.ltr b: /v

consists of the following elements:

Command   This is the name of the DOS command (in this case, COPY). It tells DOS which action you want DOS to carry out.

Delimiters   Spaces and special characters (such as /, \, and :) that break down the command line for DOS. Think of delimiters as the spaces between words in a sentence.

Parameters   Specify the objects on which you want DOS to perform the action. In the preceding example, c:\data\johnson.ltr is the parameter.

Switches   Allow you to control how the command performs its action. In this case, the /V switch tells DOS to verify the copy operation to make sure the copy matches the original.

What Kind of Computer Do You Have?

If you have DOS version 6.0 or later, you have a program called Microsoft Diagnostics that can display more information about your computer than you probably want to know. To run the diagnostic program, do this:

1. Type **msd** and press **Enter**. The Microsoft Diagnostics screen appears, as shown in the following figure.

2. To exit the diagnostic program, press **F3**, or press **Alt+F** and then X.

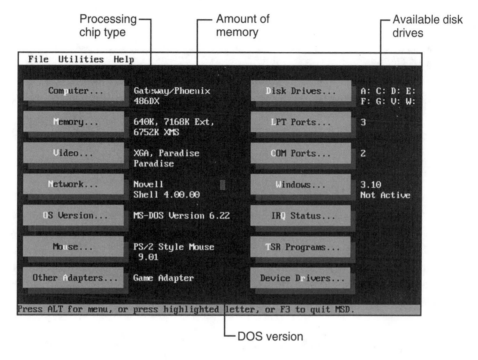

If you have DOS 6.0 or later, you can view information about your computer.

Gimme Help

DOS versions 5.0 and later include a help system (clever idea, eh?) that you can access by typing **help** and pressing **Enter**. A list of all the available DOS commands appears, as shown on the following page. Press the **Page Down** key to see more of the list. Press the **Tab** key to move from one command to another. Press **Enter** to view help for the currently selected command.

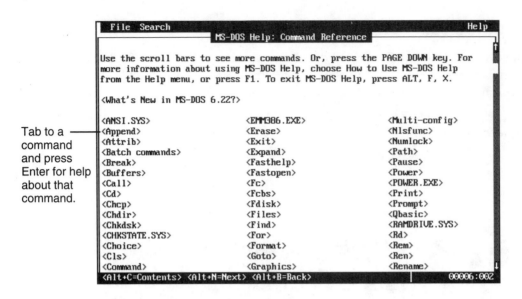

DOS versions 5.0 and later provide online help for every DOS command.

Where Have All the Files Gone?

If you're going to make it in DOS, you have to master its filing system. This system can be summed up in three words: disks, directories, and files. Each disk is capable of storing gobs of files, too many to keep track of in any single location. So, DOS uses *directories* to group the files. To figure out where DOS is hiding all your files, you have to know how to change from one drive to another, switch to a directory, and display file lists. You'll learn all this in the following sections.

Changing to a Disk Drive: The Old Shell Game

To change to a disk drive, type the letter of the drive followed by a colon (:) and press **Enter**. For example, if you have a disk in drive A, type **a:** and press **Enter**. The DOS prompt then changes to A:\>. To change back to drive C, type **c:** and press **Enter**.

Changing to a Directory: Another Shell Game

When DOS activates a disk drive, DOS automatically looks for files in the first directory on the disk: the *root directory*. If the files are in a different directory, you must change to that directory by entering the CHDIR or CD (Change Directory) command. In the next few sections, you will change back and forth between directories to get a feel for it.

Going to the House of DOS: The DOS Directory

Depending on how your computer is set up, you may have to change to the DOS directory to enter a DOS command. Here's how you do it:

1. Type **c:** and press **Enter** to change to drive C. C:\> appears on-screen.

2. Type **cd \dos** and press **Enter** (CD stands for Change Directory). C:\DOS> appears on screen. You are now in the house of DOS.

Going Back to the Root Cellar

To change back to the root directory, type **cd ** and press **Enter**. The DOS prompt changes back to C:\>.

Changing to a Subdirectory

Let's say you want to work with the files in a subdirectory (a directory that's under another directory). For example, suppose you want to work with the files in C:\DATA\BOOKS (assuming you have this directory on your hard disk). You can change to the subdirectory in either of two ways. The first way is to enter two CD commands:

1. Type **c:** and press **Enter** to change to drive C.

2. Type **cd \data** to change to C:\DATA. (The backslash tells DOS to start at the root directory.)

3. Type **cd books** to change to C:\DATA\BOOKS. (Note that the backslash is omitted here, because you don't want to start back at the root directory.)

The other way to change to a subdirectory is to use a single CD command followed by a complete list of directories that lead to the subdirectory:

1. Type **c:** and press **Enter** to change to drive C.

2. Type **cd \data\books** and press **Enter**.

Unformatted Disk Need Not Apply
Before you change to a disk drive, make sure the drive contains a formatted disk (your hard disk, CDs, and the application disks you purchase are already formatted). If you change to a drive that does not contain a formatted disk, the following error message will appear:

Not ready reading drive A Abort, Retry, Fail?

Insert a formatted disk in the drive, close the drive door, and press R for Retry.

Don't Mess with the Root Directory
The **root directory** contains a lot of important files, so don't play around too much in this directory. Move the wrong file, and you may not be able to start your computer.

In addition to moving down the directory tree, you can move up the tree. Type **cd ..** and press **Enter** to move up one directory in the tree.

So What's in This Directory?

Once you have changed to the drive and directory that contains the files you want to work with, you can view a list of the files on that drive and directory. To view a list of files, type **dir** and press **Enter**. A file list appears.

Whoa! Slowing Down the File List

If the file list contains too many files to fit on one screen, the list scrolls off the top of the screen, making you feel as though you are falling very fast. To prevent the list from scrolling off the screen, you have three options:

➤ Type **dir /w** and press **Enter**. The /W (wide) switch tells DOS to display only the names of the files and to display the file names in several columns across the screen.

➤ Type **dir /p** and press **Enter**. (The /P stands for Pause.) DOS displays only one screen of file names at a time. You can press any key to see the next screen of names.

➤ Type **dir /a:d** and press **Enter**. (The /A:D stands for Attribute:Directories.) DOS displays the names of the directories under the current directory. No file names are displayed.

Narrowing the File List

Deaing with Wild Cards
A wild-card character is any character that takes the place of another character or a group of characters. In DOS, you can use two wild-card characters: a question mark (?) and an asterisk (*). The question mark stands in for any single character. The asterisk stands in for any group of characters.

You may not want to view all the files in a directory. You may, for example, want to view only those files that end in .EXE, .BAT, or .COM (these are files that run programs). To view a group of files, you can use *wild-card characters*.

Here are some ways you can use wild-card entries with the DIR command:

Type **dir *.com** and press **Enter** to view a list of all files with the .COM file name extension (for example, HELP.COM, EDIT.COM, and TREE.COM).

Type **dir ???.*** and press **Enter** to view a list of all files that have a file name of three letters or fewer (for example, EGA.CPI, SYS.COM, and FC.EXE).

Type **dir s???.*** and press **Enter** to view a list of all files whose file name starts with S and has four letters or fewer (for example, SORT.EXE and SYS.COM).

Ditching DOS: Running Another Application

The easiest way to deal with DOS is to avoid it; run one of your applications and have DOS retreat backstage where it belongs. To run a DOS application, you change to the directory where the application's files are stored and then enter the command for running the program. For example, you may enter **wp** to run WordPerfect. For more details about running applications, see Chapter 13, "Firing Up Your Applications."

The Least You Need to Know

Until Bill Gates descends from the mountain and announces that "DOS is dead," you'll need to know the basics of working at the DOS prompt:

- ➤ The DOS prompt shows the letter of the current drive and the name of the directory.

- ➤ To change to a drive A, insert a formatted disk into drive A; type **a:** and press **Enter**.

- ➤ To change to a directory, type **cd *dirname*** (where *dirname* is the name of the directory) and press **Enter**.

- ➤ To view a list of files in a directory, type **dir** and press **Enter**. Type **dir /w** if the list flies past on the screen.

- ➤ To run an application from the DOS prompt, change to the drive and directory that contains the application's files, type the command to run the application, and then press **Enter**.

Chapter 8

Ditching DOS: Running Microsoft Windows

By the End of This Chapter, You'll Be Able To:

➤ Make DOS disappear by running Microsoft Windows

➤ Use the mouse to snoop around in Windows

➤ Get help in Microsoft Windows

➤ Run Windows' animated tutorial

➤ Use the applications that come with Windows, including a couple of neat games

Windows has given DOS a new meaning: Disabled Operating System. With Windows running, you won't even know DOS is there. In place of the DOS prompt, you get menus, pictures, and, best of all, a pointer that lets you poke at all the other stuff. In other words, you get something called a *graphical user interface* (GUI), which is designed to make your computer easier to use.

GUI
Some people joke that GUI (pronounced "GOO-ey") actually stands for "graphical unfriendly interface." As with most jokes, this one has some truth; before Windows can make your computer easier to use, you have to know how to get around in Windows.

Three Good Reasons to Do Windows

At this point, you may be saying, "Joe, why would I want to run *another* program on top of DOS before running the program I will actually use?" Fair enough. I'll give you three good reasons:

Multitasking
The capability to run two applications at the same time is called **multitasking**. Some programs such as the DOS Shell allow you to switch between two or more applications but do not allow an application to perform operations in the background. This is called **task-switching**, not multitasking.

➤ **You learn new applications faster.** Most Windows applications use a standard menu system. Once you learn how to use the menus in one application, learning to use the menus in any Windows application is a snap. For example, to leave most Windows applications, you open the **File** menu and select **Exit**.

➤ **You can run two applications at the same time.** You can print your monthly budget while typing your résumé. You can also copy information from one application to another.

➤ **Everybody is doing Windows.** I know, I know, just because everybody else is doing it is no good reason for you to do it. But most companies that are making new applications make those applications to run under Windows, so if you want to use the latest, greatest applications, you need Windows.

Bye-Bye DOS! Starting Windows

Before you can take advantage of Windows' bells and whistles, you have to do something mundane like start it from the DOS prompt. Here's what you do:

1. Change to the drive that contains your Windows files. For example, type **c:** at the DOS prompt and press **Enter**.

2. Change to the directory that contains your Windows files. For example, if the name of the directory is WINDOWS, type **cd \windows** at the prompt, and then press **Enter**.

3. Type **win** and press **Enter**. DOS starts Windows. The Windows title screen appears for a few moments, and then you see the Windows Program Manager, as shown in the following figure.

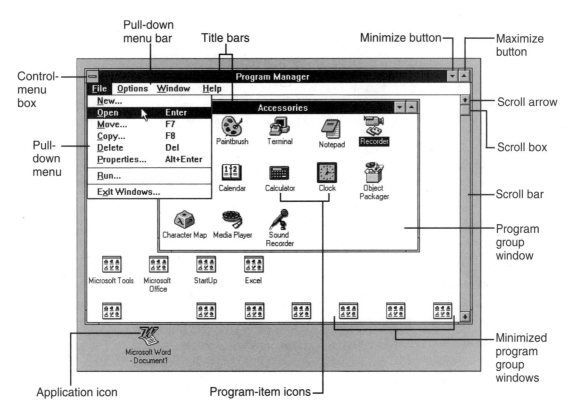

The Windows Program Manager allows you to run other applications from Windows.

Windows Anatomy 101

So, now that you know the names of all those doohickeys on the screen, you're probably wondering what each one does. Here's a quick rundown (don't be afraid to poke around on your own):

The **mouse pointer**, which looks like an arrow, should appear somewhere on the screen (assuming you are using a mouse). If you don't see it right away, roll the mouse around on your desk to bring the pointer into view.

The **title bar** shows the name of the window or application (as if I needed to tell you that).

A **program group window** contains a group of related program-item icons. What are program-item icons? Read on.

Program-item icons are small pictures that represent applications that are not running. Double-click on one of the icons now. A window should open. Double-click on the box in the upper left corner of the window to zap it.

The **Minimize button** shrinks a window down to a mere icon. To restore the window to its original condition, click on the program's icon and then click on **Restore**. Go ahead, click on any Minimize button now.

The **Maximize button** makes a window take up the whole screen. If you see a Maximize button on-screen now, click on it. The button then changes to a double-headed **Restore** button, which allows you to return the window to its previous size.

The **Control-menu box** displays a menu that allows you to close the window or change its size and location. Click on any Control-menu box now to see a list of commands. Click on the button again to close the menu.

The **pull-down menu bar** contains a list of the available pull-down menus. Each menu contains a list of related commands. Click on **Window** to open the Window menu. Click on it again to close the menu. You'll come across pull-down menu bars in all Windows applications.

Scroll bars appear on a window if the window contains more information than it can display. Use the scroll bars to view the contents of the window that are not currently shown.

An **application icon** is a small picture that represents an application that is currently running but that has been minimized. The application is still running, but it is running in the background. You can restore the application to window status by double-clicking on its application icon.

Take Windows Lessons from Windows 3.1

Most computer books keep it a secret that Windows 3.1 comes with its own animated tutorial. Why would you need a book if you can learn from the program itself? My point exactly. Here's how you run the tutorial:

1. Click on **Help** on the Program Manager button bar. The Help menu opens. (If the Windows Tutorial option is not there, either you don't have Windows 3.1 or whoever installed Windows did not install the Help files.)

2. Click on **Windows Tutorial**. The tutorial starts.

3. Read and follow the on-screen instructions.

Climbing Out of Windows

The first thing you should know about any program, including Windows, is how to get out of the program. To get out of Windows, do any one of the following:

➤ Click on the **Control-menu box** in the upper left corner of the Program Manager window, and then click on **Close**. Press **Enter**.

➤ Double-click on the **Control-menu box**. Press **Enter**.

➤ Press **Alt+F4** and then press **Enter**.

Save Your Work

If you try to exit Windows without saving your work, Windows will display a message asking if you want to save your work before leaving. Click on **Yes**, and then type a name for the file; type eight characters or fewer, and don't use any spaces or funky characters such as * or :. Stick with letters and numbers for now.

The Windows Bonus Pack

In addition to making your computer easier to use, Windows comes with several useful applications, as shown here. To run an application, double-click on its icon.

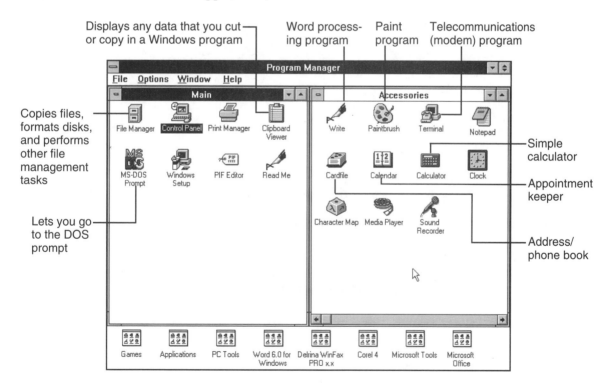

Displays any data that you cut or copy in a Windows program

Word processing program

Paint program

Telecommunications (modem) program

Copies files, formats disks, and performs other file management tasks

Lets you go to the DOS prompt

Simple calculator

Appointment keeper

Address/ phone book

Windows comes with games and several basic applications.

69

You are not limited to the applications that come with Windows. Many software companies (more than you can count on your fingers and toes) create applications that run under Windows and have the same look and feel as all Windows applications.

Launching Applications from Windows

Whenever you install a Windows application (see Chapter 12), you get one or more new program-item icons (usually inside a new program group window). To run the application, you double-click on its icon. If you can't see the program-item icon, it's probably in a shrunken group window. Double-click on the group icon to display the window, and then double-click on the program-item icon.

Mouse Practice
The Solitaire game that comes with Windows is good practice for learning how to use the mouse. That's what I tell my boss, anyway.

If the thought of running several applications at the same time flips your pickle, then minimize the application's window and double-click on another program-item icon. For you channel surfers, here's a quick list of how you switch from one running application to another:

➤ If part of the application's window is visible, click on any exposed part. The selected window moves to the front.

➤ Press **Ctrl+Esc**, and then double-click on the desired application in the Task List.

➤ Click on the **Control-menu box** in the upper left corner of any application window, select **Switch To**, and then double-click on the desired application.

➤ Hold down the **Alt** key and press the **Tab** key one or more times until the name of the desired application appears. Then release the **Alt** key.

Barking Orders at Windows

Until the geeks work out the bugs in voice activated computing, we have to settle for selecting menu commands and clicking on little on-screen pictures. The following sections will help you survive this transitional period.

Take Your Pick: Using a Pull-Down Menu

Pull-down menus work like Control-menu boxes. You click on the menu's name to pull it down from the menu bar, and then you click on the command you want to enter. What happens next depends on the appearance of the command:

➤ **Dimmed commands** are not accessible. For example, if you try to select the Copy command but have nothing selected, the Copy command appears dim.

➤ **A command followed by an arrow** opens a submenu that contains additional commands.

➤ **A command followed by an ellipsis (...)** opens a dialog box that requests additional information. Skip ahead to the next section to figure out what to do.

➤ **A command preceded by a check mark** is an option that you can turn on or off. The check mark indicates that the option is on. Selecting the option removes the check mark and turns it off.

Shortcut Keys
Notice that some commands are followed by a keyboard shortcut. For example, the Print command may be followed by Ctrl+P. You can use these keyboard shortcuts to bypass the menus. Simply hold down the first key while pressing the second key. In this example, hold down **Ctrl** while pressing **P**.

Conversing with Windows Through Dialog Boxes

If you pick a command that's followed by an ellipsis (...), Windows shoves a dialog box at you, asking for more information. You have to fill out the form and then give your okay before Windows will proceed.

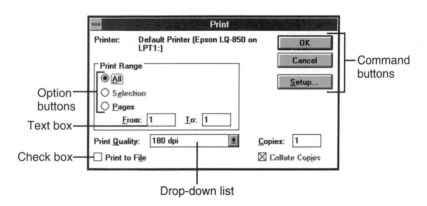

A dialog box is Windows' way of asking for more information.

Each dialog box contains one or more of the following elements:

Tabs (not shown in the picture) allow you to flip through the "pages" of options. Click on a tab to view a set of related options.

List boxes provide available choices. To select an item in the list, click on it.

Drop-down lists are similar to list boxes, but only one item in the list is shown. To see the rest of the items, click on the down arrow to the right of the list box.

Text boxes allow you to type an entry. To activate a text box, click inside it. To edit text that's already in the box, use the arrow keys to move the insertion point, and then use the **Del** or **Backspace** keys to delete existing characters. Then type your entry.

Check boxes allow you to select one or more items in a group of options. For example, if you are styling text, you may select Bold and Italic to have the text appear in both bold and italic type. To select an item, click on it.

Option buttons are like check boxes, but you can select only one option button in a group. Clicking on one button deselects any option that is already selected.

Command buttons allow you to enter or cancel your selections. Once you have responded to the dialog box by entering your choices, you click on a command button to finalize the entry. Most dialog boxes have at least three command buttons: one to give your final okay, another to cancel your selections, and one to get help.

Seeing More with Scroll Bars

Think of a window as... well, a window. When you look through a window, you don't see everything that's on the other side of the window. You see only a portion of it.

A Windows window is the same. If a window cannot display everything it contains, a scroll bar appears along the right side and/or bottom of the window. You can use the scroll bar to bring the hidden contents of the window into view, as follows:

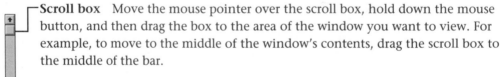

Scroll box Move the mouse pointer over the scroll box, hold down the mouse button, and then drag the box to the area of the window you want to view. For example, to move to the middle of the window's contents, drag the scroll box to the middle of the bar.

Scroll bar Click once inside the scroll bar, on either side of the scroll box, to move the view one screen at a time. For example, if you click once below the scroll box, you will see the next window of information.

Scroll arrow Click once on an arrow to scroll incrementally in the direction of the arrow. Hold down the mouse button to scroll continuously in that direction.

Dealing with Windows

Working in Windows is like being the dealer in a card game. Whenever you start an application or maximize an icon, a new window appears on-screen, overlapping the other windows. Open enough windows, and pretty soon your screen looks like you've just dealt a hand of 52-card pickup. The following sections tell you how to clean up the mess.

Moving a Window to the Top of the Deck

If you can see any part of a window, the easiest way to move the window to the top of the stack is to click on the exposed portion of the window. The window automatically jumps up front and covers anything else on-screen.

Fanning Your Cards

When you're holding a handful of cards and you want to see what you have, you fan the cards. In Windows, you can view a portion of each window on-screen by using a similar technique. You can tell Windows to display the windows side-by-side (*tiled*) or overlapping (*cascaded*). Here's how: Click on **Window** in the pull-down menu bar and then click on **Cascade** or **Tile**. Although cascaded windows overlap, you can still see the title bar of each window, so you can quickly switch to a window by clicking on its title bar.

Disappearing Windows

If you cannot see the desired window, click on **Window** in the pull-down menu bar, and then select the name of the window you want to go to. The selected window is then moved to the front and is activated. If that doesn't work, press **Ctrl+Esc** and then choose the window from the Task List.

A Fancy Card Trick: Resizing and Moving Windows

As you are rearranging windows on-screen, you may want to shrink windows that are less important or that contain fewer icons, or you may want to enlarge more important windows. You may also want to rearrange the windows. The picture on the next page shows you what to do.

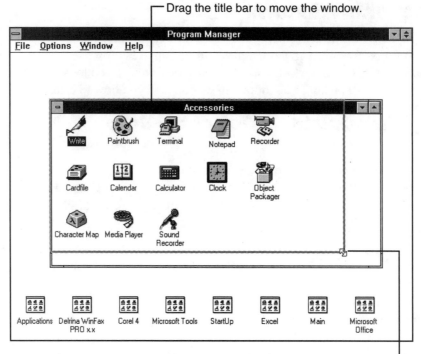

Drag the title bar to move the window.

Drag a border to change the window size and shape.

You can drag a window's border or its title bar.

What About My Keyboard?

Your keyboard isn't obsolete just yet. Although Windows works best with a mouse, you can still use your keyboard to manipulate windows. The keyboard shortcuts listed in Table 8.1 explain how.

Table 8.1 Windows Keyboard Shortcuts

Press	To
Alt+Esc	Cycle through the application windows and icons.
Ctrl+F6 (or Ctrl+Tab)	Cycle through program group icons and windows.
Alt+Spacebar	Open the Control menu for an application window or icon.

Press	To
Alt+– (hyphen)	Open the Control menu for a program group window or icon.
Arrow keys	Move from one icon to another in the active program group window.
Alt (or F10)	Activate the pull-down menu bar.
Alt+selection letter	Open a pull-down menu from the menu bar or select an option in a dialog box.
Enter	Run the application whose icon is highlighted, or restore a window that's been reduced to an icon.
Esc	Close a menu or dialog box.
Ctrl+Esc	View the task list, which allows you to switch to a different application.
F1	Get help.
Ctrl+F4	Minimize the selected program group window.
Alt+F4	Exit the active application or exit Windows.

Managing Disks, Directories, and Files... Without DOS

Disk and file management in DOS is like flying an F-1 fighter plane blindfolded. With the Windows File Manager, you get to see where you're going. File Manager displays the drive letters, directories, and file names in various windows, allowing you to select files simply by clicking on their names. For details, see Chapters 20–22.

The Least You Need to Know

Microsoft Windows comes with a book that's over 600 pages long, so there's a lot more that you can know about Windows. However, the following details will help you survive your first day on the job:

➤ To start Windows, change to the Windows directory (usually C:\WINDOWS), type **win**, and press **Enter**.

➤ To quit Windows, double-click on the Program Manager's Control-menu box.

➤ To run an application in Windows, change to the program group window that contains the application's icon and then double-click on the application's icon.

➤ To open a pull-down menu, click on the name of the menu in the menu bar.

➤ To select a command from a menu, click on the command.

➤ The buttons in the upper right corner of a window allow you to maximize or minimize a window, or restore the window to its previous size.

➤ You can bring a window to the top of the stack by clicking on any portion of the window.

➤ You can resize a window by dragging one of the window's borders.

Chapter 9

Behind the Curtains with Windows 95

By the End of This Chapter, You'll Be Able To:

➤ Start Windows without even saying "hello" to DOS

➤ Tell the difference between a Windows 3.1 screen and a Windows 95 screen

➤ Pretend you're using a Macintosh computer

➤ Pitch files and icons into an on-screen wastebasket

➤ Pick a running application from the Taskbar

Just when you started getting the hang of this Windows thing, the fine folks at Microsoft decided that you needed something new to foul up your life, something that would make your PC act more like a Mac. Welcome, Windows 95... and good-bye DOS prompt! In this chapter, you get a peek at Windows 95 (whether or not it has been released by the time you get this book). You'll learn what's in it for you, and you'll learn how to navigate this brave new operating system.

Why Switch to Windows 95?

I hate new stuff. When I buy a new shirt, I hang it in the closet for a couple of months to age. I treated Windows 3.1 the same way. I stuck it on my computer, and then I ran my

DOS programs for a good six months before firing up Windows. Windows 3.1 just didn't offer enough at the time to entice me into using it. Windows 95 is different. It offers several enhancements that make it difficult to resist:

Simplified desktop: You get a Start button that opens a menu containing a list of all the applications and utilities on your computer. In addition, if you run two or more applications, their names appear in a Taskbar at the bottom of the screen. To switch from one application to another, just select it from the Taskbar.

On-screen wastebasket: Drag files, icons, and any other objects you want to get rid of into the Wastebasket icon. If you pitch something by mistake, reach into the basket and pull it out.

Faster applications: Windows 95 is a 32-bit operating system, meaning it can take advantage of the capabilities of newer processing chips (386, 486, and Pentium). New applications are going to be designed for 32-bit systems, making them run faster under Windows 95. (Don't worry—you'll still be able to run your old Windows favorites.)

Enhanced file management: Windows 95 borrows heavily from the Macintosh way of managing files. Folder icons appear for each group of files. You double-click on a folder to view its contents. Windows 95 also lets you use long file names, so you're no longer restricted to the DOS eight-character limit.

Plug-and-play upgrades: If you've ever had the pleasure of trying to install an internal modem or a game card in a computer, you know how frustrating it can be to make everything work together. With plug-and-play, you plug the card into a slot inside the computer, and then Windows takes care of the rest.

Internet access: In the past, you had to install a separate TCP/IP (Transmission Control Protocol/Internet Protocol) program before you could even dial into the Internet. TCP/IP controls the data flow between your computer and the remote computer. Windows 95 has built-in TCP/IP, so you don't have to fiddle with it.

Multimedia support: Windows 3.1 has one big weakness: it can't play many of the niftiest games. Windows 95 supports a new WinG games subsystem and also comes with a video clip player.

Built-in networking: If your computer is on a network, you probably have a network administrator who takes care of all the hard stuff, so this doesn't really affect you.

Mobile computing: If you work at the beach all day, heading for shelter only after you've had enough sun, Windows 95 offers features that can help you connect to a docking station and create virtual briefcases.

We Now Have Control of Your TV

There's no starting Windows 95; there's no stopping it, either. Once it's installed, it comes up whenever you turn on your computer. You won't even see a DOS prompt. What you will see is the simplified Windows interface, shown in the following figure.

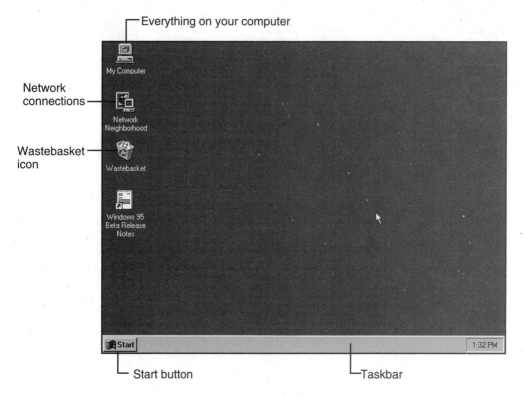

Windows 95 reduces the clutter.

Taking Off with the Start Button

Granted, the Windows 95 screen looks about as barren as the Bonneville Salt Flats. It does, however, contain the one item you need to start working: a Start button. You click on the big **Start** button, and a menu with seven options appears. Move the mouse pointer over **Programs** (you don't have to click on it), and another menu appears listing all the applications you can run. You move the mouse pointer over option after option, and then you click on the icon to run the desired application. You can even kick yourself back out to the DOS prompt for a brief reunion.

Program groups ─┐   Applications you can run

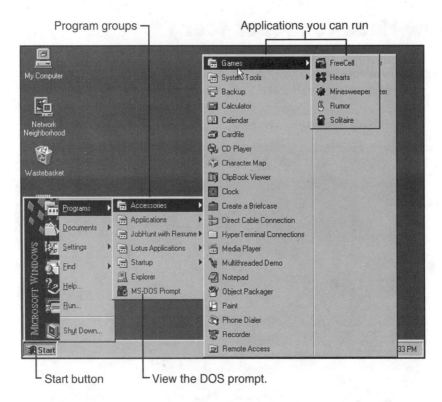

└ Start button   └ View the DOS prompt.

The Start button is your ignition key to Windows 95.

Help Is on the Way

If you get stuck in Windows 95, you don't have to flip through a book looking for help. Instead, open the **Start** menu and click on **Help**. The Help window appears, offering a table of contents and an index. Click on the **Contents** tab if you're searching for general information about how to perform a task or use Windows.

For specific help, click on the **Index** tab. This tab provides an alphabetical listing of help topics that would make the most ambitious librarian cringe. The easiest way to find a topic in this list is to click inside the first text box, and then start typing the name of the topic. As you type, the list scrolls to show the name of the topic that matches your entry.

My Computer (...Er, Your Computer)

Windows 95 gives you two ways to poke around on your computer. You can double-click on the **My Computer** icon, or you can use the Explorer. If you double-click on the My Computer icon, Windows displays icons for all the disk drives on your computer, plus three folder icons: Fonts, Control Panel, and Printers. To find out what's on a disk or in a folder, double-click on it.

The Explorer is File Manager's replacement. To run the Explorer, open the **Start** menu, select **Programs**, and select **Explorer**. You get a two-pane window, with a directory tree on the left and a file list on the right. You can use the Explorer to copy, move, and delete files and directories. For details on how to use the Explorer (or File Manager), see Chapters 20–22.

What's with the New Window Borders?

Although the new window borders sport an improved look and some strange looking icons, you can size and shape them in the same way as you did the old windows (see Chapter 8). You can drag the window's title bar to move it, or you can drag a border to alter the size and shape.

However, the icons in the title bar may throw an experienced Windows 3.1 user. The Control-menu button varies depending on which window you've opened, but it does basically the same thing, allowing you to close, move, or resize a window. However, in Windows 95, you can right-click on this button for additional options, including creating a shortcut and finding an icon. The right side of the title bar contains three buttons: the Minimize button (left), Maximize (center), and Close (the one with the X on it).

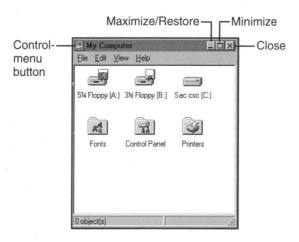

Windows' windows sport a new look.

Right-Clicking for Quick Commands

Where to Right-Click?
At first, you won't know where to right-click; the screen is pretty clueless. Try right-clicking on anything that looks as if it may have a unique identity: a window, icon, the Taskbar, or anything else floating around on the screen.

Frantically searching for a use for the right mouse button, programmers have recently developed *context-sensitive menus*. Here's how it works. You move the mouse pointer over an object (say a window's title bar, an icon, or a file), and then you click the right mouse button. Up pops a small menu that lists all the options available for that object.

For example, say you right-click on the My Computer icon. The menu you get offers options for opening the window, exploring its contents (with the Explorer), finding an item, creating a shortcut (sort of a copy of the icon), or changing the icon's properties. In short, you don't really have to know what you're doing; just right-click and pick an option.

Making Shortcuts to Your Favorite Applications

Personally, I'm not all that impressed with the Start button and its five-layer-salad menu. If I have to dig five menus deep to run an application, I probably won't run it. The Microsoft programmers must have realized this, because Windows 95 lets you clone program icons and place them right on the desktop, where you can get at them in a hurry. Windows 95 refers to these clones as *shortcuts*. To create a shortcut, take the following steps:

1. Find the icon you want to clone. You can use the My Computer icon or the Explorer to search for icons. (You can't clone an icon from the Start menu.)

Shortcut Clutter
If your desktop gets cluttered with shortcuts, you can delete the shortcut icons by dragging them over the Wastebasket icon.

2. Right-click on the icon, and then select **Create Shortcut**. In most cases, Windows 95 creates a duplicate shortcut icon in the same window as the original icon. In some cases (if you're cloning a drive icon, for example) a dialog box appears, asking if you want to create the shortcut on the desktop.

3. If a dialog box appears, click on **OK** to proceed.

4. If the shortcut icon is in the same window as the original icon, drag the shortcut icon onto the desktop.

Juggling Applications with the Taskbar

Multitasking in old Windows was like taking a Zen lesson in resignation. You click on the wrong spot, and the window you were working in disappears under an avalanche of other windows. If you're lucky, a corner of the window peeks out, allowing you to click on it and get it back.

Windows 95 displays the Taskbar at the bottom of the screen, giving you a button for each task that's running. If you happen to lose a window at the bottom of a stack, just click on its name in the Taskbar to get it back.

Slam-Dunking with the Wastebasket

The real reason to move up to Windows 95 is that it has an on-screen wastebasket into which you can slam anything you don't use—files, icons, or the latest cost-control memo from your boss. You just find the icon for the item you want to delete and drag it over to the Wastebasket.

Did you pitch something by mistake? Double-click on the **Wastebasket** icon to see what's in there. Then, drag the item back out onto the desktop or into another window. When the Wastebasket gets too full for your liking, simply open the **File** menu and select **Empty Wastebasket**.

Plug-and-Play with Windows 95

I had my first plug-and-play encounter with Windows 95 when I installed the program. Before installation, my external CD-ROM drive and my mouse were working fine. After installation, I had no mouse pointer. I plugged all right, and then I played the rest of the day—and part of the next day—trying to get all my equipment to live in harmony once again.

To be honest, I wasn't actually using plug-and-play technology. For this technology to work, your computer (and any expansion cards you install) must be designed for plug-and-play. The equipment I was using was designed more for bet-you-can't-make-this-work.

When computer manufacturers get this plug-and-play thing in gear, with Windows 95 you'll be able to add peripheral devices (modems, CD-ROM drives, and so on) by plugging in the expansion card (an integrated circuit board such as an internal modem or a sound card) and turning on your computer. Windows 95 will then identify the card for you, work out any conflicts with other cards, and configure the card for optimum performance. Even without plug-and-play expansion cards, however, Windows 95 helps you track down any conflicts and resolve them.

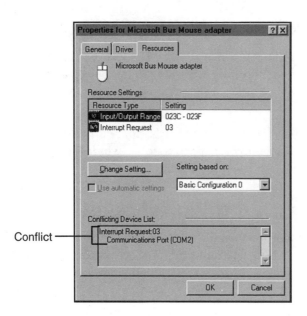

Windows 95 spots expansion card conflicts.

Conflict? Interrupt Setting? What?!

Each card that plugs into the motherboard inside the system unit has a factory-set memory address and interrupt setting. If two cards in your computer have the same settings, one of the cards won't work. With cards that don't support plug-and-play, you must flip tiny switches on the cards or move tiny jumper sleeves to change the settings. In either case, the process can cause hair loss and hives. With plug-and-play, you don't have to mess with any switches.

Had Enough? Shut It Down!

As with any operating system or application, you can't just flip the power switch on your computer when you're done. If you try that, the computer gets revenge by deleting your work and possibly refusing to start the next time. To shut down Windows 95, first exit any applications you were running, select the applications from the Taskbar, and then use their **Exit** commands to quit. After exiting all your applications, open the **Start** menu and select **Shut Down**.

A dialog box appears asking if you want to shut down the computer or reboot it. Click on the desired option, and then click on the **Yes** button. Wait until Windows tells you that it is now safe to shut down your computer. Okay, now flip the power switch (or press the button).

The Least You Need to Know

All hype aside, you will want Windows 95—whenever Microsoft gets around to releasing it. When you get your copy, keep the following in mind:

➤ Windows 95 starts automatically when you turn on your computer.

➤ To run an application, click on the **Start** button and then follow the menu system to your application.

➤ To get help, click on the **Start** button and then click on **Help**.

➤ Double-click on the **My Computer** icon to see what's on your hard disk, floppy disk(s), and CD-ROM disc(s).

➤ Right-click on an object to use a pop-up menu.

➤ The Taskbar displays buttons for all the applications you're running.

➤ To clone an icon and use it as a shortcut, right-click on the icon and select **Create Shortcut**.

➤ To exit Windows 95, click on the **Start** button and select **Shut Down**.

Chapter 10

Flying Fast with OS/2 Warp

By the End of This Chapter, You'll Be Able To:

➤ Amaze your friends with tales of the new OS/2 Warp and what makes it different from Windows

➤ Start and stop OS/2 Warp

➤ Cruise at Warp speed

➤ Coax OS/2 objects into doing what you need

➤ Play with all the neat freebies you get with Warp

By now, you've probably seen that commercial with the Catholic nuns touting OS/2 Warp and how it can do *absolutely everything*, including shampooing your dog and making perfect julienne fries. Okay, maybe that's a stretch, but when you get past all the hoopla, what exactly is OS/2 Warp?

OS/2 Warp is an operating system (like DOS), which includes a *graphical interface* (like Windows). In other words, it's like Windows 95. In OS/2 Warp, as in Windows 95, you bully your computer by poking at stuff on the screen, instead of by typing commands à la DOS, and you don't have to have DOS in order to run Warp. But don't think you have to give up Windows; OS/2 Warp can run both Windows (3.1 that is) and DOS programs with ease. Whether Warp will be able to run Windows 95 applications remains to be seen.

Why Bother with Warp, When People Will Just Make Fun?

Sure, OS/2 users take a lot of guff, especially from Windows users who think they have the best and the brightest. So why would you want to choose OS/2 Warp and suffer all that abuse? Here are some reasons:

You're tired of waiting for Windows 95 (or 96). If you have Windows but feel the need for speed that only a 32-bit operating system can give you, then Warp's the one. (Although there aren't a whole lot of 32-bit OS/2 Warp applications to choose from.)

You like getting stuff for free. OS/2 Warp comes with lots of freebies. Its BonusPak boasts IBM Works (a word processor, spreadsheet, database, chart maker, and report writer), a day planner (with an address/telephone book, appointment book, to-do list, project planner, and contact list), and software support for all those toys your wife gave you for your birthday: sound card, fax modem, and video capture board, to name a few.

You want Internet access now. OS/2 Warp is your link to the Internet. You won't have to scramble around to get software and then get the local geek to configure everything for you. And if you find the Internet too daunting, OS/2 can help you connect to various online services that provide easier Internet access.

You don't mind being laughed at. Okay, maybe you do mind a little, but when you leave at 4:00 p.m. with your work all done, you can laugh at those Windows-losers who are stuck dealing with their fourth GPF of the day.

GPF
Short for **general protection fault**, a **GPF** is what Windows throws at you when your favorite application locks up your computer. When a GPF happens, you have to restart the PC to get out of it. Warp doesn't let programs run so wild that they can crash the entire system like Windows often does.

Giving Warp the Boot (Starting Your PC)

To boot (uh, start) OS/2 Warp, you turn the computer on. Simple enough. If you don't see the OS/2 welcome screen, don't panic; this could be normal, depending on how you installed OS/2. If you picked the Easy option, OS/2 starts when you turn on the PC. If you get the DOS prompt instead, you didn't pick the Easy option. To start OS/2 from the DOS prompt, type **C:\OS2\BOOT /OS2** and press **Enter**.

If you installed something called the OS/2 Boot Manager instead, you'll need to select your operating system du jour (such as DOS or OS/2) from the menu every time your start your PC.

All Aboard the Warp Train

Starting OS/2 Warp is a horribly slow process, but at some point, your hard disk stops grinding and your screen settles into something that looks like this:

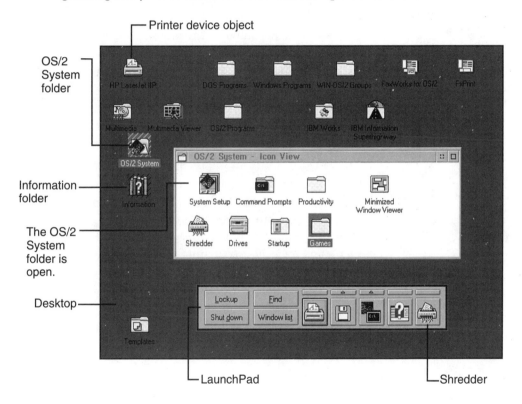

So this is what OS/2 looks like.

My Screen Looks Different
If you didn't install everything on the BonusPak and if you don't have Windows, your screen will be missing a few items when compared to the one shown on the previous page. So just ignore anything that doesn't apply.

In OS/2 Warp, your screen is basically a *desktop*. Like a real desktop, your OS/2 screen is cluttered with all sorts of junk: a telephone, notepad, clock, and calendar. OS/2 clutters its desktop with *objects* (which are the same thing as Windows icons). To do something in OS/2, you manipulate these objects.

To see how this desktop thing works, let's look at an example from history. Remember Oliver North, master paper shredder? Well OS/2 has its own electronic version of the shredder. You move the mouse pointer over the icon for the memo you want to shred, hold down the right mouse button, and drag the icon over the Shredder icon. Release the mouse button, and the memo is history (or not part of history, depending on how you look at it). If you want to print a document, you simply drag its icon over the Printer icon and release the mouse button.

More on Those Object-Thingies

Help Is on the Way
When OS/2 Warp takes you to the edge of panic, press **F1** (the 911 of computer keys). You won't get William Shatner, but you will get immediate assistance on whatever it was you were doing when you pressed F1. For a quick tutorial, click on the question mark button on the LaunchPad.

OS/2 has four types of objects: *data-file objects* (for the things you create, like letters), *program objects* (for applications such as word processors and spreadsheets), *device objects* (for your computer parts: printer, disk drives, and such), and *folder objects* (manila folders for other objects). You can usually tell what kind of object you have by how it looks. I say *usually* because folder objects often masquerade as other objects. For example, the Information folder looks like a pile of books with a question mark on top, not like the vanilla-manila you may expect.

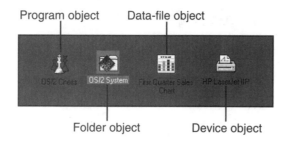

Program object   Data-file object

Folder object   Device object

These four objects make up a complete and balanced OS/2 diet.

Taking Off from the LaunchPad

At the bottom of the screen, you'll find the LaunchPad, a hangout for your favorite objects. It contains objects for your printer, floppy disk drive, the DOS prompt, help, and the Shredder. In addition, it has buttons for locking your system (with a password), shutting down your computer, looking for objects and files, and displaying a list of windows (for applications that are currently running). You can add objects to the LaunchPad simply by dragging those icons onto it.

Folder
A **folder** is nothing more than a graphic representation of a directory. It can contain other folders, program files, data files, and anything else you can store in a directory.

Taking Control with the System Folder

When you start OS/2 Warp, it opens a folder for you called OS/2 System, which contains additional objects. Think of this as the OS/2 convenience store. From here, you can configure OS/2 and your computer, display command prompts, look at your disk drives, and even play games. You can copy additional objects into this folder simply by dragging them; right-click on the object, and then drag it to the System folder object.

Where's Windows?
By the way, your Windows programs (if you have any) are tucked inside a folder called WIN-OS/2 Groups. Inside, you'll find a folder for each of the different program groups you had inside Windows. Just open one of these folders to locate your program.

Ordering Your Objects Around

If you have any Windows experience at all, you've probably mastered the mouse. You click on an object to select it, double-click to run it, and drag to move it. If you're making the transition to OS/2, you'll find that most of the mouse moves are the same. However, there are enough differences to warrant the following OS/2 mouse primer:

Click: Same as Windows; you move the mouse pointer over an object, and then press and release the left mouse button without moving the mouse. If you use the right mouse button, you get a pop-up menu, as in Windows 95.

Double-click: Same here, too. Move the mouse pointer over an object and then press and release the left mouse button twice real fast.

Drag: Big difference here. Move the mouse pointer over an object, and then hold down the *right* mouse button while moving the mouse. Former Windows users, did you get that? Here in Warpland, you drag with the RIGHT, not left, mouse button.

A Word About Object Menus

Just a special note here before we get too far into this section: when you want to change something about an object, you can probably find it on the pop-up menu that shoots out of the object's head when you right-click on it.

Opening (and Closing) Objects

To use most objects, you *open* them. To open an object, you simply double-click on it. Double-click on a folder icon, and you get a window showing the folder's contents. Double-click on a program icon, and OS/2 runs it. Double-click on the Printer icon, and OS/2 shows you what your printer is doing (in case you didn't know).

Found It!
To quickly open a document in the program you used to create it, double-click on the document's icon. OS/2 runs the required program and then loads the document into it.

When you open an object, OS/2 puts little hash marks behind it to remind you that (although you may not see the open object because of all the clutter on your desktop) it's still open—*in use*—somewhere. In the case of a folder object, the folder itself also changes to look like it's open (check out the OS/2 System folder icon in the first figure of this chapter).

To *close* an object, double-click on its *title-bar icon*. (That's the tiny snapshot of the object that's hanging around the upper left corner of the window.)

Grabbing Hold of an Object

To copy, move, or delete an object, you have to *select* it first. This is a no-brainer; just click on the object. OS/2 makes the object gray to mark it as the chosen one. To deselect an object, click on a different object or click in any blank space on the desktop.

Doing the Drag-and-Drop Shuffle

Drag-and-drop technology was developed in the caveman days as a way of capturing and transporting a potential mate. This technology has recently been applied to computers, allowing users to move objects, icons, text, and anything else that's not nailed to the screen. You've already seen drag-and-drop work with the Shredder. You simply click on the object you want to drag, and then hold down the right mouse button while moving the mouse. When the object is where you want it (in another window, over the Shredder object, over the Printer object), release the mouse button.

Selecting Multiple Objects

You can select multiple objects and perform the same task with all of them at once, such as deleting mass quantities of files. To select multiple objects that are grouped together, just drag the mouse pointer over them, or hold down the **Ctrl** key while clicking on each object.

Copying Objects

There are two ways to copy an object: a simple, straightforward *copy*, or a *shadow*. A copy is a duplicate of the original object, plain and simple. If the original object is changed somehow, the copy is not changed, because each object represents a distinctly different file on the hard disk. Unlike a copy, a shadow maintains a link to its parent. Think of a shadow as a second door to the same room. It provides convenient access to often-used programs.

To copy an object, hold down the **Ctrl** key while dragging the object where you want it. When you release the mouse button, OS/2 asks if you want to give the copy a different name. (If you drag the copy to a different folder, you can use the same name.) Type a new name, and then click on **Copy**.

To make a shadow of an object, hold down **Ctrl+Shift** while dragging the object. As you drag, a line stretches out between the original and its shadow. When you release the mouse button, the shadow object appears; the shadow sports a blue title to distinguish it from the original. OS/2 doesn't ask if you want to rename the shadow because it's linked to the original object—if you change its name, the original is changed, and vice versa.

Moving Objects

If something obscures your view of the OS/2 landscape, move it out of the way. To move an object, drag it with the *right* mouse button. To move more than one object at a time, select 'em first, as described earlier in this chapter.

Don't Delete the Original
If you delete a shadow, the original object remains intact. Delete the original, and all shadows disappear.

Use this technique to move objects from folder to folder. This is the DOS equivalent to moving files from one directory to another. However, if you're moving data-files to a *different drive* instead of a different directory, you have to hold down the **Shift** key while dragging. Otherwise, OS/2 thinks you're trying to copy the files instead. Don't ask; just do.

Do-It-Yourself Objects and Folders

If you don't have enough objects and folders strewn around your desktop, you can add more. OS/2 Warp comes with several *templates,* which are forms you can fill out to create objects (including folders). You'll learn more by doing, so go ahead and make a folder:

1. Double-click on the **Templates** folder to open it.

2. Drag a folder template off the Folder icon and onto the desktop (remember to hold down the right mouse button while dragging).

3. Release the mouse button. OS/2 creates an empty folder for you, uniquely named *Folder*, which you can rename.

4. Hold down the **Alt** key while clicking on the new folder. (Now you're going to rename it.)

5. Press the **Delete** key to erase the original name.

6. Type the new (descriptive) name, and then click anywhere on the desktop. You're done.

To create a data-file object to put in the folder, just turn to another template; for example, IBM Works comes with templates for making letters, memos, charts, worksheets, and other neat stuff. Just drag one of them from the Templates folder into your new folder, and then double-click on it to start up IBM Works. After creating your new document, exit IBM Works. You now have a data-file object in your new folder.

Playing with Windows, Menus, and Dialog Boxes

Like most graphical user interfaces, OS/2 uses windows to keep programs from spilling off your screen. If you run several programs and open a bunch of objects, you end up with a big stack of windows. You need some way to control all these windows and pick one out of the stack. You use the same basic techniques that you would use in Windows.

Move a window: Drag the window's title bar.

Change a window's size: Move the mouse pointer over one of the window's borders, and hold down the left mouse button while dragging the border.

Make it big: Click on the **Maximize** button in the upper right corner of the window.

Shrink it: Click on the **Minimize** button (just to the left of the Maximize button).

Find a window: Click on the **Window list** in the LaunchPad; then double-click on the name of the desired window.

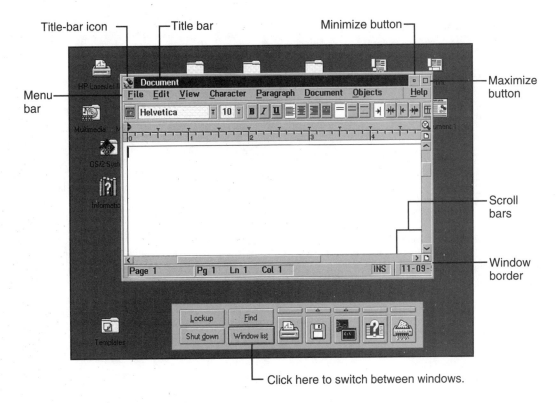

Window anatomy.

Dealing with menus and dialog boxes is also handled just like in Windows, so I won't bore you with the mundane details. Check out Chapter 8, "Ditching DOS: Running Microsoft Windows," for more information.

Dropping Out of Warp (Shutting Down)

Had enough? Say "Uncle." Okay, here's what you do to quit Warp and shut down your computer. First, go into any programs you were using, save your work, and then exit each program (open the **File** menu and select **Exit**). Now, click on the **Shut down** button on the LaunchPad, and then click on **OK**. When OS/2 says it's safe, turn off the PC. Don't just turn your computer off when you're through with it for the day; make sure you go through this shut-down procedure first.

The Least You Need to Know

You just covered OS/2 at warp speed, so if you need more help be sure to check out the *The Complete Idiot's Guide to OS/2 Warp*, available wherever neon orange books are sold. You can also use this list as a handy review:

➤ To start Warp, turn on your PC. Simple as that.

➤ To exit Warp, click on the **Shut down** button on the LaunchPad; then click on **OK**.

➤ In Warp, your screen is like a desktop: full of objects (icons). To do something such as copying a file, you manipulate these objects.

➤ To delete an object, drag it to the Shredder (remember to use the right mouse button). To print a file, drag it to the Printer.

➤ To start a program, double-click on its icon. To exit, double-click on the title-bar icon.

➤ To copy an object, hold down the **Ctrl** key while dragging the object where you want it. To move an object, just drag it. (To move an object to a different drive, hold down the **Shift** key as you drag.)

Part 3
Get to Work with Applications

You didn't buy a computer so you could watch the pretty pictures or drag icons across the screen. You got a computer so you could do some work... or play a few games. This Part provides a tour of the various applications you can run on your computer: applications for creating letters, balancing your checkbook, drawing pictures, managing your schedule, learning something, and even having some fun.

And that's not all. You'll also learn what to do when you bring a new application home: how to install it on your hard drive (or play a CD), enter commands, and use the application without flipping through the documentation. By the end of this section, you'll know how to take any application out of its box and put it to work.

Chapter 11

Application Types and What They Do

Short of tuning your car or cooking dinner, your computer can do just about anything. It can help you organize your recipes, track your budget, reconcile your checkbook, do taxes, print letters, draw pictures, keep your daily schedule, and even help you decide which video to rent.

In order to do all this, however, your computer needs the right applications: the instructions that enable it to perform specific tasks. This chapter takes you on a tour of the most popular application types and helps you decide which applications you need for work, learning, and entertainment.

Word Processing: Everybody's Doing It

Except for Studs Terkel and a couple other holdouts, few people use typewriters anymore. Instead, they use word processing applications on personal computers. A word processor essentially transforms your computer into an overpriced typewriter that gives you much more control over the look and layout of your documents. Most word processors can even handle pictures.

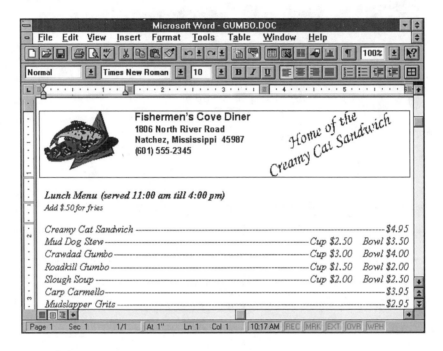

Use a word processing application to type letters and other documents.

In addition to helping you with the mundane tasks of laying text on a page and printing it, word processors commonly offer tools that can help you polish and enhance your work:

Fonts Fonts are text sizes and styles that you can use to enhance the look of your text.

Cut and paste You can quickly reorganize a document by selecting a section of text, cutting it, and then pasting it in a new location. See Chapter 16, "Making Letters, Spreadsheets, and Other Documents," for details.

Find and replace This feature hunts down all occurrences of a given word or phrase and replaces them with a new word or phrase.

Spell checker   This tool checks the spelling of each word in your document against the spellings in its dictionary. If it finds a questionable word, it marks it and displays a list of possible corrections.

Grammar checker   Grammar checkers are fairly worthless, but they do point out any overuse of the passive voice.

Thesaurus   What's another word for "blockhead?" Fire up the thesaurus for a list of suggestions.

Page numbering   Word processors are great at numbering pages—and renumbering after you've entered your changes.

Graphics   You usually get a collection of small electronic art clips that you can use to give documents a professional touch.

Mail merge   This feature enables you to combine two documents (say an address list and a form letter) and to create gobs of letters addressed to all the people on your list. You can also use mail merge to create mailing labels.

Tables   This feature can help you lay out text in columns and rows to align the text perfectly on a page. Most tables can even perform simple math, including addition, subtraction, division, and multiplication.

The three heavy hitters in word processing are Microsoft Word, WordPerfect, and Ami Pro. All these programs offer the features listed in this section.

Doing Math with a Spreadsheet

There's no mystery to spreadsheets. A checkbook is a spreadsheet. A calendar is a spreadsheet. Your 1040 tax form is a spreadsheet. Any sheet that has boxes you can fill in is a type of spreadsheet. What makes a computerized spreadsheet special is that it does math for you, and it can graph the results to help you analyze your numbers.

A spreadsheet consists of alphabetized *columns* and numbered *rows* that intersect to form boxes called *cells*. Your job is to type entries into the cells. These entries can take three forms: labels, values, and formulas. *Labels* are text that you usually enter at the top of a column or to the side of a row to indicate what's in that column or row. *Values* are numbers, and *formulas* are mathematical expressions that act on the numbers.

Cell Address
A cell address consists of a cell's column letter and row number and is used to tell the spreadsheet where a cell is located. For example, the address for the cell in the upper left corner of the spreadsheet is A1. As for the address of the cell in the lower right corner of the spreadsheet, nobody has ventured that far.

Formulas consist of *cell addresses* and mathematical symbols. The cell addresses insert values from the specified cells; for example, C25 inserts the value from the cell in column C, row 25. The mathematical symbols perform the necessary calculations: * (multiplication), / (division), + (addition), and – (subtraction). For example, if you wanted to determine the sum of the three values contained in cells C25, D25, and E25, you would use the following formula:

C25+D25+E25

Modern spreadsheets do much more than crunch numbers. Any spreadsheet worth its salt can graph your results for you and accept pieces of clip art and other graphics.

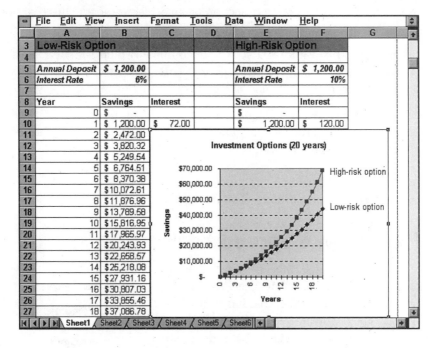

Use spreadsheets for ledgers and graphs.

Becoming an Information Superpower

Picture this. It's the year 2020. Frank Gifford has moved to FOX and is color man for Super Bowl LIV. It's the Cowboys against the Bills (yes, again), and you're in the booth with Frank. You purchased exclusive rights to the only sports trivia database on the planet, making you the most powerful (and highest paid) data broker in history. You have instant access to the most valuable information: pass completions, interceptions, third down conversions, even a complete list of who went out with O. J.'s wife! Ahh, power!

Of course, you can buy ready-made databases like the ones described here: encyclopedias, celebrity cookbooks, medical advisors, and even movie guides. However, if you're a real geek, you'll want to create your own database. How? By using a database application such as Microsoft Access or Paradox.

With a database application, you create a blank form for collecting information. As you fill out the form, the database application dumps the information into a file on your computer (keeping everything neat and tidy, of course). Each form you fill out represents a *record*; for example, one record may include the name, address, phone number, and picture of a person. A collection of these records makes up a *database*.

> **Database?**
> Don't confuse a database with a bouillabaisse. Bouillabaisse (pronounced "BOO-ya-base") is a highly seasoned fish stew made with at least two types of fish. A database has no fish, but it can list all the types of fish you may find in a bouillabaisse.

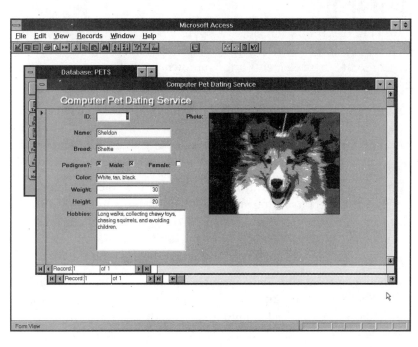

A database is a collection of records.

Of course, you can do the obvious with your database: flip through the records one-by-one or print them all out. But what makes a database a powerful information-management tool are the following features:

Search   You enter search instructions, such as "find everyone whose last name starts with L," and the database pulls up a list of all the records that match your instructions.

Sort   You can alphabetize the records from A to Z or Z to A (by last name or first name), by state, by ZIP code, or by any other system you choose.

Extract   If you want to look at only a select group of records (for example, customers who owe you money), you can have the database *extract* or *filter* those records.

Create reports   Most databases allow you to create reports that summarize and help you analyze your data. For example, if you manage a music store, you can keep track of which salesperson is selling the most piccolos.

Getting Graphical

In this age of information overload, most of us would rather look at pictures than wade through a sea of words. We want graphs, charts, moving pictures—multimedia! But how do you incorporate these elements into your own presentations and publications? With the help of graphics applications.

These applications range from software that requires no artistic talent to photo imaging and freehand drawing software that require the talents of a Vincent Van Gogh or Georgia O'Keefe. Here is a list of your options, arranged in the order of requiring the least amount of talent to requiring the most:

Clip art   This ready-made art is perfect for the lazy and untalented. Clip art often comes with word processing and desktop publishing programs, although you can purchase clip art collections separately. To drop a piece of clip art on a page, you usually enter the Insert Object command, and then select the desired image from a list. You can then drag it where you want to place it on the page.

Business presentations   Business presentation graphics applications allow you to create on-screen slide shows, overhead transparencies, 35mm slides, and audience handouts. You pick a background for your slide show, which controls the look of all the slides. You then add items to each slide, such as bulleted lists, pictures, graphs, clip art, and even sounds.

Scanners   A scanner is sort of like Silly Putty. It can lift an image from a page and convert it into an electronic form that you can insert into your documents and presentations. Table scanners are the best, because they act as copy machines. Hand-held scanners are more affordable, but take some practice in order to get high-quality images.

Paint programs   Paint programs require artistic talent (and patience). In a paint program, you use a set of tools to color your screen. For example, you might pick red, click on the spraypaint tool, and then drag the mouse pointer around to create a ribbon of red. Think of a paint program as a sophisticated Lite Brite toy; you turn on colored dots to create your pictures.

Draw programs   Draw programs allow you to assemble basic shapes (lines, rectangles, and ovals) into complex designs. Unlike paint programs, draw programs treat shapes as individual objects, allowing you to rearrange them. Draw programs are usually better for schematics, floor plans, and technical illustrations. Paint programs are better for touching up photos and creating realistic images.

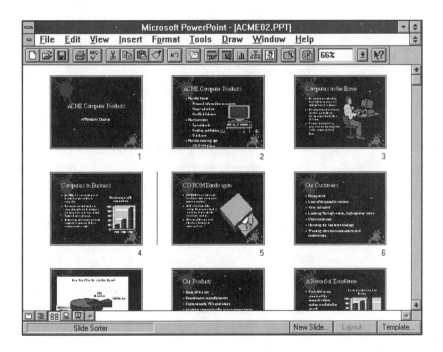

Business presentation programs help you create slide shows.

Publish It with Desktop Publishing

Newsletters, business cards, brochures, training manuals, books, flyers, signs, banners... desktop publishing does it all, by allowing you to combine text and pictures on the same page.

With most desktop publishing applications, you create a publication by combining three types of objects: text (which you type or import from your word processor), graphics (usually clip art), and drawn objects (lines, rectangles, and circles). You can drag these objects around and change their sizes and dimensions to tweak your pages to perfection.

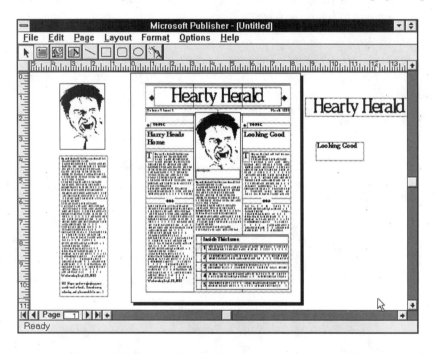

Desktop publishing applications help you combine text and graphics.

When selecting a desktop publishing program, consider what you want to do with it. If you're interested in creating greeting cards and banners, Print Shop Deluxe may be the best choice. For creating books or putting together magazines or newspapers, you might need a more powerful program, such as PageMaker. For a good general purpose program, try Microsoft Publisher (the program shown in the previous figure).

Managing Your Life with a PIM

I don't know about where you work, but where I work, about half the people tote around these small books called Franklin Day Planners. The Planner contains a calendar, a two-page spread for each day (which allows you to track appointments and tasks you must accomplish), an address book (for keeping names, addresses, and phone numbers of contacts), and a section at the back that contains all sorts of useless stuff, including a calorie counter and instructions on how to perform the Heimlich maneuver (I'm not kidding).

Believe it or not, there are several computerized versions of these day planners. My personal favorite is Lotus Organizer. Organizer is set up as a book that's divided into sections:

To Do allows you to keep a list of tasks you must perform and to prioritize the tasks.

Calendar displays the days of the month. When you click on a day, you get to see a list of appointments for that day. The Calendar also lets you set alarms that notify you of upcoming meetings.

Address acts just like the paper version of an address book. You can store names, addresses, and phone numbers for relatives, friends, and business associates.

Notepad is a scratch pad that lets you jot things down as you think of them.

Planner is a project planner that lets you keep track of the various stages of each project, vacation time, meetings, and anything else that fills up your days.

Anniversary allows you to keep track of important days, including birthdays, anniversaries, and holidays.

Free Calendar!
If you have Microsoft Windows, you already have a calendar program. Open the Accessories window and double-click on the **Calendar** icon. It ain't fancy, but it's cheap.

Keeping Track of Your Money (and Uncle Sam's)

The whole concept of money was supposed to simplify things, to make it easier to exchange goods. Instead of trading a fox pelt for a lobster dinner, you could sell the pelt to someone who wanted it and then take the money to the local seafood restaurant and pay for your lobster dinner.

Somewhere in history things got all screwed up. We now buy and sell money, store our money in banks and use checks to get at it, and even have chunks of our money removed from our paychecks before we've touched it. To help manage your money in these trying times, you can use two types of programs: personal finance (or check-writing) programs and tax programs.

Getting Personal with Your Finances

A personal finance program is useful for writing checks and helping you stick to your budget. To write a check, you simply type the payee's name and the amount on an on-screen check. The program inserts the date and the long-hand amount, copies the transaction to your register, and determines the new balance. You then print the checks whenever you plan on mailing them. If you're on a budget, you can also assign the transaction to a budget category to keep track of your expenses. In addition to check writing and budgeting, most personal finance programs offer the following advanced features:

Recurring entries   If you have a monthly bill that is the same each month (a mortgage payment, rent, or budgeted utility payment), the program issues the same payment each month.

Bill planning   You enter the information for all the bills you have to pay for the month and then mark the bills you currently plan to pay. The program compares the total amount with your current checking account balance to determine whether you have enough money. You can then prioritize your bills.

Electronic bill paying   If your computer has a modem, you may be able to pay your bills without writing a check. You'll need to subscribe to a bill-paying service to use this feature.

Reminders   A reminder feature automatically tells you when a bill is due whenever you start the program.

Income tax estimator   Compare how much you are actually paying in taxes to how much you should be paying to determine whether you are on track for the year.

Investment manager   Now that you have a budget and are saving loads of money, you may decide to invest that money. If you do, an investment manager feature can help you keep track of how your investments are doing.

Loan calculator   Some personal finance programs come with a loan calculator that you can use to determine loan payments and figure out just how much interest you will pay.

Getting Help with Your Taxes

Speaking of personal finances, you can also get programs for doing your taxes. In TurboTax, for example, you enter your name, the amount of money you made, the number of deductions you can claim, and so on. The program determines which forms you need to fill out and how much money the IRS owes you or how much money you owe the IRS. Most tax programs can perform a mock audit, help you find additional deductions, and explain tax laws in plain English.

What You Really Got a Computer for: Games

I've seen it happen. I've seen well-intentioned friends and relatives buy computers to "do work at home" and "get organized." Two weeks later, they're asking me to help them hook up a joystick and find a copy of DOOM. The next time I see them, their eyes are glazed over and their thumbs are twitching.

Due to the diversity of computer games, I can't really describe this category. Games range from action/adventure types (such as DOOM), to board games (chess and Risk), to flight simulations, war games, arcade games, and even city-management simulations (such as SimCity). You pick what you like, play until you tire of it, and then go back to the store and look for another one… or get back to work.

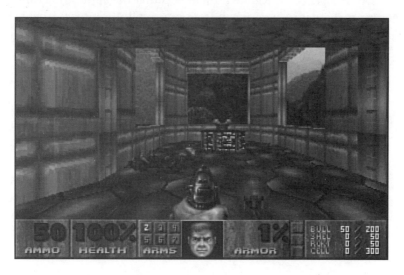

Currently, DOOM is one of the most popular computer games.

Learn Something, Will Ya?

Have you ever heard of the Nurnberg Funnel? Legend has it you can stick this funnel in your head and pour knowledge and understanding into your brain. Listening to the media, you might start to think that the computer is the Nurnberg Funnel of the '90s. If we can get all our kids to peck away at the keyboard and stare at the screen long enough, we'll have a generation of Einsteins.

Of course, this gives computers far too much credit. To learn anything requires some effort, problem solving, and critical thinking skills. However, the computer is good at presenting information, testing your knowledge of a subject, providing feedback, and helping you find information.

As with game software, educational software is too diverse to describe in 25 words or less. Kids can play *Where in the World Is Carmen Sandiego?* to learn geography, *Math Blaster* for basic math skills, and *Reader Rabbit* to get a head start on reading. Older kids and adults can prepare for college with SAT software, take on-screen piano lessons, hone their typing skills, and even learn a second language!

Gimme the Works: Integrated Software

Integrated software is the Swiss army knife of software packages. In a single package, you usually get a word processor, a spreadsheet and/or database application, a communications program (for your modem), and a draw or paint program—for one low introductory price!

The good thing about integrated software is that the applications are designed to work together, making it easy to switch from one application to another and share data between applications. The drawback is that the individual applications are not the most powerful. For example, the word processor you get with Microsoft Works is a trimmed-down version of Microsoft Word.

Da Works!
If you see an application whose last name is "Works," you can bet that it's an integrated package. Microsoft Works and Lotus Works are the two most popular integrated programs.

As a variation on the integrated package theme, software manufacturers commonly bundle several of their most popular applications and offer them as a *suite*. For example, Microsoft Office comes with Word, Excel (for spreadsheets), PowerPoint (for business presentations), and Mail (for electronic mail). Although a suite may cost as much as $500, you would pay more than twice as much if you purchased the applications separately.

Applications for Real People

Okay, we've done the business software jig and looked at the standard software categories. However, the market is packed with specialized applications that can do everything from helping you plan your next wedding to preparing for your funeral. Here's a sample of what's out there:

Street Atlas USA   A database of all the highways and byways across the United States.

JFK Assassination   A compilation of facts, video clips, interviews, and theories about the assassination of JFK.

Better Homes and Gardens Cookbook   This electronic version of one of the most popular cookbooks makes it easy to find and print your favorite recipes.

SportsWorks   A database that explains the rules and regulations governing sports that range from baseball to Sumo wrestling.

Microsoft Cinemania   An interactive movie guide that lets you look up movies by title, actor, or director. This movie guide includes reviews, clips, pictures, and sounds.

Design Your Own Home   A specialized graphics program that can help you design a custom floor plan, deck, or addition.

Home Medical Advisor   This doctor on a disk can help you cure your own minor ailments or understand your doctor's prognosis. The CD-ROM version includes video clips of common medical procedures.

Family Tree Maker   If you're interested in tracing your family roots, this is an invaluable tool. You type in names and dates, and the program draws your family tree.

The Least You Need to Know

If you want to experience the infinite variety of applications for yourself, take a trip to your local computer store. Until then, keep the following in mind:

➤ You use a word processor to type letters, books, and other documents.

➤ Spreadsheets are like accountants who can draw pretty graphs.

➤ Think of a database as a fancy Rolodex.

➤ If you have little artistic talent, you can fake it with clip art, a scanner, or a business presentation program.

111

➤ Desktop publishing applications allow you to combine text and pictures to create brochures, letterhead, greeting cards, and other publications.

➤ Use a personal finance application to reconcile your checkbook and keep track of your budget.

Chapter 12

Installing New Applications

By the End of This Chapter, You'll Be Able To:

➤ Find out whether your computer has enough disk space for another application

➤ Protect your new program disks from disaster

➤ Find a setup or install utility that does the installation for you

➤ Get a CD-ROM disc up and running

➤ Fool Windows into thinking your computer has more memory

You rush home with your copies of Print Shop Deluxe and Cinemania, log your latest VISA purchases, and start unpacking your toys. With a fistful of disks and a heart full of determination, you approach your computer.

Now what?

You can't just shove the disks in a drive and fire up your computer. You have to install the programs first. Most programs come with an installation utility that does everything for you: copying the files from the disks (or CD) to the hard disk, creating the required directories, and preparing the program for use. In this chapter, you'll learn how to run most installation programs.

Hard Disk Space: There's Never Enough

When programs such as Math Blaster gobble up 10 megabytes of disk space and a simple integrated program claims another 25 megabytes, you have to hesitate when the time comes to install a new application. After all, your computer's hard drive is not a bottom-less pit.

So, before you install a program, you should check your hard drive's free space. If you're in DOS, type **chkdsk** at the prompt and press **Enter**. Look for a line that says something like **101,000,564 bytes available on disk**. (Your number will vary.) Divide the number by 1 million to figure out how many megabytes you have.

Don't Pack Your Disk

As a general rule, keep 10 percent of your hard drive free. This gives your computer room to work and ensures that you have some space for the files you create.

If you're running Microsoft Windows, you can use the File Manager. Open the Main group window, and double-click on the **File Manager** icon. Click on the drive C icon in the upper left corner of the window. Look in the lower left corner of the window to determine how much free space you have left. This number is kilobytes, so divide by 1,000 to figure out how many megabytes you have.

Click here.

Free space

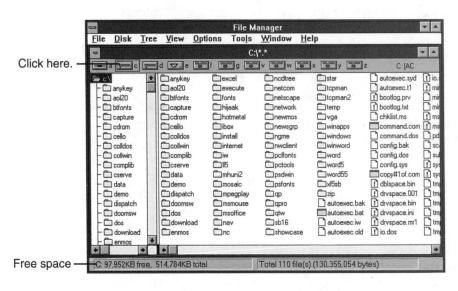

File Manager displays the amount of free space on the selected drive.

Now, check the program box to figure out how much disk space the program requires. If you don't have the necessary disk space, don't install the program; you have to remove some files first. Check out Chapters 21 and 22 to learn how to delete directories and files.

Protecting Your New Disks

Most applications come on disks that are *write-protected*. That is, your computer can read data from the disks but can't write anything to them. This prevents you from accidentally deleting or changing any of the files on the disk. If the disks are not write-protected, consider protecting them yourself. For a 3.5" disk, slide the write-protect tab so you can see through the hole, as shown below. For 5.25" disks, apply a write-protect sticker (or a piece of tape) over the write-protect notch on the side of the disk.

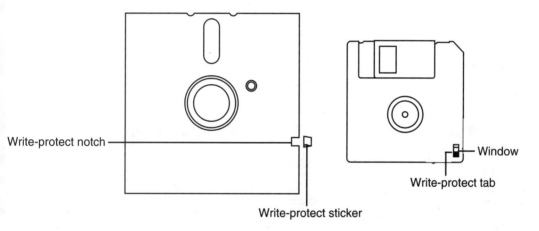

Write-protect notch

Write-protect sticker

Window

Write-protect tab

Write-protect program disks before using them.

Simple Installations Through Windows

Installing a Windows program is a no-brainer. The first disk in the set usually contains a setup or install program that leads you through the installation. All you have to do is run that program and follow the on-screen instructions:

Duplicating Application Disks
Many people recommend copying the disks before installing the application. This precaution is mostly a carry-over from the days of running applications from floppy disks. However, if you like to be extra cautious, copying all the disks can't hurt.

1. Start Microsoft Windows.

2. Display the Program Manager window.

3. Insert your application Disk 1 into drive A or B, and close the drive door, if it has one. (Or insert your CD into the CD-ROM drive.)

4. Open the **File** menu and select **Run**.

5. Type **a:** if Disk 1 is in drive A, or type **b:** if Disk 1 is in drive B. (If you're installing from a CD, use that drive letter.)

6. Click on the **Browse** button. The Browse dialog box appears, showing the *executable files* (the files you can run) on the disk, as shown below.

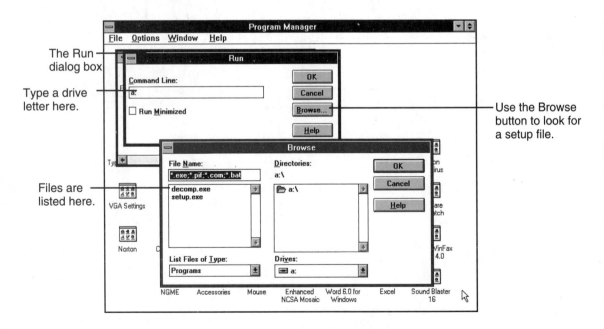

Use the Run dialog box to start the setup program.

7. Click on the **Install** or **Setup** file in the File Name list.

8. Click on the **OK** button. You are returned to the Run dialog box, and the name of the file you selected appears into the Command Line text box.

9. Click on the **OK** button. Windows runs the Setup or Install program and displays its initial screen.

10. Follow the installation instructions that appear on-screen.

DOS Applications: They're All Different

As soon as you buy a computer, all your friends and relatives start clearing their shelves and giving you a bunch of obsolete DOS programs to help you get started. If you're lucky, they include the documentation. If not, then you have to figure out how to install the program on your own. The following steps will work for nine out of ten installations:

1. Insert the first disk of the set into floppy drive A or B, and close the drive door if there is one. (Or insert your CD into the CD-ROM drive.)

2. Type **a:** or **b:** and press **Enter** to activate the drive that contains the floppy disk. (If you're installing from a CD, use that drive letter.)

3. Type **dir /w** and press **Enter** to see what's on the disk.

4. Look for a file name such as INSTALL.BAT, SETUP.BAT, INSTALL.COM, or something similar. The file name must have a .BAT, .COM, or .EXE extension.

5. Type the install or setup file's name without the extension, and press **Enter**. The installation program starts and usually displays a screen indicating what's going on or asking you to do something.

6. Read the instructions on the screen, answer any questions as best you can, and do what the screen tells you. You will probably have to feed the computer floppy disks until you reach the last disk.

Read the Label
Most software companies print installation instructions on the first disk in the set.

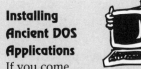

Installing Ancient DOS Applications
If you come across an application that has no setup or install utility, make a directory for the program, and then copy the files from the floppy disks to that directory. See Chapters 21 and 22 for details.

Special CD-ROM Considerations

Installing CD-ROM applications isn't much different from installing applications that come on floppy disks. You insert the disc, run the setup or install utility, and follow the instructions. However, there are a couple differences:

➤ Most CD-ROM applications run from the CD (not from the hard drive). For Windows applications, the setup utility creates an icon that you can double-click on to run the application.

➤ Some CD-ROM applications require you to install the application on your hard disk. This usually takes up a lot of disk space, which sort of defeats the purpose of having a CD-ROM drive.

➤ If you get a CD with several applications on it, each application is usually stored in a separate directory. To install one of the applications, you'll have to change to its directory and run its setup or install utility.

➤ CD-ROM games and educational programs are notorious for causing problems. They often have trouble working with certain sound cards and joysticks, and they just can't get enough memory. Invite the neighborhood geek over to help you.

➤ If you want to play a music CD on your CD-ROM player, you have to install a special program. Most CD-ROM players come with the program you need.

When Four Megabytes of RAM Just Isn't Enough

The guy who sold you your computer said that four megabytes of RAM would be plenty. The truth is that four megabytes is a mere hors d'oeuvre for most Windows applications. Some applications won't even blink unless you feed them six megabytes. Other memory hogs lock up your computer at the first command. If you're having trouble with a Windows application, try the following to free up some memory:

➤ Press **Ctrl+Esc** to see a list of running applications. Switch to those applications and exit them.

➤ If you have a screen saver program running, switch to it, and then click on the **Disable** option.

➤ Open the **Main** group window, double-click on the **Clipboard Viewer** icon, press the **Del** key, and then click on **Yes**. This deletes the Clipboard contents, which are stored in memory.

If you still have problems, there is a way to get more memory: *virtual memory*. Virtual memory is disk space that Windows treats as RAM. Although this type of memory is much slower than real RAM, it can help get a memory-hungry application up and running and prevent crashes. Here's what you do:

118

1. Open the **Main** group window.

2. Double-click on the **Control Panel** icon.

3. Double-click on the **386 Enhanced** icon.

4. Click on the **Virtual Memory** button. The Virtual Memory dialog box appears, showing the drive used for the swap file and the file's size and type. Keep in mind that one megabyte equals 1,024 kilobytes.

5. Click on the **Change** button. A **New Settings** area appears in the dialog box, allowing you to specify a new drive and a swap file size and type.

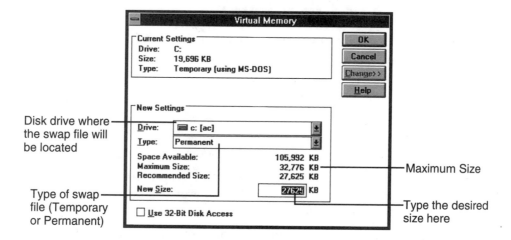

Using virtual memory.

6. (Optional) Open the **Type** drop-down list and select one of the following options:

   Temporary is the safest option. Windows uses any free space on the disk for swap files. However, a temporary swap file can be stored in several places on the disk, making it slower than a permanent swap file.

   Permanent creates a swap file using the largest block of free space on the selected drive. Because the swap file is in one location on the disk, Windows can read and write to it more quickly.

7. In the **New Size** text box, type the desired size for the swap file. This number must be less than or equal to the **Maximum Size** listed.

386 Enhanced? I Have a 486!
Don't freak if you see references to 386 processors on your 486 computer. The 386 ushered in some advanced memory handling options, so many options still refer to it. These options are available for 486 processors and Pentiums, as well.

8. Click on the **OK** button. A confirmation message appears, asking if you're sure you want to make these changes.

9. Click on the **Yes** button. This returns you to the 386 Enhanced dialog box.

10. Click on the **OK** button.

If you still have memory problems (not you personally, but your computer), you may have to break down and have an additional four megabytes of memory installed on your system.

The Least You Need to Know

Once you've installed two or three applications, you start feeling pretty confident. You may even start ignoring the installation instructions. Until you reach that point, here's what you need to know:

➤ Most applications come with a setup utility that installs the application for you.

➤ To run the setup utility at the DOS prompt, insert Disk 1, change to the drive that contains the disk, type **install** or **setup**, and press **Enter**.

➤ To run the setup utility in Windows, insert Disk 1, open the Program Manager's **File** menu, and select **Run**. Use the **Browse** button to find the setup or install file, and then click on the **OK** button twice.

➤ For all practical purposes, CDs are big floppy disks that usually contain a setup or install utility.

➤ If a Windows application says it needs more memory, set up Windows to use disk space as virtual memory.

➤ To change the virtual memory setting in Windows, open the **Control Panel**, double-click on the **386 Enhanced** icon, and click on the **Virtual Memory** button.

Chapter 13

Firing Up Your Applications

By the End of This Chapter, You'll Be Able To:

➤ Wake up a Windows application with your mouse

➤ Snoop around for the command you need to start a DOS application

➤ Run your favorite DOS applications from Windows

➤ Make Windows icons for your DOS applications

➤ Play an application off a CD-ROM

You don't need a big brain to run applications. You double-click on the application's icon (in Windows) or enter its startup command at the DOS prompt. The only time you may run into problems is when you can't find the application's icon, you don't know its DOS command, or you want to run a DOS application from Windows. When you encounter those difficulties, turn to this chapter for help.

Taking Off with Executable Files

Each application consists of gobs of files. Fortunately, you can ignore most of them. The only ones that concern you are the *executable files*—files that you can run. If you're ever asked to pick out an executable file in a police lineup, it's easy; all executable file names end in .BAT, .EXE, .COM, or .PIF.

With DOS, you actually have to know the name of the executable file that runs the program. You enter the file's name at the DOS prompt (dropping the .BAT, .EXE, or .COM off the end). Windows, on the other hand, gives you an icon that represents the executable file. When you double-click on the icon, Windows enters the command for you.

All Those Other Files...

An application's directory is a menagerie of exotic files, most of which control the application's look and function. You may see file names that end in WAV (sounds), CFG (configurations), DLL (shared program instructions), INI (initialization), TXT (text), HLP (help), OVL (overlays for display), LST (lists), and much more. You don't need to worry about most of these files; the application uses them to do its job.

Finding and Running Windows Applications

Running a Windows application is easy, assuming you know where its icon is hiding. However, as you install applications and open program group windows, your desktop clutter can bury the icon you need. Here are a few ways to reduce the clutter and root out the desired program group window:

➤ To find an errant program group window, open Program Manager's **Window** menu. A list of program group windows appears at the bottom of the menu; if you see the one you want, click on it. If you don't see it, click on **More Windows** for a complete list.

➤ If the program group window has a scroll bar, use it to bring other icons into view. The icon is probably in the window, but you can't see it.

Recovering Lost Groups

If you delete any of Windows' original program group windows (Applications, Main, StartUp, or Games), you can get them back. Open the Program Manager's **File** menu and select **Run**. Type **setup /p** and press **Enter**.

➤ Minimize all your program group windows (see Chapter 8). Open the **Window** menu and select **Arrange Icons**. You can now double-click on the icon for the desired program group.

➤ Make a program group window for all the applications you use daily: Open the Program Manager's **File** menu, select **New**, select **Program Group**, and click on **OK**. Type a name for the group window and click on **OK** again. To move icons into this new window, drag them from other windows. To copy icons, hold down the **Ctrl** key while dragging.

122

➤ To have an application run automatically when you start windows, hold down the **Ctrl** key while dragging the application's icon to the StartUp program group window or icon.

➤ When your desktop is just as you want it, freeze it. Open the **Options** menu and select **Save Settings on Exit** to remove the check mark next to it. Now, hold down the **Shift** key while double-clicking on the Program Manager's **Control-menu box** (in the upper left corner of the window).

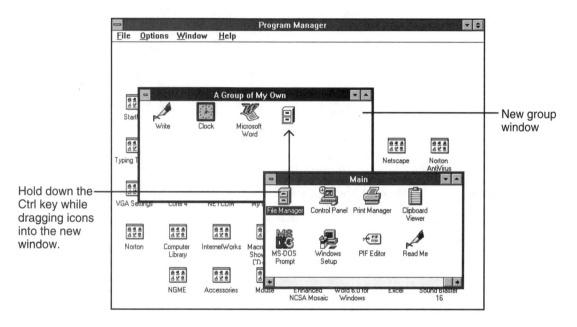

You can make your own group window in Windows.

Once you find the icon for the application you want to run, simply double-click on the icon to run it.

Launching a DOS Application

With DOS applications, you don't get a pretty picture of your program. You get the dour DOS prompt that provides no clue as to what you need to type. Check the documentation, type what it says, and then press **Enter**. Usually, the command you type is an abbreviation of the application's name. Table 13.1 lists the startup commands for several popular applications.

Table 13.1 Try the Following Commands for Some of the More Popular Programs

To Run This Program	Type This Command and Press Enter
America Online	aol
Carmen Sandiego	carmen
dBASE	dbase
Harvard Graphics	hg
Lotus 1-2-3	123
Microsoft Windows	win
Microsoft Word	word
Microsoft Works	works
Paradox	paradox
PC Tools	pcshell OR pctools
PFS: First Choice	first
PFS: First Publisher	fp
PRODIGY	prodigy
Professional Write	pw
Q&A	qa
Quicken	q
TurboTax	ttax
WordPerfect	wp

Bad Command or File Name

You read the documentation. It said, "Type WP and press Enter." Been there, did that, and all you get is **Bad command or file name**. Maybe you had a typo, so you enter the command again and once again get **Bad command or file name**. If you're like most people, you start to wonder if you messed up the installation. You probably didn't.

You simply need to change to the directory that contains the application's executable file. Try this:

1. Change to the drive on which you installed the application. For example, type **c:** and press **Enter**.

2. Type **cd** and press **Enter** to climb to the top of the directory tree.

3. Type **dir /a:d /w** and press **Enter**. This gives you a list of the directories on your disk.

4. Scan the list for the directory that you think might contain the program's files. For example, WordPerfect 5.1 stores its files in the WP51 directory.

5. Change to the directory that contains the application's files. For example, type **cd \wp51** and press **Enter**.

6. Now try typing the command.

> **Calling All Executables**
> If you don't know which command to type, enter **dir *.bat, dir *.com**, and **dir *.exe**. This gives you a list of all the executable files. Find one that looks promising, and then enter its name (leaving off the .BAT, .COM, or .EXE).

Making an Application Run from Any Directory

When you install some applications, they add their directory to the AUTOEXEC.BAT file's PATH statement. This tells DOS where the application's files are stored, so you don't have to change to its directory to run it.

To add a directory to the PATH statement, type **edit c:\autoexec.bat** at the DOS prompt and press **Enter**. Use the down arrow key to move down to the line that starts with PATH, and then press the **End** key. Type a semicolon and then the drive letter and directory; for example, type **;c:\wp51**. Open the **File** menu and select **Save**. Open the **File** menu and select **Exit**. You have to reboot your computer to put the change into effect.

> **AUTOEXEC.BAT**
> Stands for automatic execution batch file. This file contains a bunch of commands that DOS reads whenever you start your computer. Don't delete this file, and be careful when editing it.

125

Doing DOS Applications from Windows

Windows does DOS applications, sometimes better than DOS does. To run a DOS application, open the **File** menu, select **Run**, type the command needed to run the application, and press **Enter**. You can also click on the **Browse** button in the Run dialog box to poke around your hard disk looking for the executable file.

When you installed Windows, it gave you the option of creating icons for your DOS applications. Windows then sniffed out executable files, created icons for them, and dumped them in an Applications window. If you don't find the icon (or an Applications window, for that matter), you can have Windows do a repeat performance:

1. Open the **Main** group window.

2. Double-click on the **Windows Setup** icon.

3. Open the **Options** menu and select **Set Up Applications**.

4. Click on **Search for applications** and then click on **OK**. A dialog box appears prompting you to specify which drives you want to search for applications.

5. Click on each drive you want to search, and then click on the **Search Now** button.

6. Follow the on-screen instructions until the search is complete.

7. In the **Applications found on hard disk(s)** list, click on each application you want to set up. (If the application you want to set up is not in the list, Windows Setup cannot handle it. Skip ahead for details.)

8. Click on the **Add** button.

9. Click on the **OK** button. Program Manager creates the icons and places them in the Applications group.

DOS Games Don't Do Windows

DOS games typically like to take control of your computer, and they don't like Windows getting in the way. For example, Microsoft's Flight Simulator locks up most computers when running under Windows. If your computer keeps locking up, exit Windows and then run the DOS game.

If Windows can't create an icon for your DOS application, you have to do it yourself. Open the program group window in which you want the new icon (or make a window as explained earlier). Open the Program Manager's **File** menu, select **New**, select **Program Item**, and then click on **OK**. Type a description for the icon, and press the **Tab** key. Click on the **Browse** button, and use the dialog box that appears to select the executable file for the desired application. Click on **OK** once... twice... you now have an icon.

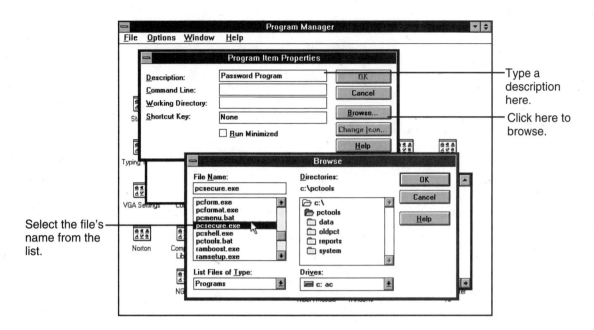

You can create your own program-item icons.

Although this is a foolproof way to create icons for DOS applications, it's not the best way. Using the Windows Setup utility (as described earlier) works better because Windows Setup creates a PIF for the DOS application. PIF (short for program information file) contains information that helps Windows run the application more smoothly. However, Windows Setup cannot create PIFs for all applications.

Running a CD-ROM Application

CD-ROM applications don't differ much from the applications on your hard disk or from applications that come on floppies. They are all either DOS or Windows software, and you install them and run them the same way. However, there are a few differences of which you should be aware:

➤ If you get a disc that has two or more applications on it, each application is stored in a separate directory. You must change to that directory in order to run the application or run its setup utility.

➤ When you install a Windows CD, the setup utility usually creates an icon for the application, but the icon points to an executable file on the CD. You need to insert the CD before double-clicking on the icon.

➤ Some CDs come with special helper applications that may play sounds or help display moving pictures. Usually, the setup utility installs all this stuff, but sometimes you have to run a separate setup utility. If you run into problems, read the setup documentation before chucking your computer out the window.

The Least You Need to Know

In this chapter, you learned some fairly advanced techniques for finding, running, and managing applications. However, you don't have to know all that to run an application. Here's all you really need to know:

➤ In Windows, double-click on an application's icon to run it.

➤ If you can't find the group window that contains the application's icon, use the Program Manager's Window menu to search for it.

➤ With some DOS applications, you have to change to the drive and directory where the application's files are stored before you can start the application.

➤ To start a DOS application, type its startup command at the DOS prompt and press **Enter**.

➤ Windows can create icons for your DOS applications. Double-click on the **Windows Setup** icon in the Main group window.

GO! GO FIND A MENU, BOY! GWAN!!

Chapter 14

Barking Out Commands

By the End of This Chapter, You'll Be Able To:

➤ Quit almost any application (without reading the documentation)

➤ Find out where an application hides its menus

➤ Bypass menus by pressing shortcut keys

➤ Tell the difference between a speed button and a speed bump

➤ Use your right mouse button (in some applications)

Your computer is essentially an interactive television set. Press **F1**, and you get the Help channel. Press **Alt+F4**, and you exit your Windows application. You even get on-screen menus and buttons you can use to do everything from printing a file to zooming in on a page. The only thing you can't do is buzz in ahead of the other *Jeopardy* contestants. In this chapter, you'll learn how to take control of your television set (er... computer) with your keyboard and mouse.

Pick One: Entering Menu Commands

In the late '80s to early '90s, menus started popping up on all application screens. Some-times, a big menu would appear front and center at startup. Other times, the menus would be hidden inside a *menu bar* near the top of the screen. If Windows 95 is any indication, menus will soon be migrating south, to the bottom of the screen. But no matter where they hide, the following steps will help you flush them out and make them do something useful:

➤ **Click on a menu name.** If you can't find the menus, they're probably hidden in the menu bar. Look around the top of the screen for a horizontal bar that has names in it like File and Edit. To open one of these hidden menus, click on its name. To select a menu item, click on it, or use the arrow keys to highlight the item and then press **Enter**.

➤ **Press the Esc key.** In some older DOS applications (including Microsoft Word), pressing **Esc** displays a menu. Use the arrow keys to highlight the desired option, and then press **Enter**. This usually opens another menu and then another. Follow the menu trail until you get what you want.

Quick Windows Menu Selections
To quickly select a menu option in Windows, move the mouse pointer over the desired menu name. Hold down the mouse button while dragging the mouse pointer over the desired option on the menu. When you release the mouse button, Windows executes the high-lighted command.

➤ **Hold down the Alt key.** If you hold down the Alt key in some applications, the selection letters in the menu names appear highlighted. To open the menu, hold down the **Alt** key while typing the highlighted letter.

➤ **Press F10.** In Windows applications (and some DOS applications), the F10 key activates the menu bar. Use the arrow keys to highlight the desired menu name, and press **Enter**.

➤ **Cancel the menu.** You can usually cancel a menu by clicking somewhere outside the menu or by pressing the **Esc** key.

130

Click on an
option.

Click on a
menu name.

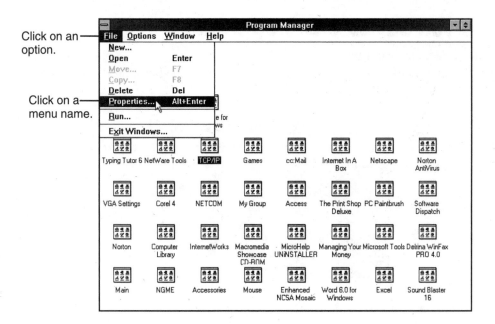

*In Windows and most menu-driven programs, you can click on a
menu to open it.*

All Menu Items Are Not Created Equal

As you flip through any menu system, you might start to notice that some of the menu
options look a little strange. One option may appear pale, others might be followed by a
series of dots, and still others may have arrows next to them. Their appearance tells all:

Light gray options are unavailable for what you are currently doing. For example, if
you want to copy a chunk of text and you have not yet selected the text, the Copy
command will not be available.

An option with an arrow opens a *submenu* that requires you to select another
option.

An option with a check mark indicates that the option is currently active. To turn
the option off, select it. This removes the check mark, although you won't know it,
because selecting the option also closes the menu.

An option followed by a series of dots (...) opens a *dialog box* that requests additional information. For more about dialog boxes, keep reading.

What Do You Say to a Dialog Box?

If you choose a command that's followed by a series of dots (...), the application displays a *dialog box* that essentially says, "WHAT D'YA WANT?!" You click a few buttons, check a few check boxes, and then give your okay.

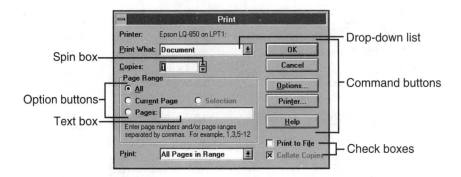

A typical dialog box.

Trouble is, you'll rarely meet a typical dialog box. As developers search for the perfect box, they continue to add items and alter the box design. However, in any dialog box, you can expect to find one or more of the following items:

 Tabs: One of the newest dialog box innovations, the tab allows a dialog box to contain two or more "pages" of options. To switch to a set of options, click on its tab.

 Text boxes: A text box stands for "fill in the blank"; it allows you to type text such as the name of a file. To replace an entry in a text box, double-click inside it and then type your entry. To edit an entry, click inside the text box, use the arrow keys to move the insertion point, and then type your correction.

 Option buttons: Option buttons (alias radio buttons) allow you to select one option in a group. Click on the desired option.

 Check boxes: Check boxes allow you to turn an option on or off. Click inside a check box to turn it on if it's off, or off if it's on. You can select more than one check box in a group.

 List box: A list box presents two or more options. Click on the option you want. If the list is long, you'll see a *scroll bar*. Click on the scroll bar arrows to move up or down in the list.

132

Drop-down list box: This list box has only one item in it. It hides the rest of the items. Click on the arrow to the right of the box to display the rest of the list, and then click on the item you want.

 Spin box: A spin box is a text box with controls. You can usually type a setting in the text box or use the up or down arrow to change the setting.

 Command buttons: Most dialog boxes have at least three buttons: OK to confirm your selections, Cancel to quit, and Help to get help.

To get around in a dialog box, you can click on items with the mouse, use the **Tab** key to move from item to item (**Shift+Tab** to move back), or hold down the **Alt** key while typing the underlined letter in the option's name.

Quick Keyboard Commands

If your boss still thinks WordPerfect 5.1 is the best word processing application in the world, you may find yourself having to memorize a long list of keyboard commands: Shift+F7 to print, F3 for help, and so on. Most of these keystrokes are not intuitive; you have to memorize the keystroke-command combination. To help you get up to speed, you can purchase a keyboard template that contains a complete list of the commands and corresponding keystrokes.

Like the Great White whale and the Siberian tiger, function key commands are disappearing fast. Most applications now use Ctrl+key combinations that allow you to bypass their pull-down menus. For example, you might press Ctrl+P to print, Ctrl+S to save a file, and Ctrl+C to copy selected text. These Ctrl+key combinations are a bit easier to memorize, and most applications use the same combinations for identical commands.

Command-Driven Programs
Programs that depend on special keystroke commands are called "command-driven," as opposed to "menu-driven." However, menu-driven programs usually contain *keyboard shortcuts* that allow you to bypass the menu system.

Button Bars, Toolbars, and Speed Buttons

In an effort to give you even less room to do your work, software developers have added buttons to the screen. The idea behind these time-savers is that it's faster to click on a button than to pull down a menu and select a command... assuming, of course, that you know what each button does. If you're wondering what I'm talking about, take a look at

133

the button bar for America Online, an online service that has won awards for usability.

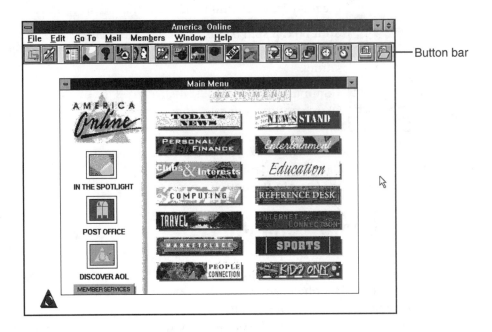

Button bars are often as clueless as the DOS prompt.

Recently, programmers have figured out a way of telling you what these buttons are for. In most new applications, if you move the mouse pointer over the button in question and let it rest there for a couple of seconds, a box appears, indicating what the button is for.

A Surprise in Every Click: Pop-Up Menus

Button Bars, Speedbars, and Other Names

Each application has its own name for these button bands. The most popular names are **button bar**, **speedbar**, **toolbar**, and **palette**.

I always thought that the second mouse button was there in case the first one broke or got tired... sort of like a reserve gas tank. You never used it, but you were glad it was there.

Recently, however, applications have been using the reserve button to do real work. You right-click on some text, and you get a pop-up menu that lets you copy, cut, or style the text. Right-click on the window's title bar, and you get a menu that lets you print or save the file. Right-click on the button bar, and you can turn it off (or turn a different one on).

134

Although I'm not a big fan of pop-up menus, they do give you a quick look at what's available. Each pop-up menu contains only those options that pertain to the object you clicked on, so you don't have to search the whole menu system to find your options.

Recording and Playing Back Commands with Macros

Unlike humans, computers can perform the same tasks over and over without getting bored or acquiring carpal tunnel syndrome. Humans, on the other hand, detest repetition. That's why we need progressively better commercials to keep us interested in the Super Bowl.

Whenever you notice yourself performing the same computer task over and over, it may be a sign that you need to delegate this task to your computer. You may need to create a *macro*.

Macro
A **macro** records a series of keystrokes and/or menu selections and allows you to play them back with a single selection or keystroke.

Most applications have a macro feature that can record your actions or keystrokes for you. You enter the command to record a macro, and then you perform the task as you normally would. When you finish, enter the command to stop recording. The application then asks you to name the macro and assign it to a keystroke. To play back the macro, you select it from a macro list, or press the unique keystroke you assigned to it. Many applications even let you create a button for the macro... assuming you're into buttons.

What About Voice-Activated Computers?

The Jetsons popularized voice activated computing. George Jetson barks a command at his kitchen appliance, and it dutifully serves up his meal. In reality, voice-activated computers are not so quick to carry out your commands. If you strained your voice the night before, or you developed a cold since you "trained" your computer, it won't recognize your voice. Sure, it'll carry out a command, but it may not be the command you wanted.

If I haven't discouraged you yet, and you want to try this relatively new technology, get yourself a 16-bit sound board, a microphone, and a voice activation program (try VoiceAssist). Once you've installed the program (and the sound board), you have to train it. This consists of recording and assigning voice commands to menu selections, macros, and keystrokes.

The hardest part of this process is to speak naturally. If you record clearly spoken, articulate commands one day, and then slur your words (as you normally would) the next, the voice activation program won't understand your normal speech.

Good luck!

The Least You Need to Know

Although each application sports its own command system and shortcut keys, you can usually navigate by knowing a few tricks:

➤ In most applications, you can get by with its menu bar and a couple of memorized keystrokes.

➤ If you select a menu command that's followed by a series of dots, you get a dialog box asking for more information.

➤ Many menu commands have a corresponding keystroke combination that allows you to bypass the menu system.

➤ In many applications, you can right-click on an object to view a pop-up menu.

➤ A macro is a record of keystrokes or actions that you can play back with a single keystroke.

Chapter 15

Surviving Without Documentation

By the End of This Chapter, You'll Be Able To:

- ➤ Get late-breaking information about your programs

- ➤ Find and read a Help file in Windows and DOS

- ➤ Search for specific help in most Windows applications

- ➤ Get immediate help for the task you're trying to perform

- ➤ Skip around a Help system for additional information

Worst case scenario—you get a program, and there's no documentation. None of your friends knows how to use the program, and the local bookstore doesn't have a book on the topic. What do you do? The following sections provide some tactics for dealing with such situations. Although they won't work for all programs, they will work for most.

Looking for Help in README Files

Most programs come with a Help menu of some type, which is the most logical place to look for help. However, if you can't even get the program running (or running right), you won't be able to get into the Help system. When that happens, the first thing you should do is look for a README file.

A README file usually contains information about installing and running the program, details about how the program works, information about new features, and descriptions of known bugs.

In Search of README

If you're at the DOS prompt, change to the drive and directory that contains the program's files. Type **dir read*.*** and press **Enter**. If you get a message saying **File not found**, you're out of luck; there is no README file. If all goes well, you get one or two file names such as README.EXE, README.TXT, or README.DOC. Skip ahead to the next couple of sections to learn what to do.

If you're in Windows, use the File Manager to search for wandering READMEs. To find all README files on drive C, take the following steps:

1. To run File Manager, open the Main program group window and then double-click on the **File Manager** icon.

2. Open the **File** menu and select **Search**. The Search dialog box appears.

3. Type **read*.*** and press the **Tab** key to move to the Start From text box.

4. Type **c:** in the Start From text box.

5. Click on the **OK** button. File Manager finds all the README files on drive C and displays a list of them.

Running a README Executable File

If you find a file called README.BAT, README.COM, README.EXE or a similar name with the extension .BAT, .COM, or .EXE, you can run the README file as you can run any executable file. Type its name at the DOS prompt (without the extension .BAT, .EXE, or .COM) and press **Enter**. The program will then display the information for you.

Bug
A **bug** is a problem in a program that causes it to behave erratically, lock up your system, and make you want to smash your computer with a baseball bat.

To run an executable README file from File Manager, double-click on it. File Manager runs the README program for you and displays the information on-screen. In most cases, you can use the Page Up and Page Down keys to move through the document.

Taking a Peek at a README Text File

If a README file has the extension .DOC, .TXT, or .WRI (or the name READ.ME), you can't run it. You have to open it in a word processing program or use the DOS TYPE command to display its contents. If you're at the DOS prompt, here's what you do:

1. Change to the drive and directory that contains the README file.

2. Type **type** *readme.txt* **| more** where **type** tells DOS to display the contents of the file on-screen, *readme.txt* is the name of the README file, and **| more** tells DOS to pause after displaying each screen of information.

3. Press **Enter**. DOS displays the first screen of information.

4. Read the information and then press **Enter** to see the next screen.

5. Repeat step 4 until you are returned to the DOS prompt.

> **README in Print**
>
> An easy way to view the contents of the README file is to print the file. Type the following command (remember to substitute the actual file's name in place of *readme.txt*) and press **Enter**:
>
> **copy** *readme.txt* **> prn**

File Manager *associates* most README file types to specific applications, so you can display the README file simply by double-clicking on its name in File Manager. For example, if you double-click on a file called README.WRI, File Manager runs the Windows Write application and opens README.WRI. If you double-click on a README.TXT file, File Manager will try to open it in Windows Notepad. If the file is too big for Notepad, run Write (from the Accessories group), and use Write to open the README.TXT file.

Help Yourself: Online Documentation

Some people enjoy reading documentation from cover to cover. These are usually the same people who date themselves on Friday night. Those of us who have lives expect a program to be simple enough so we don't have to read 600 pages of technical material. We would rather figure things out on our own, seeking help only when all else fails.

For people like us, there are online Help systems. You open the **Help** menu, click on **Contents** or **Index**, and then follow a trail of topics until you find the answer.

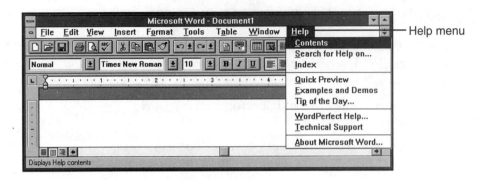

Most programs have a Help menu.

What? No Help Menu?!

If you can't find a Help menu, don't give up. Some programs like to hide their Help systems behind a keystroke. Try the following to chase the Help system out of the bush:

➤ **Press the F1 key.** The F1 key is the 911 of the computer industry. Most programs use this key to call up the Help system.

➤ **Press the F3 key.** If you need help with WordPerfect older than version 6.0, try pressing the **F3** key. WordPerfect likes to buck the system.

➤ **Look for a Help button.** Some programs display a Help button in a button bar or in dialog boxes (it usually has a question mark on it). Click on the **Help** button.

Skipping Around with Hypertext Links

No matter how you get into a program's Help system, you need some way to get around in the system once you're there. Most Help systems contain *hypertext links* that let you jump from one topic to another. The hypertext link is a highlighted word or phrase that, once selected, displays a definition of or additional information concerning that word or phrase. You usually have to click or double-click on the hypertext link to display the additional information, or you can tab to the link and press **Enter**.

Context-Sensitive Help One of the best ways to use a Help system is to start performing the task and then press **F1** when you get stuck. In most programs, this displays a context-sensitive Help screen that provides the specific information you need to continue.

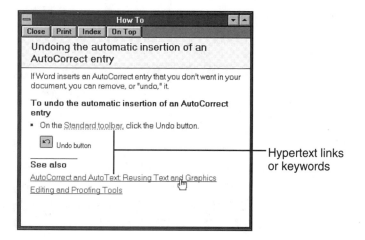

Hypertext links let you jump from one topic to another.

Most Help systems that allow you to jump from one topic to another also provide a way for jumping back. Look for the Back and History options. The Back option usually takes you back one topic at a time. The History option provides a list of topics you have looked at and allows you to select a topic from the list.

Working with the Online Librarian

Advanced help systems usually provide a way for you to search for information on a specific topic or task. For example, you may want to search for information about setting margins or printing. Here's what you do:

1. Open the **Help** menu and select **Search**, or enter the Search command in the Help system.

2. Start typing the name of the term or topic. As you type, a list of available topics that match what you type scrolls into view.

3. When you see the desired topic, double-click on it, or highlight it and press **Enter**. A list of subtopics appears.

4. Double-click on the desired subtopic. A Help window appears, showing information that pertains to the selected subtopic.

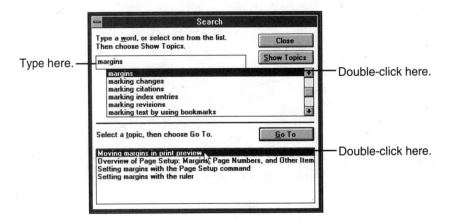

Type here.

Double-click here.

Double-click here.

A Built-In Tutor? You've Struck Gold

Some programs come with a tutorial that leads you through the process of using the program's major features. You may have already encountered such a tutorial in Chapter 8, "Ditching DOS: Running Microsoft Windows."

Help File Reader
Windows comes with a program that can read any Windows Help (.HLP) file. If you see a file that ends in .HLP in the File Manager, double-click on it. Windows runs the reader and opens the Help file. (Some .HLP files are for DOS applications, so the reader can't display them.)

In Windows and most Windows applications, you can get to the tutorial through the Help menu. In DOS applications, you usually have to run a separate program. Display a directory of the program's files and look for a file such as TUTOR.EXE, TUTOR.COM, LEARN.EXE, or LEARN.COM. If you find such a file, try running it.

The Least You Need to Know

As you become accustomed to using a computer, you'll be more and more tempted to try using each program without looking at the documentation. As you take on greater and greater challenges, keep the basics in mind:

➤ Some programs contain a README file or another text file that may contain instructions on how to install and use the program.

➤ If you find a README file that ends in .COM, .BAT, or .EXE, run it.

➤ If you find a README file that ends in .TXT, .DOC, or .WRI, double-click on it in File Manager, or enter the **DOS TYPE** command followed by the complete name of the README file.

➤ For online documentation, run the application and open its **Help** menu.

➤ F1 is the universal Help key.

Part 4
Your Turn to Create

Face it; you can't spend all your time playing Solitaire and checking out the latest multimedia CDs. Occasionally, you have to get some work done… to keep up appearances and pay your bills. Maybe you have to write a letter, do some data entry, or update schedules. Maybe your boss just caught you playing Solitaire, and you have to slap together a quick résumé and cover letter.

No matter what your ultimate goal, you need to know a few basics. You at least have to know how to type, style your text, save files, set margins, and print. In this Part, you'll learn everything you need to know to become productive in any application. As a bonus, you'll get quick answers to common problems you are sure to encounter along the way: when the printer won't print or the computer refuses to save your file. By the end of this section, you'll have what it takes to stare down any problem.

Chapter 16

Making Letters, Spreadsheets, and Other Documents

By the End of This Chapter, You'll Be Able To:

➤ Type in a word processing application without going insane

➤ Zoom in on a page

➤ Skip around in a spreadsheet

➤ Select, cut, copy, and paste chunks of text

➤ Undo mistakes

From the time you get your first box of Crayolas until you draw up your last will and testament, you're driven to create. Maybe this drive comes from some primitive need to further the species. Perhaps the hostile natural environment forces us to invent, or maybe we're just trying to avoid boredom.

Computers further drive us to create. When you run an application, it presents you with a blank page, daring you to make something. In this chapter, you'll learn how to transform those blank pages into letters, ledgers, and other types of documents, and how to use special tools to edit your documents.

Type Away!

Most applications start you out with a blank "sheet of paper" or a work area. The screen is about a third as long as a real sheet of paper, and it may be black instead of white, so you'll have to use your imagination. The application also displays a *cursor* or *insertion point*; anything you type will be inserted at this point.

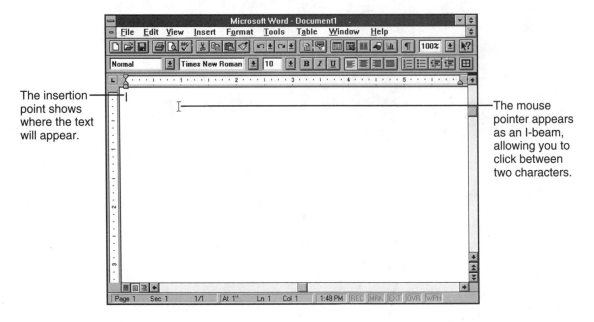

The insertion point shows where the text will appear.

The mouse pointer appears as an I-beam, allowing you to click between two characters.

You start with a blank page.

All Applications Differ

To type in a word processing application, you pretty much just do it. You type as you normally would, pressing the **Enter** key at the end of each paragraph. In other applications, typing is a little more complicated:

➤ In a spreadsheet, you tab to or click inside the cell into which you want to type an entry. When you type, your entry appears on an *input line* near the top of the spreadsheet. Press **Enter** to move the entry from the input line into the cell.

➤ In a database application, you type each entry into a *field*—in a box or on a line. You typically press the **Tab** key to move from one field to the next, or click inside the field with your mouse.

➤ In desktop publishing, graphics, and presentation applications, you have to draw a text box before you can type anything. To draw a text box, click on the **text box**

148

button, and then use the mouse to drag a text box onto your work area. An insertion point appears in the text box, and you can start typing.

Easing the Transition

Moving from a typewriter to a keyboard can be a traumatic experience. I've known several people who developed nervous tics during the transition. To prevent you from going stark raving mad during your transitional phase, I'll give you some free advice:

Press Enter only to end a paragraph. The application automatically *wraps* text from one line to the next as you type. Press **Enter** or **Return** only to end a paragraph or break a line.

Don't move down until there is something to move down to. If you press the down arrow key on a blank screen, the cursor usually will not move down. If you want to move the cursor down on a blank screen, you have to press **Enter** to start new paragraphs.

Text that floats off the top of the screen is NOT gone. If you type more than a screen of text, any text that does not fit on the screen is *scrolled* off the top of the screen. You can see the text by pressing **PgUp** or by using the up arrow key to move the cursor to the top of the document.

Use the arrow keys or the mouse to move the cursor. Many people try to move the cursor down by pressing the Enter key. This starts a new paragraph. Worse, some people try to move the cursor left by pressing the Backspace key. This moves the cursor, but it deletes any characters that get in its way. To move the cursor safely, use the arrow keys.

Delete to the right; Backspace to the left. To delete a character that the cursor is on (or under) or a character to the right of the insertion point,

Starting with a Template
Some applications come with a bunch of *templates*, which are starter documents that are already laid out for you. For example, spreadsheet applications usually come with a budget spreadsheet, and word processing applications come with templates for business letters and newsletters. You can then customize the document for your own use.

Field
A fill-in-the-blank area on a database form. You type entries into the fields to create a record. Records make up the database. Think of a record as a single card in a Rolodex.

press the **Del** (Delete) key. To delete characters to the left of the cursor or insertion point, press the **Backspace** key.

Just do it! Once you've grasped the behavior of word processing applications, typing is easy—just do it.

Insert or Overstrike?

In most applications, if you move the cursor between two words or two characters and start typing, whatever you type is inserted at the cursor. Any surrounding text is bumped to the right to make room for the new kids. This is known as *Insert mode*, and it is the mode that most applications work in (unless you specify otherwise).

You can switch to *Overstrike mode* in order to type over what's already on-screen. If you want to replace one word with another, you simply type over the word you want to delete. In most applications, you can switch back and forth between Insert and Overstrike modes by pressing the **Ins** key.

Zooming In and Zooming Out

Nothing is more annoying than text that's too small to read or so large that it runs off the right edge of the screen. You could, of course, change the size of the text (as explained in Chapter 17, "Giving Your Document a Makeover"), but that changes the size on the printed copy as well.

The solution is to change the display size. Most applications offer controls that allow you to zoom in on a document so you can see what you're typing, or zoom out to get a bird's eye view. Check the menus and the button bar for zoom controls.

Skipping Around in a Document

Being in a document is like squeezing your way through a crowded city. You have all these characters on-screen elbowing each other for a peek at the parade. You are the cursor, attempting to weave your way through the crowds. To move the cursor (or insertion point), you have several options:

Mouse pointer   To move the cursor with the mouse pointer, simply move the pointer to where you want the cursor or insertion point, and then click the left mouse button.

Arrow keys   The arrow keys let you move the cursor up, down, left, or right one character at a time.

Ctrl+Arrow keys   To move faster (one word at a time), most applications let you use the Ctrl (Control) key along with the arrow keys. You hold down the Ctrl key while pressing the arrow key to leap from one word to the next.

Home and End keys   To move at warp speed, you can use the Home and End keys. The Home key usually moves the cursor to the beginning of a line. End moves the cursor to the end of a line.

PgUp and PgDn keys   Use the PgUp key to move up one screen at a time, or use PgDn to move down one screen at a time. Remember, a screen is shorter than an actual page. Most applications also offer a scroll bar, as shown below, that lets you page up or down.

> **Default Mode**
> When an application starts in a certain mode, that mode is referred to as the **default mode**. Because nothing was specified, the application defaults to a particular setting, usually the safest or most common setting.

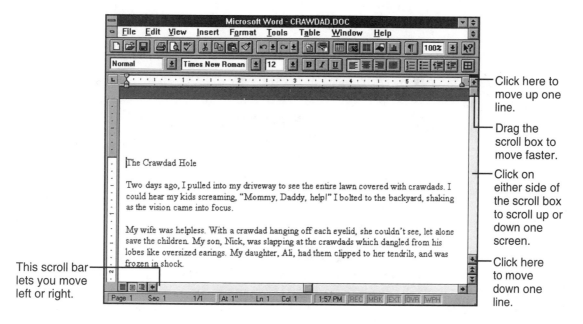

Click here to move up one line.

Drag the scroll box to move faster.

Click on either side of the scroll box to scroll up or down one screen.

This scroll bar lets you move left or right.

Click here to move down one line.

Use the scroll bar to bring scrolled text into view.

Selecting Text and Other Data

After you've entered text, you may want to *select* it to cut it, move it, or change its look. If you have a mouse, selecting text is fairly easy:

1. Click in the upper left corner of the area you want to select.

2. Hold down the left mouse button and drag the pointer to the lower right corner of the selection area.

3. Release the mouse button.

Click the
pointer here.

Hold down the
mouse button
while dragging
the pointer here.

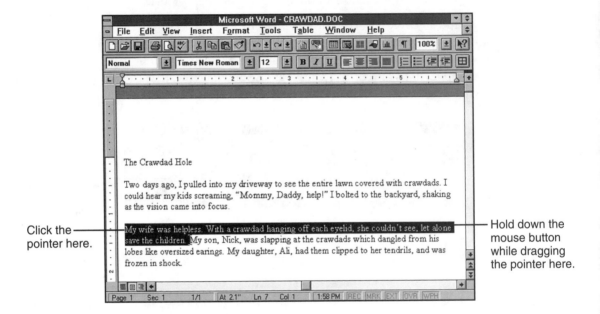

Drag over text to select it.

If you don't have a mouse, selecting text can be slightly less intuitive. Most applications offer several keyboard selection options, such as pressing the F10 key to select a paragraph or Alt+F4 to anchor the highlight so you can "stretch" the highlight over the desired selection using the arrow keys. In most Microsoft applications, you can hold down the Shift key and use the arrow keys to stretch the highlight, or Ctrl+Shift and the arrow keys to stretch the highlight over entire words.

Chopping, Copying, and Pasting

What's cool about electronic documents is that you can juggle the content. Don't like a particular sentence? Snip—it's gone. Want to move a paragraph from page four to page 20? Select it, cut it, and plop it down on page 20. The application takes care of adjusting any surrounding text and reestablishing page breaks. The procedure for cutting and pasting text is fairly standard:

1. Select the text that you want to move or copy.

2. Open the **Edit** menu.

3. To move the text, select **Cut**. To copy the text, select **Copy**. The selection is placed in a temporary holding area in your computer's memory (called the *Clipboard* in Windows).

4. Move the insertion point to where you want the cut or copied data inserted.

5. Open the **Edit** menu and select **Paste**.

> **Shortcuts**
> In most Windows applications, you can bypass the Edit menu by using shortcut keys: **Ctrl+X** for Cut, **Ctrl+C** for Copy, and **Ctrl+V** for Paste.

Oops! Undoing Your Changes

If you happen to vaporize your entire document or lose a few choice words, you may be able to recover. Most applications offer an Undo feature that lets you take back your most recent change. The Undo command is usually on the Edit menu, the same menu that probably got you in trouble in the first place.

Don't rely too much on the Undo feature, though, because most applications save only your most recent change. If you delete two sections of text, you may be able to recover only the second one.

The Least You Need to Know

Although every application requires you to learn a few new commands and techniques, you can usually start creating documents by knowing a few basics:

➤ If you see a cursor or insertion point, you can start typing.

➤ In a word processing application, press **Enter** only at the end of a paragraph or to insert a blank line.

➤ In a graphics or desktop publishing application, you usually have to create a text box before you can type anything.

153

➤ In Overtype mode, you can type over existing text.

➤ The quickest way to select text is to drag over it with the mouse.

➤ The Cut, Copy, and Paste commands (usually on the Edit menu) let you quickly delete and reorganize text.

➤ If you accidentally nuke some text, use the Undo feature to get it back.

Chapter 17

Giving Your Document a Makeover

By the End of This Chapter, You'll Be Able To:

➤ Widen your margins to fill the page length requirement for your next assignment

➤ Control the line spacing within and between paragraphs

➤ Make text big and bold like in newspaper headlines

➤ Make your application number your pages

➤ Use styles to quickly change the look of your text

Plain text just doesn't cut it anymore. People aren't satisfied with a typed page, no matter how ingenious its contents. If it doesn't look like the front page of *USA Today*, they probably won't even pick it up. You need to add some character, some attitude. You need to *format* your text.

Messing with Margins

In most cases, margins are preset at about an inch, which is sufficient for business letters and other standard documents. However, if you're printing a poem, or if you need to stretch a four-page report to five pages, you have to make some adjustments.

Format
To improve the look of your document. Formatting includes changing the margins and line spacing, changing text size and style, adding lines and shading, and numbering the pages.

Margin settings often hide behind the Page Setup command, which is usually on the File menu. If you can't find the margin settings there, look for a similar command on the Format menu. When you find and select the command, you should get a dialog box that prompts you to enter new settings for the left, right, top, and bottom margins. Double-click inside the text box whose setting you want to change, and enter your change.

Another way to set margins is to choose the Print Preview command, available in most applications (try the File menu). This displays an aerial view of the page. Drag the margin markers to where you want the new margins placed.

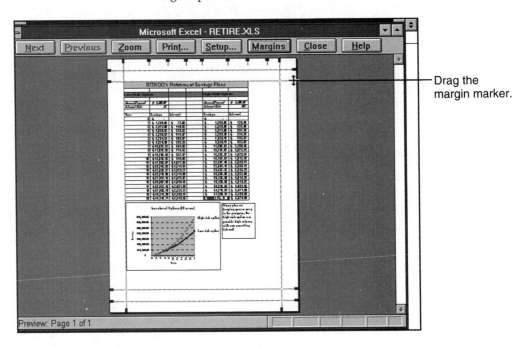

Drag the margin marker.

Use Print Preview to set your margins.

Primping Your Paragraphs

It's tempting to do most of your paragraph formatting with the two universal formatting keys: the Spacebar and the Enter key. Double-space? No problem, just hit Enter twice at the end of each line. Need to indent a paragraph? Just press the Spacebar five times. The trouble with this approach is that it's sloppy, it makes it difficult to adjust text later, and people will laugh at you.

Word processors come with special paragraph formatting commands. To format an existing paragraph, click inside the paragraph first; to format several paragraphs, select them. In most applications, you enter the **Format Paragraph** command, and you get a dialog box that allows you to enter all your preferences:

Line spacing   You can single-space, double-space, or select a fraction (for example, 1.5 for a line and a half). In addition, you can specify the amount of space between this paragraph and the next one. For example, you can single-space the lines within a paragraph, and double-space between paragraphs.

Indents   Normally, you indent the first line of each paragraph five spaces from the left margin. However, you can also indent the right side of a paragraph, or set a long quote off by indenting both sides. In addition, you can create a *hanging indent* for bulleted or numbered lists.

Alignment   You can have text left-aligned (as normal), centered, right-aligned (pushed against the right margin), or fully justified (spread between margins as in newspaper columns).

Tab settings   Tab stops are typically set at every five spaces, so whenever you press the **Tab** key, the cursor moves five spaces to the right. You can change the tab stop position and *type*. The tab stop type determines how the text is aligned on the tab stop, as shown on the next page.

Gutter Margin
Some applications let you enter a setting for the **gutter margin**. Use this setting only if you intend to bind the pages in a book. The gutter margin adds space to the right side of left-hand pages, and to the left side of right-hand pages.

157

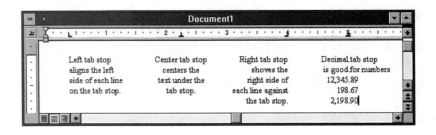

Different tab stop types.

Giving Your Characters More Character

Coloring Your Text
As the price of color inkjet and laser printers plummets, more and more people are adding color to their documents. And most applications make it just as easy to change colors as it is to change your socks; perform the same steps you would perform to change fonts, and then select the desired color from a list.

To emphasize key words and phrases, many word processing programs let you select from various fonts and typestyles. In other words, you can make the letters look big and fancy like in a magazine.

So, what's a font? A *font* is any set of characters of the same *typeface* (design) and *type size* (measured in points). For example, Helvetica 12-point is a font; Helvetica is the typeface, and 12-point is the size. (Just for reference, there are 72 points in an inch.) A *typestyle* is any variation that enhances the existing font. For example, boldface, italics, and underlining are all typestyles; the character's design and size stay the same, but an aspect of the type is changed.

To change fonts or typestyles, you select the text you want to change, and then enter the **Format Fonts** command. This opens a dialog box that allows you to select the typeface, size, and typestyles you want to use.

Cell Formatting in Tables and Spreadsheets

Spreadsheets and tables have additional formatting needs. Not only can you change the fonts and text color for your entries, but you can also add lines and shading to the cells, and display values as dollar amounts or percents. The following list provides a rundown of the most common table and spreadsheet formatting options.

➤ **Alignment:** You usually want labels aligned left within a cell. Dollar amounts are usually aligned along the decimal points.

➤ **Lines and shading:** You can add lines around the cells to help mark rows and columns.

158

➤ **Column width and row height:** If a column isn't wide enough for your entries, the spreadsheet might cut off the entry or display a value as a series of asterisks (*******). When this happens, you have to widen the column. You can usually do this by dragging the right side of the letter box that appears at the top of the column.

➤ **Value formatting:** When you type a number in a spreadsheet, it usually appears as a plain number (without a dollar sign or percent sign). To display these signs, select a value format.

Right-Click for Formatting Options
Most new applications support the right mouse button. Drag over the text you want to format, and then right-click on the selected text. If you get a pop-up menu, you're in business. Select the desired format option, and enter your preferences.

Quick Formatting with Rulers and Toolbars

To give you quick access to commonly used formatting tools, applications typically provide a formatting toolbar near the top of the screen. To apply a format, select the text you want the format to affect, and then click on the **format** button or select the desired setting from a list. On-screen rulers help you quickly indent text and change margins and tab stop settings.

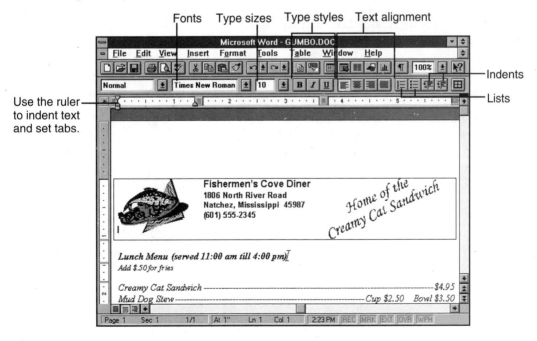

The formatting toolbar gives quick access to common formats.

Topping It Off with Headers and Footers

Long documents often need some text that repeats at the top or bottom of every page. This text may include the document's title, a chapter name and number, and the page number. You can add such text in the form of *headers* (printed at the top of every page) or *footers* (which appear at the bottom).

Don't count on finding the Header or Footer command on the Format menu or even on the Insert menu. Different applications have different hiding places for these commands. In Microsoft Word 6.0 for Windows, the command is on the View menu.

When you enter the command, you usually get some sort of text box that allows you to type the text that you want to appear in the header or footer. In addition, you can enter special codes for inserting the date or page numbers.

Saving Time with Styles

Formatting is probably one of the most time-consuming and frustrating parts of making documents. You may spend hours tweaking your design before it looks just right, and when you're done, you don't want to put on a repeat performance. Because of this, applications allow you to save your format settings and quickly apply them to other text in other documents. You do this with *styles*.

You are creating a book and each chapter title is to be set in 24-point New Century Schoolbook font, set in italic, and centered. Rather than change the font, style, point size, and indentation each time you type a chapter title, you can create a style called Chapter Title. This style would contain all the specified format settings. The next time you need to format a chapter title, you highlight the chapter title and choose the Chapter Title style.

The biggest advantage of using styles is that you can quickly change the formatting of all the text formatted with a particular style. Suppose (in the preceding example) that you decide the chapter title should be larger, say 36-point type. Because you formatted all the chapter titles with the Chapter Title style, you can edit the style's definition, changing the point size from 24 to 36. This changes all the chapter titles that were formatted with the Chapter Title style to 36-point type.

The Least You Need to Know

Although all applications handle formatting a little differently, you can usually get by with a few basics:

➤ To format new text, enter your format preferences, and then type the text.

➤ To format existing text, select the text before entering your preferences.

➤ In most applications, use the **File, Page Setup** command to set the page margins.

➤ You can set the margins for individual paragraphs by using indents.

➤ Most applications have a format toolbar you can use to quickly apply formatting.

Chapter 18

Saving, Closing, and Opening Files

By the End of This Chapter, You'll Be Able To:

➤ Save what you've been typing

➤ Give your files legal names

➤ List five reasons why DOS may refuse to save a file

➤ Open a saved file

➤ Dig up a misplaced file

As you smugly type away, your thoughts dancing across the screen, the computer stores your priceless creations in a very tentative area: RAM. If a squirrel fries himself on your power line, or someone trips the circuit breaker by running the toaster and microwave at the same time, your data is history. Why? Because RAM stores data electronically; no electricity, no data. That's why it's important to save your work to a disk—a permanent storage area.

File
A collection of information stored as a single unit on a disk. Each file has a name that identifies it.

There's a First Time for Everything

The first time you save a file, your application asks for two things: the name you want to give the file and the name of the drive and directory where you want the file stored. Here's the standard operating procedure for saving files in most applications:

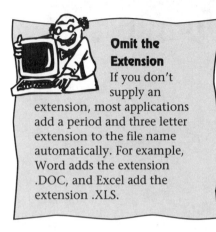

Omit the Extension
If you don't supply an extension, most applications add a period and three letter extension to the file name automatically. For example, Word adds the extension .DOC, and Excel add the extension .XLS.

1. To save the file to a floppy disk, insert a formatted disk into the floppy disk drive. (Make sure the disk is not write-protected.)

2. Open the **File** menu and select the **Save** command. A dialog box appears asking you to name the file.

3. Inside the **File Name** text box, type a name for the file, up to eight characters (skip ahead to the section called "File Name Rules and Regulations" for more information).

4. If desired, select the drive and directory where you want the file saved. If you don't specify a directory, the application picks a directory for you. To pick a drive and directory:

Click on the arrow to the right of the **Drives** list, and then click on the letter of the desired drive.

In the **Directories** list, double-click on the desired directory. (To move up the directory tree, double-click on the drive letter or directory name at the top of the list.)

5. Click on the **OK** button. The file is saved to disk.

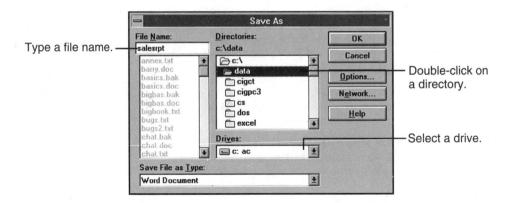

The Save As dialog box asks you to name the file.

From now on, saving this file is easy; you don't have to name it or tell DOS where to put it. The application saves your changes in the file you created and named. You should save your file every five to ten minutes, to avoid losing any work. In most applications, you can quickly save a file by pressing **Ctrl+S**.

When you save a file, most applications create a backup file (usually using the same name but adding the .BAK extension). The new version of the file (the one with your changes) replaces the old version; the old version then becomes the .BAK file. If you really mess up a file and save it, you can open the .BAK file and use it to restore your file to its original condition (before you messed it up).

When There Is No Fancy Directory Tree

With some DOS applications, you won't get a dialog box that lets you select a drive and directory from a list. You may simply be prompted to name the file. In such a case, if you want to save the file to a particular drive and directory, you must type a complete path. Following are some examples:

a:sales.rpt saves the file called SALES.RPT to the disk in drive A. (Make sure there's a disk in drive A first.)

c:\sales\1993\salefigs.xls saves a file called SALEFIGS.XLS to drive C in the \SALES\1993 subdirectory.

d:\personal\bookidea.doc saves a file called BOOKIDEA.DOC to drive D in the \PERSONAL directory.

Directory Must Exist
You can save a file only to a directory that already exists. You can use the DOS MD (Make Directory) command or the Windows File Manager to make a directory. See Chapter 21, "Making and Deleting Directories," for details.

File Name Rules and Regulations

When Windows 95 arrives, you'll be able to give your files just about any name you can dream up: everything from LETTER.DOC to "Who came up with these numbers?!" Until then, DOS has some rules you have to follow:

➤ A file name consists of a *base name* (up to eight characters) and an optional *extension* (up to three characters), for example, CHAPTER9.DOC.

➤ The base name and extension must be separated by a period.

➤ You cannot use any of the following characters:

" . / \ [ ] : * < > | + ; , ? space

(You can use the period to separate the base name and extension, but nowhere else.)

➤ Although you cannot use spaces, you can be tricky and use the underline character (_) to represent a space.

What D'Ya Mean, Can't Save File?!

Occasionally, your application may refuse to save a file, rarely telling you what you're doing wrong. It could be something simple such as a mistyped file name, or maybe the disk is so packed it can't store another file. If you get a cryptic error message, use the following list to decipher it:

Invalid file name   Retype the file name following the DOS file name rules given earlier.

Invalid drive or directory   You probably tried to save the file to a drive or directory that does not exist. Save the file to an existing directory, or create the directory before trying to save to it. If you are trying to save the file to a floppy disk, make sure there is a formatted disk in the drive.

Error writing to device   You tried to save the file to a drive that does not exist or to a floppy drive that has no disk in it. Make sure you've typed the correct drive letter. If saving to a floppy disk, make sure there is a formatted disk in the drive and that the disk is not write-protected.

Disk full   The file you're trying to save is too big for the free space that's available on the disk. Save the file to a different disk, or delete some files from the disk you're using.

Closing Up Shop

When you're done with a file, you should close it. This takes it out of your computer's memory (RAM), making that space available for other files and applications. Before closing a file, save it one last time; open the **File** menu and select **Save**. To close a file in most applications, open the **File** menu and select **Close**. In Windows applications, you can close a file by double-clicking inside the document window's **Control-menu box**.

Most applications have a safety net that prevents you from nuking your files by mistake. When you choose to exit such applications, they ask you if you want to save the changes to your files. Once you've given your okay (or choose not to save your changes), the application closes itself down. The worst thing you can do to your data is to flip the power off before exiting your applications; doing this is a sure way to lose data.

Opening Saved Files

Saved files are essentially stapled to your disk drive. They stay there, waiting to be called into action. To open the file, here's what you do:

> **Two Control-Menu Boxes**
> Don't confuse the document window's Control-menu box with the application window's Control-menu box. Double-clicking on the document window's Control-menu box closes the file. Double-clicking on the application window's Control-menu box exits the application.

1. Run the application you used to create the file. (Most applications allow you to open files that were created using other applications, too.)

2. If the file you want to open is on a floppy disk, insert the disk into the drive.

3. Open the **File** menu and select **Open**. (If you are using a DOS application, the command may be different.) A dialog box appears, asking you to specify the name and location of the file you want to open.

4. Click on the arrow to the right of the **Drives** list, and then click on the letter of the drive where the file is stored.

5. In the **Directories** list, double-click on the desired directory. (To move up the directory tree, double-click on the drive letter or directory name at the top of the list.)

6. To view the names of only those files that end with a specific extension, click on the arrow to the right of the **List Files of Type** list, and then click on the desired file type. The application displays a list of files.

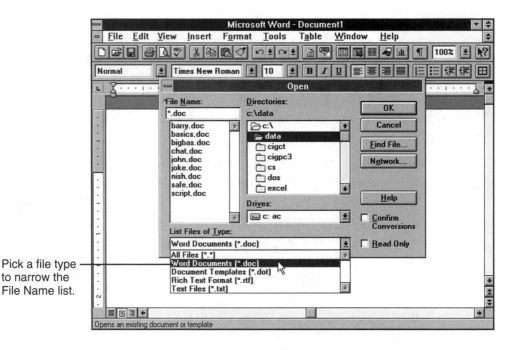

Pick a file type to narrow the File Name list.

Select the drive, directory, and name of the file you want to open.

Can't Find the File?

If your file doesn't show its face, chances are that the file is on a different drive or directory than you think it's on. Use the drive list and directory tree to poke around for it. Try looking in the directory where the application's program files are stored. If you still can't find the file, skip ahead to Chapter 22, "Copying, Moving, and Deleting Files," for some advanced file-finding tactics.

7. Click on the desired file in the **File Name** list, or type its name in the **File Name** text box.

8. Click on the **OK** button. The application opens the file and displays its contents on-screen.

Windows applications commonly add the names of the most recently opened files to the bottom of the File menu. To open one of these files, open the **File** menu and click on the file's name.

168

The Least You Need to Know

Assuming you don't encounter any error messages and your files don't get lost in the directory tree, working with files is fairly easy:

➤ Always save your work before exiting an application or turning off the power.

➤ To save a file, open the **File** menu and select **Save**.

➤ Legal file names start with up to eight characters followed by a period and an extension of up to three characters.

➤ In general, use only letters and numbers in a file name. Never use spaces.

➤ To close a file, open the application's **File** menu and select **Close**.

➤ In most applications, you can open a file by selecting **Open** from the **File** menu.

Chapter 19

Printing Your Creations

By the End of This Chapter, You'll Be Able To:

➤ Tell your application which printer to use

➤ Figure out what all the lights on your printer are for

➤ See how easy it is to print (most of the time)

➤ Track down the causes of most printing problems and fix them

➤ Resume printing after you've fixed the problem

When printing goes as planned, nothing is simpler. You open the **File** menu, select **Print**, click on the **OK** button, and then make yourself a pastrami sandwich while the printer spits out your document. However, rarely does a print job proceed without a glitch. You come back with your pastrami sandwich only to find a stack of paper covered with foreign codes, or you get an error message saying the printer's not ready. After hours of cussing and fiddling, you find and correct the problem only to face a new problem: getting your printer back online. In this chapter, you'll learn all you need to know to print glitch-free and recover from the occasional catastrophe.

Installing a Printer Driver

You can't just plug your printer into the printer port and expect it to work with all your applications. No, that would be far too easy. Each application needs a *printer driver* that translates the application's print commands into a language that the printer can understand. When you install an application, its setup utility asks you to select a printer driver and specify where you plugged in the printer:

➤ **Printer make and model.** The setup utility presents a list of the printers you can use. Select your printer from the list. After you select a printer, the program copies the specified printer driver to your hard disk.

➤ **Printer port.** This is the connector at the back of the system unit into which you plug the printer. Most printers connect the LPT1 port. If you're not sure, try LPT1.

Parallel and Serial Printers

All printers are commonly categorized as either *parallel* or *serial*. Parallel printers connect to one of the system unit's parallel printer ports: LPT1 or LPT2. A serial printer connects to the system unit's serial port: COM1, COM2, or COM3. Most people use parallel printers because they're faster; a parallel cable can transfer several instructions at once, whereas a serial cable transfers them one at a time. However, serial communications are more reliable over long distances, so if you need to place the printer far from your system unit (over 20 feet), a serial printer may be a better choice.

Dealing with Unlisted Printers

If you bought a popular printer, such as Epson, Hewlett-Packard, or Canon, you'll probably find your printer in the list of drivers. If you find the manufacturer name, but not the exact make and model number, select the closest driver you can find. For example, if you have an HP DeskJet 520, you might try the HP DeskJet 500 driver (assuming it is in the list).

If you went cheap and bought some off-brand printer, check the documentation that came with the printer to see if it *emulates* (acts like) a more popular brand. Then, select the printer driver for the printer that your printer emulates. In most cases, you also have to pry open a panel on the printer and flip some DIP switches to turn on the emulation. The printer documentation tells you how to get to the switches, which switch you need to flip, and which position it has to be in.

One Printer Driver Serves All (In Windows)

In Windows, all Windows applications use the default printer driver that you selected when you installed Windows. To check which printer driver is currently the default or to select a different default printer driver, here's what you do:

1. Double-click on the **Main** icon in the Windows Program Manager. This opens the Main group window.

2. Double-click on the **Control Panel** icon. The Control Panel window appears.

3. Double-click on the **Printers** icon. The Printers dialog box appears, showing a list of the installed printers.

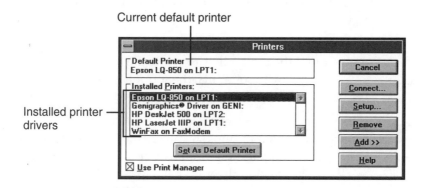

The Printers dialog box.

4. To select a different printer, click on the desired printer driver, and then click on the **Set As Default Printer** button. Be sure to select the correct printer driver for your printer.

5. Click on the **Close** button.

If you get a new printer and you want to install a new printer driver in Windows, display the Printers dialog box, and then click on the **Add** button. After you select your printer from the list, you must insert one of the Windows setup disks in the drive. Make sure you have the disks handy. Sometimes, the printer comes with the Windows printer driver you need, in which case, you use that disk rather than the Windows setup disk.

Where Do Fonts Come From?

Please pardon the following long digression. In Chapter 17, "Giving Your Document a Makeover," you learned a little about how to apply fonts to your text to make the text look happy or sad, big or small, and so on. You can usually style text in this way without giving it much thought. The application, the printer driver, and the printer work out all the details and produce the font you specified.

However, you should know where your fonts are coming from: what makes one font more flexible than another, why some fonts print faster than others, and why your co-worker has more fonts than you do.

Soft Fonts and Printer Fonts

The first font fact is that you usually deal with two types of fonts: printer fonts and soft fonts. *Printer fonts* are built into the printer. Most printers have a set of buttons you can use to pick the font. Printer fonts usually print faster, but they don't give you the variety or flexibility of soft fonts.

Soft fonts are styles and sizes that come with an application. The software (your application or Windows) tells the printer how to create the font. If you style your text with soft fonts, the soft fonts override the printer fonts; so pressing the buttons on the printer won't do any good.

Getting More Soft Fonts
You usually get fonts with every application. If you just can't seem to get enough fonts, you can purchase additional soft fonts. They come on a disk, just like applications.

Several years ago, Windows came out with its own font technology called TrueType fonts. (In Windows applications, font lists display TrueType fonts with a TT next to them.) What makes these fonts so special is that most printers can handle them, and the fonts are *scalable*. That means that you can specify any type size. With unscalable fonts, you can select only those sizes that are listed: for example, you can select 10-point or 12-point, but not 11-point (if it's not listed).

Cartridge Fonts

If you prefer the speed of built-in fonts, but your printer doesn't have the fonts you need, consider purchasing cartridge fonts for your printer. Many printers have one or more cartridge slots into which you can plug a cartridge that has additional fonts or more printer memory (more about printer memory later).

Screening Your Fonts

With some fonts, you have to install two versions of the font: one to control the printing and one to display the font on-screen. In Windows, if a font has no screen font, Windows uses the most similar screen font it can find. One of the advantages of Windows TrueType fonts is that the same font is used for both the printer and the screen.

Advanced Users Only!

In Windows, you can see which fonts are installed by double-clicking on the **Control Panel** icon in the Main group and then on the **Fonts** icon. You can use the dialog box that appears to preview fonts, remove them (they take up disk space and memory), and to add fonts (most installed fonts are in the WINDOWS\SYSTEM directory). Whatever you do, don't remove the font called MS Sans Serif; Windows uses it for menu names and other text it has to display.

Before You Print

You can avoid nine out of ten printing problems by making sure your printer is ready. Is it connected and turned on? Does it have enough paper to finish the job? Is the On Line light lit (not blinking)?

When the On Line light is on, the printer has paper, is turned on, and is ready to print. You can usually make this light come on by filling the printer with paper, and then pressing the On Line button or the Reset button or the Load button... what the heck, press all the buttons.

Printing's Easy... When It Works

Once your printer is installed and online, printing is a snap. Here's what you do in most applications:

1. Open the document you want to print.

2. Open the **File** menu and select **Print**. The Print dialog box appears, prompting you to enter instructions.

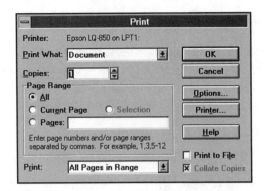

The Print dialog box lets you enter specific instructions.

3. In the Print Range section, select one of the following options:

   All prints the entire document.

   Current Page prints only the page that currently contains the insertion point.

   Selection prints only the selected portion of the document, assuming you dragged over some text before selecting the Print command.

   Pages prints only the specified pages. If you select this option, type entries in the **From** and **To** boxes to specify which pages you want to print.

4. Click on the arrow to the right of the **Print Quality** option, and select the desired quality. (**High** prints sharp but slow. **Low** prints faint but fast.)

5. To print more than one copy of the document, type the desired number of copies in the **Copies** text box.

6. Click on the **OK** button. The application starts printing the document. This could take awhile depending on the document's length and complexity; documents that have lots of pictures take a long time.

7. Go make yourself a pastrami sandwich.

Common Printing Woes (and How to Correct Them)

Although printing usually proceeds trouble-free, you may run into some problems. When that happens, check the following:

➤ **Is the printer turned on, does it have paper, and is the On Line light lit?** I know; I said this before. Humor me and check again.

➤ **Is the printer printing strange symbols?** If so, chances are you picked the wrong printer driver for your printer. The application is sending codes to your printer that your printer does not understand.

➤ **Is the correct printer port selected?** If you just set up your printer and it is not working, maybe you selected the wrong printer port. If your printer is on port LPT2 and LPT1 is selected, the printed document will never reach the correct destination.

➤ **Did you get only part of a page?** Laser printers are weird; they print an entire page at one time, storing the whole page in memory. If the page has a big complex graphic image or lots of fonts, the printer may be able to store only a portion of the page. The best fix is to get more memory for your printer. The quickest fix is to use fewer fonts on the page and try using a less complex graphic image.

➤ **Are you having problems in only one application?** If you can print from other applications, the problem is with the printer setup in the problem application.

➤ **Is it a printer problem?** To determine if the printer has a problem, type **dir > lpt1** at the DOS prompt and press **Enter**. This prints the current directory list. If it prints okay, the problem is in the Windows printer setup or the application's setup. If the directory does not print or prints incorrectly, the problem is probably with the printer.

Oh yeah, there's one more problem you might encounter. I recently came across a Windows CD-ROM application that wouldn't print (even though it had a Print button). The help file contained the convoluted solution: you click on the Print button, and then choose the option to print the file to disk. When you click on OK, Windows asks you to name the file (just as if you were saving it). Then, Windows saves the file as a text file (with the .TXT) extension. You can then open the file in Notepad or Windows Write (or your word processing application) and print it.

Copycat Printer Setup

If you can print from one application but not from another, check the printer setup in the application that's working. Write down the settings and then use the same settings in the application that's giving you trouble.

Try, Try Again

Once you correct the printing problem, you may have another problem: the print job may be waiting in the queue for your final okay. What's a *queue*? It's a waiting line. Applications commonly send printed documents to disk and then feed them from disk to the printer. If something goes wrong, the document has to stand in line until the printer is ready. If you keep entering the Print command over and over, you end up with a long line of documents. Once you've corrected the original problem, you have to deal with the queue.

In Microsoft Windows, a program called Print Manager handles the printing for all your applications. To view the Print Manager's queue, here's what you do:

1. Press **Ctrl+Esc**. The Task List appears, showing the names of all the applications. If documents are waiting in the queue, Print Manager should appear in the list.

2. Click on **Print Manager**.

3. Click on **Switch To**. The Print Manager window appears, showing a list of files waiting in the print queue.

Documents waiting hopelessly to be printed

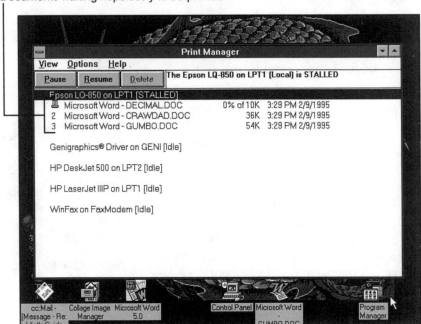

Documents can get backed up in the print queue.

4. Click on the printer you're using. It should be marked **[Stalled]**.

5. Click on the **Resume** button. Printing should start.

If you're working with a DOS application, it probably has its own print queue or *spooler* that handles background printing. Check the documentation to find out what the application calls its queue and where it stores the command to get to it.

The Least You Need to Know

Once your printer is connected and online, you can pretty much forget about it. Until then, brush up on the following printer facts:

➤ Most printers are parallel printers, which connect to the LPT1 port.

➤ When you install an application (or Windows), you have to pick a printer and specify which port it's connected to.

➤ Fonts are typestyles and sizes which are built into the printer or come with the application.

➤ Before you print, make sure your printer is turned on, has plenty of paper, and that the On Line light is lit (not blinking).

➤ To print in most applications, open the **File** menu and select **Print**.

➤ Most applications print the document to a print queue on disk and then feed the document to the printer.

Part 5
Managing Disks, Directories, and Files

*You're a slave to your computer. You install applications where it tells you to.
You save your document files to the default drive and directory, and even when
you stop using a program, you leave its files on your hard drive, afraid that any
deletion will bring your system to a grinding halt.*

*In this Part, you'll learn how to take control of your disks, directories, and files.
You'll learn how to format floppy disks, create your own directories, rearrange
files, and even remove some of the vagrant files that are cluttering your hard disk.
And you'll learn how to do all this in both DOS and Windows.*

Chapter 20

Formatting and Copying Floppy Disks

By the End of This Chapter, You'll Be Able To:

➤ Format brand new floppy disks, so you can store files on them

➤ Figure out what kind of floppy disk drives you have

➤ Reuse a floppy disk

➤ Duplicate disks for fun and profit

In addition to acting as second-rate frisbees and first-rate drink coasters, floppy disks store files and enable you to transfer files from one computer to another. Before you can use them in this capacity, however, you need to know how to format the disks (prepare them to store data) and copy disks.

Making a Floppy Disk Useful

You buy a brand-new box of disks. Can you use them to store information? Maybe. If the disks came preformatted, you can use them right out of the box. If they are not format-ted, you'll have to format them yourself, with the help of DOS.

Formatting divides a disk into small storage areas and creates a *file allocation table* (FAT) on the disk. Whenever you save a file to disk, the parts of the file are saved in one or more of these storage areas. The FAT functions as a classroom seating chart, telling your computer the location of information in all of its storage areas.

Before You Begin

Before you start formatting disks, ask yourself a couple of questions:

What kind of floppy disk drives do I have? What capacity is each disk drive? Is it high-density (1.2MB or 1.44MB) or double-density (360K or 720K)? The documentation that came with your computer will tell you whether you have high- or double-density drives. If you have DOS 6.0 or later, enter **msd** at the DOS prompt; this runs the Microsoft Diagnostics program, which tells you the floppy disk drive types you have.

Format a Disk Only Once
You normally format a disk only once: when it is brand new. If you format a disk that contains data, that data is erased during the formatting process. Before you format a disk, make sure the disk is blank or that it contains data you will never again need.

What kind of floppy disks do I want to format? Do you have high-density or double-density disks? Check the disks or the box in which the disks came.

Why does this matter? There are two reasons. First, you can't format a high-density disk in a double-density disk drive. For example, you cannot format a 1.2MB disk in a 360K drive. Second, you can format a double-density disk in a high-density drive if you tell DOS specifically to do that. For example, you can format a 360K disk in a 1.2MB disk drive if you know what you're doing.

Formatting Diskettes with Windows File Manager

As with most tasks, formatting floppy disks is much easier in Windows than in DOS. In Windows, you simply select the Format command and pick the correct disk capacity from a list. Here's how you do it:

Low-Density Drives Are Rare
If you have a new computer, you can safely assume that you have high-density drives. However, low- or double-density disks are still common.

1. Start Windows and double-click on the **Main** group icon.

2. Double-click on the **File Manager** icon. The File Manager window appears.

3. Insert a blank disk in drive A or B, and close the drive door, if necessary.

4. Open the **Disk** menu and select **Format Disk**. The Format Disk dialog box appears.

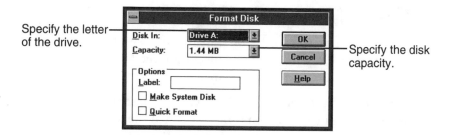

Specify the letter of the drive.

Specify the disk capacity.

The Format Disk dialog box.

5. Click on the arrow to the right of the **Disk In** option, and select the drive that contains the blank disk.

6. Click on the arrow to the right of the **Capacity** option, and select the capacity of the disk.

7. Click on the **OK** button. The Confirm Format Disk dialog box appears, warning you that formatting will erase any data on the disk and asking if you want to proceed.

8. Click on the **Yes** button. File Manager formats the disk. When done, File Manager displays a message asking if you want to format another disk.

9. Click on **No** to quit or **Yes** to format another disk.

> **Disk Capacity, Not Drive Capacity**
> If you are formatting a double-density disk (360K or 720K) in a high-density drive (1.2M or 1.44M), make sure you select the capacity of the *disk*, not the drive.

Using the DOS FORMAT Command

If the DOS prompt is displayed, you can format a disk using the DOS FORMAT command. Insert the new, blank disk you want to format in the floppy drive, and then perform one of the following steps:

➤ **If the disk and drive capacities match**, type **format a:** (if the disk is in drive A) or **format b:** (if the disk is in drive B), and press **Enter**. Follow the instructions that appear on the screen.

➤ **If you're formatting a double-density disk in a high-density drive**, use the /F switch to specify the disk capacity. For example, to format a 360K disk in a 1.2MB drive, type **format a: /f:360** and press **Enter**. To format a 720K disk in a 1.44MB drive, type **format b: /f:720** and press **Enter**.

Reusing Disks Without Losing Data

Once you've formatted a floppy disk, you usually don't have to format it again. If you want to reuse the disk, make sure you no longer need the files it contains, and then delete those files (see Chapter 22, "Copying, Moving, and Deleting Files").

If you start having problems with a disk, you may be able to fix it by reformatting the disk. Perform the same steps given earlier to format the disk in Windows or DOS. Keep in mind that formatting destroys any data on the disk, so if the disk contains files you need, copy those files to another floppy disk or your hard disk before reformatting.

Disk Errors

Several factors may cause disk errors. The read/write head inside the disk drive may go out of alignment over years of use, storage areas on the disk itself might start to go bad, or the data on the disk may have become corrupted by dirt or some magnetic field. If you get disk errors with several floppy disks, have the disk drive repaired or replaced. If you're having trouble with a single disk and reformatting doesn't seem to help, trash the disk.

Copying Disks for Friends and Colleagues

Although illegal, it seems that the main reason people copy floppy disks is to pirate software. For ten bucks, you can make Christmas presents for the entire family! I'm not going to lecture you on the evils of this practice. You know it's wrong. However, I will say that the only reason you *should* copy floppy disks is so you can put the original program disks in a safe place and use the copies for installing and using the program. Having done my duty for the software industry, let us proceed.

Get Some Blank Disks

To copy disks, first obtain a set of blank disks that are the same *size* and *density* as the program disks you want to copy. You can't copy low-density disks to high-density disks or vice versa, and you can't copy a 5.25" disk to a 3.5" disk either. Don't worry about formatting the disks; DOS can format the disks during the copy operation. However, the copying will go faster if the disks are formatted.

Copying Disks with DOS

Once you have the blank disks, making copies is easy (but not very interesting). Here's what you do:

1. Type **diskcopy a: a:** (or **diskcopy b: b:**) and press **Enter**.

2. Insert the original program disk into the drive you specified (A or B), and close the drive door if there is one.

3. Press any key. DOS reads the information from the disk and stores it in memory.

4. When DOS prompts you, insert one of the blank disks in the specified drive and press any key. DOS writes the information stored in memory onto the blank disk.

5. Follow the on-screen messages until you've created a copy of each program disk.

Format Plus Drive Letter

Always follow the FORMAT command with the letter of the drive you want to use. With some versions of DOS, if you enter the FORMAT command without specifying a drive letter, DOS will attempt to format drive C, your computer's hard drive. This could destroy your hard drive data.

Copying Disks with the Windows File Manager

If you have Windows, here's an easier (although equally uninteresting) way to copy disks:

1. Open the **Main** program group window, and double-click on the **File Manager** icon.

2. Insert the original disk into drive A or B, and close the drive door if there is one.

3. Open the **Disk** menu and select **Copy Disk**. If you have two floppy drives, the Copy Disk dialog box appears, asking you to specify the source drive and destination. If you have only one floppy drive, skip to step 7.

4. From the **Source In** list box, select the letter of the drive that contains the original disk.

5. Select the same drive from the **Destination In** list box. (Don't worry, File Manager will tell you to switch disks at the appropriate time.)

6. Click on **OK**. The Confirm Copy Disk dialog box appears.

7. Select **Yes** to continue.

The Double-Drive Copy

If you have two floppy disk drives of the same size and capacity, you can use both drives to speed up the disk copying. Insert the original program disk into drive A and the blank disk into drive B. Type **diskcopy a: b:** and press **Enter**.

187

8. When you are instructed to insert the Source diskette, click on **OK** since you already did this in step 2. The Copying Disk box appears, and the copy process begins.

9. When you are instructed to insert the target disk, remove the original disk from the drive and insert the blank disk. Then click on **OK** to continue. The Copying Disk box disappears when the process is complete.

The Least You Need to Know

Few people use floppy disks anymore. They buy everything on CD-ROM and store all their data on the hard disk. When you can't avoid working with a floppy disk, keep the following important points in mind:

➤ You can't use a new floppy disk until you've formatted it.

➤ Formatting destroys any data on the disk, so avoid reformatting disks.

➤ To format a disk with DOS, insert the disk and type **format a:** or **format b:**.

➤ To format or copy disks in Windows, run File Manager and find the appropriate command on the Disk menu.

➤ Disk copies make great Christmas presents, but they're illegal.

Chapter 21

Making and Deleting Directories

By the End of This Chapter, You'll Be Able To:

➤ List the similarities between a landfill and a hard disk

➤ Jump from directory to directory in DOS and Windows

➤ Make your own directories for storing files

➤ Wipe out entire directories with a single command

➤ Name a directory after your favorite actor

Right now, you may be thinking of your hard disk as a data landfill. Each time you install an application, you can almost hear the dump truck beeping as it backs up to your disk, your hard disk grinding under the added burden. You start to wonder where future generations are going to dump their files.

Without directories, this image might be accurate. However, directories help organize the files into logical groups, making them much easier to find and manage... assuming you know what you're doing.

Climbing the Directory Tree

Before you lay your fingers on any directories, you should understand the basic structure of a directory tree. Shake that landfill analogy out of your mind, and start thinking of

Path
A map to the desired drive and directory. For example, in the figure, the path to the MEGHAN directory is C:\HOME\MEGHAN. Backslashes (\) are used to separate the directory names.

your disk as a big, sterile filing cabinet, stuffed with manila folders. Each folder represents a directory that stores files and/or additional directories.

The structure of a typical hard disk is shown here. The monkey at the top of the tree is the *root directory*; other directories branch off from the root. In the figure, the HOME directory branches off from the root directory (C:\) and includes four *subdirectories*: MEGHAN, RYAN, MEDICAL, and TAXSTUFF. Each of these subdirectories contains files. (And don't ask me why the root is at the *top* of the tree; that's just the way it is.)

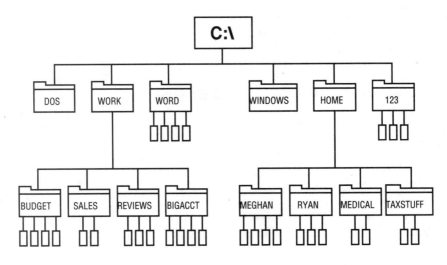

A typical directory tree.

Do-It-Yourself Directories

You rarely have to create your own directories. When you install an application, it usually makes the directories it needs or uses existing directories. However, you will need to make directories for your own data files, so they don't get mixed up with all your program files.

When creating directories, try to follow one rule: *keep it shallow*. If you bury a file eight subdirectories deep, you're going to have to do a lot of digging to get it out. On my drive, I have one directory for everything I do. It's called DATA. Under it, I have a subdirectory for each book I write, a subdirectory for personal files, and a subdirectory for tax records. I go only two levels deep; every file I create is only two directory changes away.

Directory Name Rules

You can't use just any name for a directory. A directory name can consist of up to eight characters and an optional three-character extension (just like a file name). You can use any characters except the following:

" . / \ [ ] : * < > | + ; , ?

Don't use the extension—it'll just complicate things later.

Grafting Directories in Windows

The Windows File Manager is ideal for creating new directories, because it displays a graphic image of the directory tree. Here's what you do:

Floppy Factoid

If you want, you can make directories on a floppy disk, too. Most people choose not to do this, because floppies store so few files.

1. Run Windows, and open the **Main** group window.

2. Double-click on the **File Manager** icon. The File Manager window appears.

3. Hold down the **Shift** key while clicking on the drive letter icon for the drive on which you want the new directory. This displays all the directories and subdirectories on the selected drive.

4. Click on the directory under which you want the new directory or click on the drive letter at the top of the directory tree (to make the directory under the root directory).

5. Pull down the **File** menu and select **Create Directory**. The Create Directory dialog box appears.

6. Type the name of the new directory in the dialog box, and then click on the **OK** button or press **Enter**.

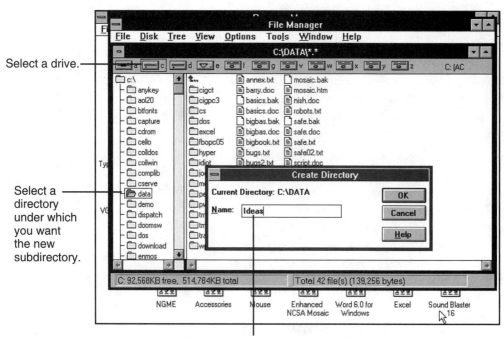

Select a drive.

Select a directory under which you want the new subdirectory.

Type the new directory's name here.

Creating a directory in File Manager.

Making Directories with DOS MD

Making directories with DOS is like trying to get dressed in a dark closet (not that I've ever done that). DOS doesn't display a directory tree, so you pretty much have to know your existing directories' names in order to get the job done. Here, try it:

1. Change to the disk on which you want the new directory. For example, type **c:** and press **Enter**.

Displaying a Directory List
To display a list of directories under the current directory, type **dir /a:d** and press **Enter**.

2. Change to the directory under which you want the new directory. For example, type **cd \dos** and press **Enter** to change to the DOS directory. To create a directory under the root (first) directory, type **cd ** and press **Enter**.

3. Type **md** *dirname* where *dirname* stands for the name of the new directory. For example, type **md mylife** and press **Enter**. DOS creates the new directory, but it won't show you it unless you ask.

192

4. To change to the new directory, type **cd *dirname*** (where ***dirname*** is the name of the new directory) and press **Enter**.

If you ever get really good at this, you can stop using the CD command. Just type something like **md c:\mylife\taxes** and press **Enter**. This creates the subdirectory TAXES under the MYLIFE directory.

Nuking Directories

Directories are like federal spending programs; they're easy to make, but tough to get rid of. In DOS, for example, you have to delete all the files and subdirectories before DOS lets you zap the directory. Once you've done that, you change to the directory that's above the one you want to delete, type **rd *dirname***, and press **Enter**. (Remember to type the directory name in place of ***dirname*.)

The Dangerous DELTREE Command

If you have DOS 6.0 or later, you can delete directories that contain subdirectories or files. Change to the directory above the one you want to delete, type **deltree *dirname***, and press **Enter**. You'll get a warning message; type **Y** to confirm or **N** to cancel.

Windows makes it a little easier to delete directories, but you have to be careful, because Windows will delete directories that contain files. In File Manager, click on the directory you want to delete, and then press the **Del** key (or open the **File** menu and select **Delete**). You'll get a series of confirmation boxes; just follow the instructions and make your picks.

Renaming and Moving Directories (Windows Only)

DOS doesn't offer any easy ways to rename or move directories. You basically have to make a new directory, copy all the files from the old directory to the new one, and then delete the old directory and all its files.

With Windows File Manager, moving a directory is as simple as dragging its icon from one directory to another. Renaming a directory is almost as easy:

1. Click on the icon of the directory you want to rename.

2. Open the **File** menu and select **Rename**.

3. Type a new name for the directory.

4. Click on the **OK** button or press **Enter**.

A Kinder, Gentler DOS (Which You May Not Have)

If you like File Manager, but you're holding out on Windows until the next version comes out, you may have a *DOS Shell*: a file management utility that looks and acts like File Manager. At the DOS prompt, type **dosshell** and press **Enter**. If you get something that looks like this, you're in business.

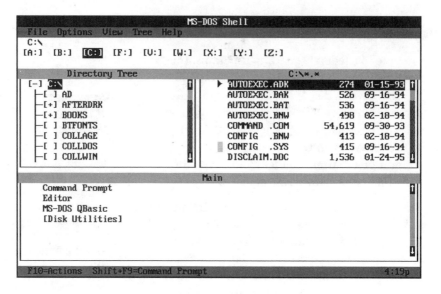

The DOS Shell is File Manager's grandpa.

DOS Shell Last Rites

The DOS Shell was born in version 4.0 and died in version 6.0. According to Microsoft, most users rarely used DOS Shell, so they removed it from DOS versions after 6.0. However, if you upgraded from a version of DOS between 5.0 and 6.0, you still have the DOS Shell. Also, Microsoft will send you the DOS Shell if you have a DOS version after 6.0.

The Least You Need to Know

Consider this chapter basic training for Chapter 26, "Keeping Your Computer in Tip-Top Shape," where you'll use your directory and file management skills to optimize your hard disk. Until then, here are a few of the more important points:

➤ You disk *is* a big data landfill; it's just a little better organized.

➤ Hard disks and CDs typically group files in directories to make them more manageable.

➤ You create directory names the same way as file names, except you don't usually add extensions.

➤ To make a directory in File Manager, open the **File** menu and select **Create Directory**.

➤ To make a directory at the DOS prompt, use the **MD** command.

➤ Use the RD (Remove Directory) command to delete directories at the DOS prompt.

Chapter 22

Copying, Moving, and Deleting Files

By the End of This Chapter, You'll Be Able To:

➤ Pick a peck of files in DOS or Windows

➤ Duplicate files on hard disks or floppies

➤ Move files from one disk or directory to another

➤ Find misplaced files and other interesting relics

To take control of your computer, you have to deal with files. To share a file with someone, you may have to copy it to a floppy disk. To reorganize files, you have to move them to different drives or directories. To do any of these file management tasks, you have to find the files in the first place. If all this sounds fun to you, you probably enjoy whacking your funny bone on your armrest, too. However, these chores are essential if you want to share files and rid your disks of useless trash.

Pick a File, Any File

If you're copying, deleting, or moving a single file, picking a file is about as easy as picking a losing lottery number. In DOS, you just enter the desired command followed by the file's name. In Windows File Manager, you click on the file. If you want to work with a group of files, however, things start to get a little tricky. In the following sections, you'll learn how to handle the complexities.

Using DOS Names and Wild Cards

To select a single file in DOS, you follow a command with the name of the file you want the command to act on. To select multiple files, you use wild-card entries. I'll give you some examples, so you won't have to flip back to Chapter 7:

➤ ***.com** specifies all files whose names end in .COM. This may include WINDOWS.COM, FORMAT.COM, and EDIT.COM.

➤ **chpt??.doc** specifies all files that start with CHPT, have two or fewer additional characters, and end in .DOC. This may include CHPT01.DOC, CHPT14.DOC, and CHPT4.DOC.

➤ **g*.???** specifies all files that start with G and end in three characters or fewer. This may include GO.BAT, GERSHWIN.DOC, GAGGLE.BK, and GLOO.M.

Merely typing a wild-card entry at the DOS prompt won't do anything; you need a command to go with it. For example, you can enter **copy *.com a:** to tell DOS to copy all files that have the .COM extension to the disk in drive A. Later in this chapter, you'll learn more about combining wild-card entries with commands.

Poke and Pick in Windows File Manager

Windows File Manager makes it easy to select one file; you click on it. You would think if you clicked on another file, you'd select that one, too, but it doesn't work that way. Picking another file unpicks the first one. This can be maddening to anyone who doesn't know the tricks for selecting groups of files:

Contiguous
Fancy name for "neighboring." Files that are next to each other in a list are said to be *contiguous*. Neighboring storage areas (sectors) on a disk are also said to be contiguous—not to be confused with "contagious."

➤ To select neighboring files, click on the first file, and then hold down the **Shift** key while clicking on the last file in the group.

➤ To select non-neighboring files, hold down the **Ctrl** key while clicking on the name of each file.

➤ To deselect a file, hold down the **Ctrl** key while clicking on its name.

Shift+click to select a group of neighboring files.

Ctrl+click to select non-neighboring files.

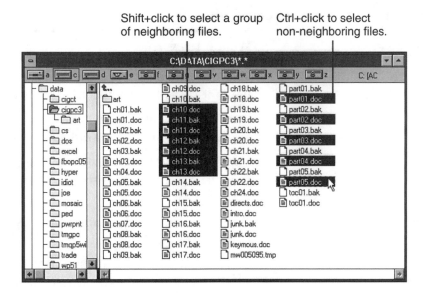

You can select neighboring or non-neighboring files.

If you love working with wild-card entries, File Manager provides that service as well. Change to the drive and directory that contains the files you want to select. Then, open the **File** menu and choose **Select Files**. Type your wild-card entry, click on the **Select** button, and then click on **Close**.

Cloning Files

Your computer moonlights as a high-speed copy machine. Does your friend or colleague need a file? Simply drag it from your disk to a floppy disk. Do you need to modify a file without changing the original? Just copy the file under another name or in a different directory. You can even copy entire drives or directories.

Copying Files at the DOS Prompt

To copy files with DOS, first change to the drive and directory that contain the files you want to copy. Then type **copy** *file1.ext d:\directory*, where *file1.ext* is the name of the file you want to copy, and *d:\directory* is the drive and directory to which you want the file copied. (See the examples listed in Table 22.1.) Press **Enter**. DOS copies the file(s).

Table 22.1 Sample Copy Commands

Command	What It Does
copy *.doc a:	Copies all files that have the .DOC extension from the current directory to the disk in drive A.
copy chap09.doc b:	Copies only the file named CHAP09.DOC from the current directory to the disk in drive B.
copy *.doc c:\samples	Copies all files that have the .DOC extension from the current directory to a directory named C:\SAMPLES.
copy *.* c:\samples\books	Copies all files from the current directory to C:\SAMPLES\BOOKS.
copy chap09.* c:\samples	Copies all files named CHAP09 (CHAP09.DOC, CHAP09.BAK, etc.) from the current directory to C:\SAMPLES.

A quick way to copy a directory and its contents from one drive to another is to use the XCOPY command. For example, to copy all the files and subdirectories of the C:\DATA directory to drive A, you would type **xcopy c:\data a:** and press **Enter**.

Copying Files Using File Manager

The only reason to use DOS to copy files is if you don't have Windows. The Windows File Manager makes copying much easier by laying all the files, disks, and directories on a single desktop. You can then copy files simply by dragging them from the file list to one of the drive or directory icons on the screen. If you are copying the files to a different directory on the same disk, hold down the **Ctrl** key while dragging.

Copy Errors
If you try to copy a file to a drive and directory that contain a file of the same name, you'll get a message asking if you want to replace the file. Before answering yes, make sure the file you are replacing is one you will never need. Otherwise, rename one of the files (as explained later in this chapter) before copying.

When you release the mouse button, File Manager displays a confirmation dialog box. Click on **Yes** to confirm, and File Manager copies the selected files. If the destination contains a file that has the same name and extension as one of the files you are copying, you'll get a warning box that asks if you want to overwrite the existing file. Click on **No** to skip this file and proceed copying the other files, or click on **Yes** to overwrite the existing file with the copy.

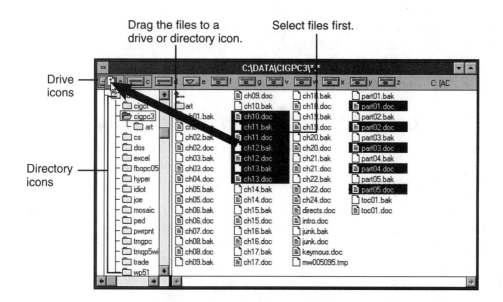

Drag the files to a drive or directory icon.

Select files first.

Drive icons

Directory icons

Drag any one of the selected files to a drive or directory icon.

Some people prefer to create two windows in File Manager and drag the files from one window to the other. To create a new window, double-click on a drive icon; File Manager creates a new window for this drive. Open the **Window** menu and select **Tile** to display both windows. In the source window, select the files you want to copy. In the destination window, change to the drive and directory into which you want the copies placed. Then, drag the files from the source to the destination window.

Giving Your Files New Names and Locations

If you need to place a file in the witness relocation program, you can give it a new name and location. In DOS, you change to the drive and directory that contain the file, and then use the RENAME or REN command followed by the current file name and the new file name or location. For example, you can enter **ren myfile.doc yourfile.doc**. Or if you want to rename and move the file to drive A, you could enter **ren myfile.doc a:yourfile.doc**.

> **Moving the Masses**
> When you need to rename or move a bunch of files, use wild-card entries. For example, you can type **ren *.doc *.old** to change the extension on a group of files from .DOC to .OLD.

201

In File Manager, you move files by dragging them. If you want to move files from one disk to another, hold down the **Shift** key while dragging. To rename a file, click on the file's name, and then open the **File** menu and select **Rename**. Type the new name you want to give the file, and then click on the **OK** button.

Wiping Out Duplicates and Other Useless Files

I'm beginning to think that files procreate. I can't have created all those files that are populating my hard drive; I just don't work that hard. If you get the same feeling about your disks, you may need to do a little housekeeping. Get your shovel, and meet me in File Manager.

Undeleting Files

You may be able to recover accidentally deleted files. In DOS, change to the drive and directory that contained the file, type **undelete**, and press **Enter**. In File Manager, open the **File** menu and select **Undelete**. If these commands are unavailable, you have an early version of DOS that did not offer undelete capabilities.

In Windows File Manager, you delete files by selecting them and pressing the **Del** key (or opening the **File** menu and selecting **Delete**). You'll get one dialog box asking if you're sure you want to delete those files. After confirming, you may get another dialog box asking if you're really, really sure. Just answer to the best of your knowledge. You can turn off the confirmation dialog boxes by opening the **Options** menu, selecting **Confirmation**, and then entering your preferences.

At the DOS prompt, you can delete a file by changing to the drive and directory that contain the file, and entering the DEL command followed by the name of the file you want to delete. For example, you might type **del myfile.doc** and press **Enter**. To delete a group of files, use a wild-card entry; for example, to delete all files with the .BAK extension, enter **del *.bak**.

The Land of the Lost: Finding Files

If you don't have Windows or at least the DOS Shell, finding files is about as easy as finding a snowball in an avalanche. You change drives and directories and dig through directory lists trying to find a familiar name. Good luck.

Both File Manager and the DOS Shell provide file searching tools. (To run the DOS Shell, enter **dosshell** at the prompt.) Open the **File** menu and select **Search**. A dialog box appears, asking for the name of the file you want to find and the drive and directory where you want to search for it. Type the name of the misplaced file, or type a wild-card entry in the Search for text box; for example, you can type **read*.*** to find all the README files on the disk.

In DOS Shell, make sure there is an X in the **Search entire disk** check box; this tells Shell to search all directories on the drive. In File Manager, tab to the Start from text box, and type the letter of the drive you want to search followed by a colon and backslash (for example, c:\). Make sure there is an X in the **Search All Subdirectories** text box. Once you've set your options, click on the **OK** button to begin the search. You'll get a list of files that match your search instructions.

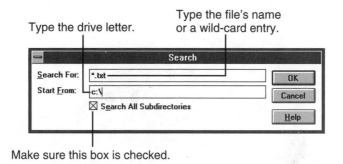

File Manager helps you search for files.

The Least You Need to Know

Now that you can find, copy, move, rename, and delete files, you have all the tools you need to clean house. As you're cleaning and rearranging, you'll keep returning to the basics:

➤ In DOS, use COPY to copy files, DEL to erase them, and REN to rename or move files.

➤ Follow each DOS command with the file name you want it to act on or with a wild-card entry.

➤ To select a file in File Manager, click on it; hold down the **Ctrl** key while clicking on files to select more.

➤ To copy files in File Manager, hold down the **Ctrl** key while dragging any one of the selected files to a drive or directory icon.

➤ To move files in File Manager, hold down the **Shift** key while dragging.

➤ To find files with the DOS Shell or File Manager, open the **File** menu and select **Search**.

Part 6
Reaching Out and Touching Other Computers

How would you like to play a computer game against a friend in another town? Get the latest news, weather, and sports without taking your fingers off the keyboard? Connect to an online encyclopedia, complete with sounds and pictures? Order items from a computerized catalog? Send a letter and have it arrive at its destination in a matter of seconds? Or even transfer files from your computer to a colleague's computer anywhere in the world?

In this Part, you'll learn how to do all this and more. You'll learn how to buy a modem that can keep up with traffic on the Internet (and how to install it). You'll get a taste of the big three online services, and you'll get a quick tour of the Internet. With this section, a modem, and the right software, you'll be well-primed to master the information age.

Chapter 23

Buying, Installing, and Using a Modem

By the End of This Chapter, You'll Be Able To:

➤ Name the three things your computer needs in order to communicate with another computer over the phone lines

➤ Read a modem ad or box and understand what it says

➤ Compare the speeds of two modems and tell which is faster

➤ Figure out which type of software you need to do what you want to do

➤ Hook up an internal or external modem—and get it to work

Okay, I admit it, the section opener was a teaser. I wanted to tell you all the neat stuff you could do with a modem, so you would start thinking that you simply can't live without one. I conveniently left out all the complicated information about shopping for a modem, hooking it up, and figuring out what software you need. Now that I've sucked you in, I'll hit you with the hard stuff.

Shopping for a Modem

Before you start shopping for a modem, you need a brief lesson in modem-ese, the language of modem ads. Do you think I'm exaggerating? Then read the following ad I lifted from my favorite computer catalog:

> **SupraFaxModem V.32bis External**
> The SupraFaxModem V.32bis features 14,400 bps communications with up to 57,600 bps throughput with another modem that supports both V.32bis and V.42bis data compression. And of course, it also maintains downward compatibility with millions of V.32, 2,400, and 1,200 bps modems already in use. With any fax software that supports Class 1 or Class 2 fax commands, you'll be able to send and receive high-quality faxes without ever leaving your desk. Includes a status display with 25 different messages and DOS and Windows software.

If you're in shock, try to calm down. You'll be able to translate this gobbledygook by the time you finish this section. Take it slow, and read on.

Inside or Outside: Internal and External Modems

Motherboard
Inside your computer is the mother of all circuit boards, appropriately called the *motherboard*. This board contains some openings called *expansion slots* that allow you to plug expansion boards into the motherboard. Common expansion boards include sound cards (for speakers), game cards (for joysticks), and controller cards (for hard drives and CD-ROM drives).

Modems come in two types: *internal* and *external*. An internal modem is a board that plugs into an expansion slot inside your computer. To use an internal modem, you must have an open expansion slot on the motherboard inside your computer. An external modem plugs into a *serial port* (a receptacle) on the back of your computer. To use an external modem, you must have an extra serial port; if some other device (such as a mouse) is using the serial port(s), you have to unplug the device or install a board that provides another serial port.

Which is better? Internal modems are less expensive, take up less desk space, and require only one connection (the phone line). If you have an open expansion slot inside your computer, get an internal modem. External modems have a couple advantages: they are easy to install, and most come with indicator lights that show you what the modem is doing (these can help you troubleshoot common problems).

Go Hayes-Compatible

The Hayes modem, made by a company called Hayes Technologies, has set the standard in the modem market. Hayes modems use a set of commands that allow you to tell the modem what you want it to do and how you want it to operate. (For example, to dial the phone number 567-1234, you would enter the Hayes command ATDT followed by the phone number.) This set of commands is called the *Hayes command set*. When a modem is advertised as being Hayes-compatible, it means that it understands Hayes commands. Make sure the modem is Hayes-compatible, or you may have trouble running the more popular telecommunications software.

Get a Speedy Modem

Modems transfer data at different speeds, commonly referred to as *baud rates* or *bits per second*. The higher the baud rate, the faster the modem can transfer data. Common baud rates include the following: 2,400; 9600; 14,400; and 28,800 bps. Although you pay more for a higher baud rate, you save time and decrease your phone bill by purchasing a faster modem. 14,400 bps modems are probably your best buy; you won't want to do the Internet on anything slower.

In the ad at the beginning of the chapter, you may have noticed that the modem was said to be *downward-compatible*. This means that if you connect the 14,400 bps modem with a slower modem (say 2,400 bps), the two modems can still communicate. Most modems are downward-compatible.

Baud and bps, What's the Difference?

Baud is the maximum number of times per second a modem can change the signal it sends. **Bits per second** refers to the number of bits of information transferred per second. A modem may send more than one bit of information for each change in the electrical signal. For example, a modem operating at 300 baud may be transferring at 1,200 bps. So if you are comparison shopping, you would do better to compare rates based on bits per second.

V.32bis, V.42bis, and Throughput

Nothing perks up a modem ad like a list of standards: V.32bis, V.42bis, MNP 2-4. You don't know what these standards represent, but you must have them. To understand the standards, keep in mind that they fall into three categories: modulation, data compression, and error correction. (*Modulation* is a way of sending signals; sort of like AM or FM radio signals, but through the phone lines.) Table 23.1 lists common standards.

Table 23.1 Modem Standards of the Rich and Famous

Category	Standard	What It Does
Modulation	V.22	Transfers up to 1,200 bps
	V.22bis	Transfers up to 2,400 bps
	V.32	Transfers up to 9,600 bps
	V.32bis	Transfers up to 14,400 bps
	V.32terbo	Transfers up to 19,200 bps
	V.Fast	Transfers up to 28,800 bps
Error Correction	MNP 1, 2, 3	Checks for phone line noise and corrects transmission errors
	MNP4	Checks for transmission errors and adapts to phone line conditions
	LAPM	Prevents transmission errors
	V.42	Combines MNP 2, 3, and 4 with LAPM
Data Compression	MNP 5 and 7	Compresses data 2:1
	V.42bis	Compresses data 4:1

Modems that come with data compression are able to squish data before sending it. This allows the modem to send more data per second. Trouble is, both modems (the caller and receiver) must use the same data compression standard in order for it to work. If you know that you'll be communicating with another modem using a specific data compression standard, make sure you get a modem with a matching standard. For online services, you don't need to worry too much about data compression.

Oh yeah, and don't let the term *throughput* confuse you. Throughput is simply a measure of how much data a modem can transfer given its speed and data compression capability. For example, in the ad I mentioned earlier, the throughput was advertised as 57,600 bps. That means that when the modem is operating at maximum speed (14,400 bps) using V.42 data compression, the modem can transfer data at 57,600 bps.

To Fax or Not to Fax?

Some modems, called *fax modems,* come equipped with the added capability either to simply send faxes or to both send and receive faxes. Like fully equipped fax machines, a fax modem allows you to dial a number and transmit pages of text, graphics, and charts to a conventional fax machine, or to another computer that has a fax modem. You can also use the fax modem to receive incoming calls.

Shop carefully. Many fax modems are able only to send faxes, not to receive them. If you want to be able to receive faxes, make sure the fax modem can handle incoming faxes. Also, make sure your modem supports Class 1 and 2 Group III fax machines. Nearly 90 percent of faxes in use today are of the Group III variety.

Voice Support

If you plan on having your computer answer the phone and take messages, make sure the modem offers voice support. Without voice support, your modem can answer the phone, but it can only make annoying screeching noises... which is useful for making tele-marketers back off.

Do You Need Another Phone Jack for the Modem?

If you already have a phone jack near the computer, but your phone is plugged into it, you don't need to install an additional jack. Most modems come with two phone jacks: one that connects the modem to the incoming phone line and another one into which you can plug your phone. When you are not using the modem, you use the phone as you nor-mally would. If your modem doesn't have two phone jacks, you can purchase a split phone connector from an electronics store. The split phone connector allows you to plug both your phone and your mo-dem into the same jack.

If your computer is far from an existing phone jack, get a long phone cable or have an additional phone jack installed. If you're good with a screw-driver and pliers, you can probably do it yourself in less than an hour.

When the Line Is Busy

If your modem and phone are on the same line, your modem will try to answer the phone when it rings. (This drives my wife crazy.) To get around this problem, you can buy a voice/data switch that routes the call to either your computer or your phone. If the incoming call is one of those high-pitched computer squeals, the switch routes the call to the computer. If the call is a normal phone call, your phone rings so you can pick it up and start talking.

Installing a Modem

Modem installation varies depending on whether you are installing an internal or external modem. With an internal modem, you must get under the hood of your PC, plug the modem into an open expansion slot, and plug the modem into the phone jack. If you're a rank beginner, get an experienced person to coach you through it.

Just about anyone can install an external modem. All you have to do is turn off the computer and make the following three connections:

Modem to serial port: Connect the modem to the serial port (usually marked COM) on your computer using a serial cable.

Modem to power source: Plug the modem's power cord into a receptacle on your wall or into your power strip or surge suppressor.

Modem to phone line: Connect the modem to the phone jack. This is just like plugging a phone into a phone jack. (You may also want to connect your phone to the modem, as shown here.)

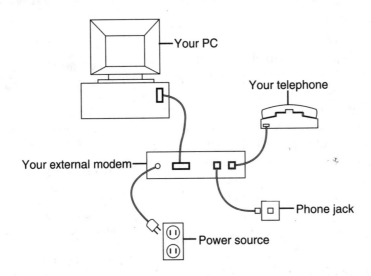

An external modem requires three connections.

Before You Call

Before you begin using your modem, you may need some additional software. To determine what software you need, ask yourself what you want to do with the modem. The following paragraphs describe some of the common uses for a modem and the type of program required for each use.

Online information services: If you want to connect with an online service (such as PRODIGY or America Online), you have to purchase a special program and pay the subscription price to the service. Skip to the next chapter for details.

Games in two-player mode: If you have a game such as Populous that allows you to play games in two-player mode using a modem, the program probably contains all the tools you'll need to play the game over the phone lines. Refer to the user manual that came with the game.

Transfer files between two computers or connect to a bulletin board system: You will need a communications program. Most modems come with a simple communications program. If you have PC Tools, Windows, or some other integrated program, it may come with a communications program. You can also purchase advanced programs such as ProComm Plus.

Remote computing: Say you have a computer at work and one at home. You can purchase a special remote computing program that lets you control your computer at work from your computer at home and vice versa.

Surf the Internet: This is sort of like connecting to an online service. You must find an *Internet service provider* who can connect you to the Internet. The service provider usually equips you with the software you need and any other instructions you need to get started. See Chapter 25, "Test Driving on the Internet."

Bulletin Board System

A bulletin board system (BBS for short) enables a computer to automatically answer the phone when other computers call. The BBS allows the calling computer to copy files to it (*upload* files) and copy files from it (*download* files). Although you can purchase a BBS program to set up your own BBS, most users work with BBSs set up by computer companies and professional associations.

Know Your Telecommunications Settings

If you connect your computer to another computer or to an online service, you must make sure both computers are using the same *communications settings*. Otherwise, errors may result during data transfer. For example, if one modem is talking at 14,400 bps and the other is listening at 2,400 bps, it's likely that some information will get lost. Common communications settings include the following:

Baud rate   The transfer rate can be only as fast as the *slower* of the two modems allows.

COM port   The COM port setting tells the telecommunications program where to look for your modem. (The COM port setting applies only to your computer; the settings do not have to be the same on both computers.) If you get a message saying that the program could not find your modem, try changing the COM port setting.

Parity   Tests the integrity of the data sent and received. Common setting is None or No Parity.

Data bits   Indicates the number of bits in each transmitted character. Common setting is Eight.

Stop bits   Indicates the number of bits used to signal the end of a character. Common setting is One.

Duplex   Tells the computer whether to send and receive data at the same time (Full), or send data or receive data but not both at the same time (Half). Common setting is Full.

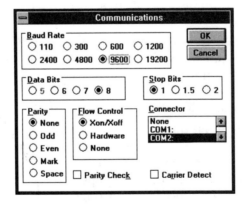

You can change most communications settings using a single dialog box.

The important thing to remember is that the communications settings must be the same on both computers. Once the settings are right, you can enter a command to have the modem call the other computer. The communications program dials the number and establishes the connection between the two computers.

214

What Went Wrong?

Rarely do modem communications proceed error free the first time. Any minor problem or wrong setting can cause a major disruption in the communications between your computer and the remote computer. The following list can help you solve the more common problems:

➤ **"Modem not responding" or "Cannot find modem."** If nothing happens or if your communications program displays a distress signal saying that it cannot find the modem, the COM port setting for the modem may be wrong. First, if you have an external modem, make sure the power is turned on. Then, enter the Modem Settings command, and make sure the correct COM port is selected (usually COM 2). Keep trying to dial with different COM port settings until the modem dials or you run out of COM port settings to try. If you have an internal modem, it has tiny switches that you can flip to give the modem a different COM port setting. Make sure the COM port setting in your communications program matches the COM port setting on your modem.

➤ **Busy signal.** You may not hear it, but if a message appears on-screen saying the lines are busy, the computer you're calling is all tied up with incoming calls. Enter the Hangup command, and try again later.

➤ **Voices from your modem.** You dialed the wrong number. Some poor sap on the other end answered and is wondering who the jerk is who woke him up and refuses to talk. Check the phone number you typed earlier, and pray that this guy doesn't have Caller ID.

➤ **On-screen garbage.** First, check the baud rate setting in your communications program. Make sure the setting matches the fastest setting that both your modem and the service provider can handle. Next, check the terminal emulation to make sure it conforms to the emulation required by the computer you're calling.

➤ **Seeing double.** Both your computer and the remote computer are echoing back what you type. Try turning Local Echo off, so your computer will stop echoing echoing.

➤ **What you type is invisible.** Try turning Local Echo on.

➤ **Single line of text.** Turn on Inbound CR/LF. This tells your computer to place a carriage return after each line of text as it arrives.

➤ **Blank lines between text.** If you get blank lines between what you type, try turning off Outbound CR/LF. If you get blank lines between incoming text, turn off Inbound CR/LF.

The Least You Need to Know

The most difficult aspects of telecommunications are in picking out a good modem and getting it set up. Once you get the modem working for at least one program, the rest is easy. As you struggle, keep the following in mind:

➤ In order for you to use a modem, you need three things: the modem itself, a communications program, and a connection to your phone jack.

➤ The speed at which a modem transfers information is measured in bits per second (bps).

➤ When shopping for a modem, look for one that transfers data at 14,400 bps or faster.

➤ Modems that have fax capabilities can transfer faxes to or from a fax machine or another computer that is equipped with a fax modem.

➤ The telecommunications program you need depends on what you want to do. When you subscribe to an online service, you usually get the program you need in order to connect to the service.

Chapter 24

PRODIGY, CompuServe, and America Online

By the End of This Chapter, You'll Be Able To:

➤ Connect to one of the big-three online services

➤ Pick a local access number (to avoid long-distance charges)

➤ Send and receive mail electronically

➤ Chat live with friends and strangers

➤ Get games, pictures, and other files for free

One of the first things most people do with a modem is connect to one of the big-three online services: PRODIGY, CompuServe, or America Online. When you subscribe to the service (usually for about 10 bucks a month), you get a program that allows you to connect locally to the service (assuming you live near a major town), and you get access to what the service offers. This includes electronic mail, news, research tools, magazines, university courses, and much, much more.

What's the Cost?

What's the price you pay for all of this? When you're shopping for an online service, compare subscription rates and consider the focus of each service. Here's a rundown of the three biggies:

PRODIGY offers two membership plans. The Basic plan gives you five hours of usage per month for $9.95 ($2.95 an hour if you go over that). The Value plan gives you unlimited access to core services (news, weather, sports, and general information) for $14.95 a month, and you get five hours of Plus services (including bulletin boards and chat rooms). Special services (such as travel and financial services) also cost extra. PRODIGY is a family-oriented online service. Call 1-800-PRODIGY for a startup kit.

Canceling Your Membership Online services typically waive the first month's usage fee. If you choose to no longer use the service, be sure you cancel your membership.

America Online charges a flat rate (about $10) for five hours a month, and $3.00 for each additional hour at any time of the day or night. You can send as many e-mail messages as you like. America Online is the online information service for the Me generation. Call 1-800-827-6364 for a startup kit.

CompuServe charges $9.95 for unlimited connect time to many basic services, including news, weather, and business information. Special services cost extra. E-mail charges vary depending on the length of the message and the speed of your modem; however, you can send over 200 pages per month free. CompuServe has traditionally been more technical- and business-oriented.

When you first connect to any of the online services, keep tabs on your phone bill. If you use a modem to call long distance, your friendly neighborhood phone company charges you long-distance rates—so keep this in mind when you are playing with your modem. Most online information services, however, provide you with a local number for connecting to the service. You can then communicate with other people in different states by way of the local connection.

Starting Your Online Account

Extra Charge for Fast Service? Although most services currently charge the same amount for 2,400 and 9,600 bps service, you may have to pay more for a higher speed connection.

When you subscribe to an online service, you get a startup kit that includes the software you need to connect to the service, an account number and password, and documentation that teaches you how to start. You install the software just as you install any new software—by running the installation or setup program on the first disk.

The installation program copies the necessary files to your hard disk and then asks you to specify which COM port and type of modem you are using. Some installations test the COM port and modem settings for you, and simply ask for your confirmation.

The installation program then uses the modem to dial a toll-free number that gives you access to local connections in many cities. By selecting a local number, you avoid long-distance charges. Once you select a local number (and usually an alternate number, in case the first number is busy), the installation program disconnects from the toll-free connection.

Modem speeds

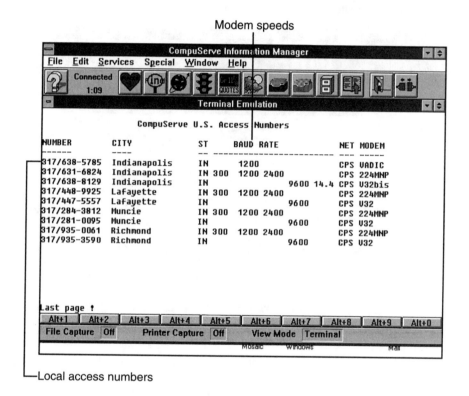

Local access numbers

Search for a city close to you, and then pick your modem's maximum speed.

Connecting for the First Time

Once you have a local number to dial, you can sign on to the service and start using it. To sign on to PRODIGY or America Online, you simply click on an on-screen button. The service dials the local access number and then asks for your screen name (online nickname) and your password. With CompuServe, you must select a feature (for example, News or Mail)

Phone Charges
If you dial a long distance number, or if your phone service charges for local calls, keep in mind that you will be charged for your modem calls just as you are charged for any phone calls.

before you sign on; CompuServe then dials the local access number, connects to the service, and takes you immediately to that feature.

When you are done with the service, you hang up. You usually do this by opening the **File** menu and selecting **Disconnect** or **Exit**.

Button bar offers quick access to several popular services.

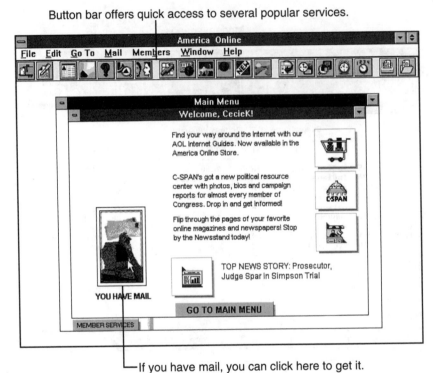

If you have mail, you can click here to get it.

The screen that greets you when you sign on to America Online.

Navigating the Service

Online Help
To get help on America Online, press **Ctrl+K**, type **Help**, and press **Enter** (the Help area is free). On CompuServe, press **Ctrl+G**, type **Practice**, and press **Enter**.

Although each online service offers different tools for moving around in the service, the tools are very similar. Most services display buttons and menus that allow you to use popular features such as mail, news, and games. In addition, you can use keywords to quickly access a feature. For example, on America Online, you can press **Ctrl+K**, type the name of the feature you want to use (**news**, **mail**, **help**), and press **Enter**. On CompuServe, you can use keywords by pressing **Ctrl+G**; and on PRODIGY, you press **F6**.

Postage-Free Mail, Same Day Delivery

How would you like to send a letter and have it reach its destination in less than a minute? With electronic mail (e-mail for short), you can enjoy warp-speed delivery at a fraction of the cost.

To send an e-mail letter, you first enter the Compose Mail command (or its equivalent). This brings up a dialog box that allows you to compose and address your correspondence. Type the e-mail address of the person to whom you want to send the message (this is usually the person's screen name, if he is a member of the same service). Click inside the Description area, and type a brief description of your message. Finally, type your message (or paste it) in the Message area, and then click on the **Send** button. In a matter of seconds (or minutes), the message appears in your friend's mailbox. When your friend connects to the service, your message appears in his mail box.

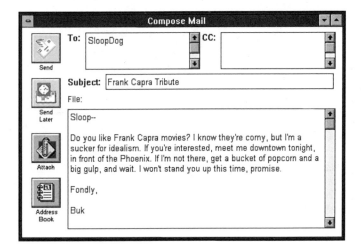

You can send messages electronically.

Everyone (including you) on your online service has an electronic mailbox. Whenever you sign on, the application indicates in some way if you have mail waiting. To get your mail, you enter the **Get Mail** command or click on the **Mail** button. This displays a list of waiting messages. Double-click on the message you want to read. The message appears inside a dialog box, which usually contains a Reply button, allowing you to respond immediately to the message.

Conversing in Chat Rooms

If you don't like waiting for mail, you can converse with your friends and colleagues on the service. You pick a room in which 20 or so people are hanging out and then start typing. Your messages appear on the screens of the other people in the room, and their messages appear on your screen. If you prefer to talk in private with one or more other users, you can create your own private room and invite other users to join you.

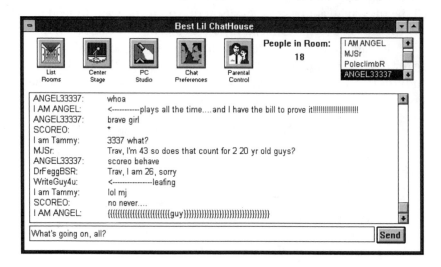

Chat rooms let you converse with other members.

Sharing Common Interests

Sordid Conversations
If you have children who may be using the service, you must be careful with mail and chat rooms. Although most service members attempt to be civil, some members may be a bit unruly.

Online services started as computerized community centers where people could share their ideas, problems, and solutions. This tradition is still alive in online *forums* and *boards*. You can find a forum or board for almost any special interest—from gardening and parenting to computers and automobiles. If you have a question, you simply post a message on the board. In a day or so, other members will post answers in an attempt to help you out. You can get free legal advice, information on how to grow prize roses, and even help finding long lost relatives.

Reading Online Newspapers and Magazines

Electronic publishing is big these days. In addition to publishing paper periodicals, publishers are placing their articles in electronic format on online services. You can get the latest headline news, read popular magazines (such as *Time* and *Newsweek*), and search newspapers and magazines for information on specific topics.

Downloading Files and Programs

Online services contain huge vats of files, offering everything from game files to digitized photographs of members. You can download (copy) any of these files to your computer using your modem. The procedure is fairly simple:

1. Sign on to the service and go to the area that contains the file you want to download. In America Online, you can go to the Download area (the Software Center). In other services, you normally must enter a special interest forum to download files related to that forum.

2. Enter the command to search for a particular file or application. A dialog box usually appears asking you to specify the type of file you want.

Quick Go To Command

Online services commonly offer a keyboard or menu command that allows you to quickly use a specific service. In America Online, you press **Ctrl+K**. In CompuServe, you press **Ctrl+G**. A dialog box prompts you for the name of the service. Type the name (for example, **encyclopedia** or **news**), and press **Enter**.

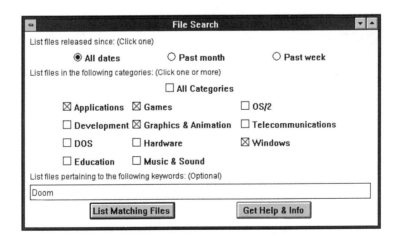

Specify the desired file or application type.

3. Follow the on-screen instructions or prompts to find the file you want to download.

4. Select the file, and then enter the command to download the file. A dialog box usually appears, prompting you to specify a name and a drive and directory for the file.

5. Enter the requested information, and press **Enter**. The service sends the file to your computer and stores it in the specified drive and directory. This could take minutes or hours depending on the file size and modem speed.

Other Compression Programs

PKZip is one of the most pop-ular compression programs on the market, but it's not the only one. A different compression program may have been used. If that's the case, you can usually download that compression program (and the documentation for using it) from your service.

Nabbing the file is only half the story. You may have to download additional files in order to work with the file you just downloaded. For example, if you downloaded a picture of your friend, and the file's name ends in .GIF, you need a GIF viewer in order to display the picture on your screen. You can usually find the file you need using the same techniques just described.

You may also encounter compressed *(zipped)* files that end in .ZIP. Services commonly store large files in a compressed format, so the files take up less space and require less time to download. If you find one of these files, you'll need a program called PKZip to decompress the file and make it usable. You can usually download this file from the same service where you obtained the .ZIP file.

Decompressing a .ZIP File

To decompress a .ZIP file, first copy the .ZIP file and the file PKUNZIP.EXE to a directory on your hard disk. Change to the drive and directory that contains the .ZIP file. Type **pkunzip** *filename***.zip** (where *filename* is the name of the zipped file) and press **Enter**. PKUnzip decompresses the file. Delete the .ZIP file from your hard disk so it doesn't take up disk space.

Decompressing Self-Extracting .ZIP Files

PKZip can also create self-extracting .ZIP files that have the .EXE extension. You simply copy the file to an empty directory and then run it; it decompresses itself. You can then delete the .EXE file from your hard drive.

How can you tell if the .EXE file is a zipped file? You can't until you try to run it. If you run it, and it shows on-screen that it is unzipping itself, you just hit pay dirt. If not, you haven't hurt anything. Give it a shot.

Internet Access

You'll learn all about the Internet in the next chapter. However, before you leave, you should know that most online services offer limited access to some Internet features. Although you won't experience the full, intimidating effect of the Internet, online services give you a good first encounter.

The Least You Need to Know

Okay, you've read enough. Now, get hold of a couple free online trial membership kits, and get connected. As you're cruising your online service, be sure you try everything:

➤ Send an e-mail message to a friend or colleague.

➤ Visit a chat room.

➤ Check out a board or forum.

➤ Find the hourly news service.

➤ Read a couple articles from online magazines.

➤ Download a file or two.

➤ Check out the Internet access.

Chapter 25

Test Driving on the Internet

By the End of This Chapter, You'll Be Able To:

➤ Describe the Internet in 25 words or less

➤ Name three ways you can connect to the Internet

➤ Poke around in computers all over the world

➤ View pictures, movies, and sounds

➤ Get free legal and financial advice

➤ Write a complete sentence using only Internet acronyms

Unless you've set up permanent residence in the New York subway, you've probably heard the terms *Internet* and *information superhighway* (which are basically the same thing). The Internet is a massive computer network connecting thousands of computers all over the world, including computers at universities, libraries, businesses, government agencies, and research facilities.

By connecting to the Internet, you can tap many of the resources stored on these computers. You can copy files from them, use their programs, send and receive electronic mail (*e-mail*), chat with other people by typing messages back and forth, get information about millions of topics, shop electronic malls, and even search for a job or a compatible mate.

Finding an Entrance Ramp

Before you can navigate the Internet, you have to find an entrance ramp—a way onto the Internet. You have several options:

E-mail gateway   Most online services (America Online, PRODIGY, and so on) provide an Internet connection called a mail gateway, which allows you to send and receive electronic mail. When you send mail, you type your letter and then enter the person's online mail address. You'll learn about Internet e-mail addresses later.

Internet Quick Start
To quickly connect to the Internet, get *The Complete Idiot's Guide to Internet for Windows* or *The Complete Idiot's Guide to the Internet.* These books come with the software and information you need to connect to the Internet and tap its resources. You won't even have to shop around for an Internet service provider.

Online service connection   Most online services are currently developing ways to connect their subscribers directly to the Internet to offer more than just e-mail. These services provide the tools you need to easily navigate the Internet. However, because most services currently support 9,600bps and slower connections, this type of Internet access is slow.

Permanent connection   If your company or university has a network that is part of the Internet, and your computer is connected to the network, you have access to the Internet through the network. This is the least expensive (and fastest) way to go. Your network administrator can tell you if you're connected.

Internet service provider   One of the most practical ways to connect to the Internet is through a service provider. For a monthly (or hourly) fee, you use your modem to connect to the service provider's computer, which is hooked into the Internet.

What to Expect

To sign onto the Internet, you typically use your modem to dial the phone number of your Internet connection. The process for navigating the Internet depends on the connection you have. If you use a typical online service, it probably offers several Internet tools for sending mail and doing research.

If you connect through an Internet service provider, there's no telling what you'll get. With some connections (called *terminal connections*), you get a texty-menu that lists your options. With other services, you get a bushel full of programs for using various Internet features; for example, you may get an e-mail program, Web browser (more about this later), an FTP program (for grabbing files), and a newsgroup reader (for reading messages in special interest areas). Each program has a unique look and feel, because each program deals with a different aspect of the Internet. You'll learn about these programs in the following sections.

Browsing the World Wide Web

The easiest way to do the Internet is to connect through the World Wide Web. The Web is a collection of "documents" stored on computers all over the world. Each computer that has Web documents is called a *Web server*; it serves up the documents to you and other users on request.

What makes these documents unique is that each document contains a link to other documents contained on the same Web server or on a different Web server (down the block or overseas). You can hop around from document to document, from Web server to Web server, from continent to continent, with a click of a button.

And when I say "document," I don't mean some dusty old text document like you'd find in the university library. These documents often contain pictures, sounds, and even video clips. When you click on one of these multimedia links, your modem pulls the file into your computer, where another (*helper*) application "plays" the file. All you have to do is tilt your chair back, nibble on popcorn, and watch the show.

Server
In the politically incorrect world of the Internet, the server is the computer that serves up all the data. The other computer, the **client** (your computer), acts as a customer, demanding specific information and complaining about the prices and service.

Click on a hyperlink to follow the trail.

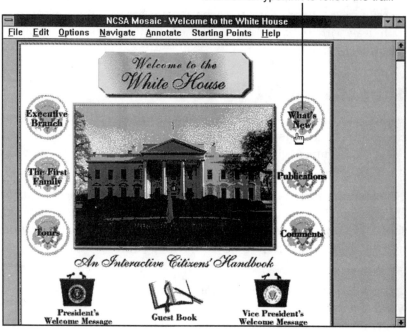

A Web document with hyperlinks.

To do the Web, you need a special program called a *Web browser*, which works through your service provider to pull documents up on your screen. You can choose from any of several Web browsers, including Mosaic, Netscape, Cello, and (my personal favorite) InternetWorks. You also need the *helper applications* that play the picture, sound, and movie files. Your service provider usually supplies a free Web browser and shareware helper application to get you started.

Doing Electronic Mail

Because the Internet connects computers all over the world, it's ideal for transmitting messages electronically. You can sit in front of your computer and jot notes to your friends across town, across the country, or in exotic foreign lands. And these messages arrive in a matter of minutes or hours rather than days.

The procedure for sending messages over the Internet varies, depending on the e-mail program or online service you're using. In most cases, however, you get a dialog box that asks you to enter the person's e-mail address, a description of the message, and the message itself.

The e-mail address typically consists of two parts: the person's *login name* and *domain name*. For example, Bill Clinton's e-mail address is **president@whitehouse.gov**. The login name is the name that the person uses to connect to the Internet (for example, **president**). The domain name is the address of the computer the person connects through (for example, **whitehouse.gov**). Type the address in all lowercase characters, and use an @ sign to separate the login and domain names.

If you're sending messages from a commercial online service such as PRODIGY or America Online, you have to specify that the message is going to someone outside the service. For example, on CompuServe, you type **INTERNET:** before the e-mail address. If you sent a message from CompuServe to a member of America Online, the address might look something like this:

      INTERNET: jsmith@aol.com.

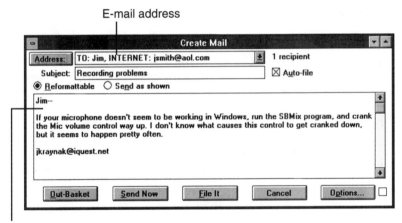

Sending mail with a typical Internet e-mail program.

Sharing Interests in Newsgroups

A *newsgroup* is a discussion group, an electronic bulletin board on which users exchange messages. For example, you can post a message on a body-art newsgroup asking the best way to remove the tattoo of your ex's name from your left biceps. Another user (more experienced in such matters) will read your message and post a reply, which you can then read.

Reading on the Web

If you have a Web browser, you can use it to read newsgroup postings. However, most Web browsers do not allow you to post your own messages. You need a specialized newsgroup reader to do that.

The Internet supports over 10,000 newsgroups covering everything from gardening to desktop publishing. Whatever your interest, you can find a newsgroup (maybe three or four) where you can swap information with others.

To read newsgroup postings (and post your own messages), you need a newsgroup reader. When you connect to the Internet with the reader, it displays the names of all the newsgroups your service provider subscribes to. After you pick a newsgroup, the reader displays a list of recent postings from which you can choose.

Fetching Files with FTP

When the Internet started out, it wasn't much more than a gigantic file warehouse. Businesses and individuals stored files on various Internet servers, where other people could come and copy (download) those files. It was like a huge swap meet for computer nerds.

As the Internet grew and diversified, it had to assign specific jobs to different servers. World Wide Web servers were given the task of storing hyperdocuments, newsgroups were set up to act as bulletin boards, and FTP servers became the file warehouses. What does this have to do with you? You can connect to many public-access FTP servers and copy programs, text files, graphics, and anything else that can be stored electronically.

FTP

Short for *File Transfer Protocol*, FTP is a set of rules that governs the transfer of files between computers. True nerds use this acronym as a verb. For example, "You can ftp to the NSCA site and download the latest Mosaic."

As with most Internet sites, you can access FTP sites most easily by using a Web browser. When you connect to the site, you get a list of files and directories that are displayed as links. To grab a file, you usually have to turn on the browser's **Load to Disk** option, and then click on the link.

If the Web browser idea doesn't appeal to you, you can use a special FTP program to transfer files. These programs are usually set up something like the Windows File Manager, allowing you to copy files by dragging them from one window to another.

Using Gopher Menus to Navigate

Gopher is an indexing system that enables you to access various Internet services through menus. Whenever you connect to a Gopher site, it presents you with an opening menu. When you select a menu item, the server presents you with *another* menu containing additional options and/or files. These options may send you off to another Gopher site, an FTP site, a newsgroup, or other Internet sites. You proceed through the menus until you find the file or information you want—or reach a dead end.

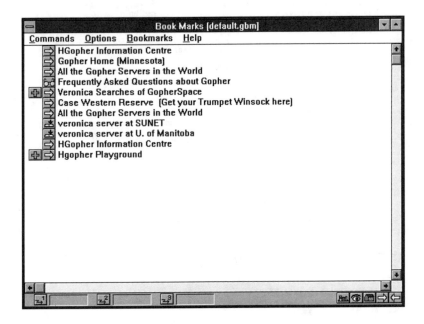

Gopher lets you surf the Internet using menus.

Telnetting (When Your Computer Just Isn't Enough)

Have you ever tried using someone else's computer? You never know what you're going to find. Maybe a menu system, maybe some fancy graphical interface such as Norton Desktop. Maybe you even get... horror of horrors... a DOS prompt! That's sort of what telnetting is like. You connect to another computer, and you enter commands just as if you were sitting at its keyboard. However, you're never sure what you're going to encounter: a texty menu system, a prompt, or a spiteful warning explaining what will happen to you if you go any further.

With most telnet sites, you can log in as a guest. The site then displays a crude menu system that allows you to ferret out the information you're looking for.

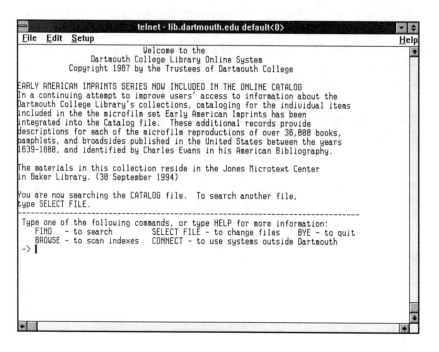

Telnetting lets you use other computers.

Searching with WAIS

If you have a research project, the last thing you want to do is wander the Web or follow a trail of menus through Gopher. You've nailed down the subject, and now you want some specific information. The best tool for you at this point is WAIS.

WAIS (pronounced "ways") stands for *Wide Area Information Server.* WAIS is a system that allows you to search various databases on the Internet for specific articles and other resources. For example, you can connect to a WAIS server and find a list of 500 or more databases for everything from stocks to cooking. You pick the database you want to search, and type your subject title or other unique search text. WAIS finds the articles and other resources that match your entry and lets you know where you can find them. In most cases, you can even view the articles immediately.

The Least You Need to Know

This chapter provides a mere smattering of what you'll find on the Internet. To experience this vast resource for yourself, get a fast modem and an Internet connection, and start playing. Here are some tips to get you started:

➤ Use a 14,400 bps or faster modem.

➤ Try the World Wide Web first; you can do most of the other stuff from the Web. (You'll need a Web browser.)

➤ Internet e-mail allows you to send messages to anyone who's connected to the Internet.

➤ Use newsgroups to communicate with other users.

➤ You can FTP using your Web browser much more easily than by using an FTP program.

➤ Use WAIS to find information about a specific topic.

Part 7
Becoming a Power User

You know the basics. You can get by in any application, rearrange your files, and even connect to an online service. But what happens when something goes wrong? Can you figure out the problem? Can you fix it? Can you make sure it never happens again?

In this Part, you'll get the advanced tools you need to prepare for, prevent, and recover from common disasters. You'll also learn how to keep your computer in tip-top shape and optimize it for peak performance.

Chapter 26

THIS WON'T HURT A BIT...

Keeping Your Computer in Tip-Top Shape

By the End of This Chapter, You'll Be Able To:

➤ Extract dust balls from your mouse

➤ Run a Windows screen saver utility

➤ Remove Windows files and fonts that you no longer need

➤ Make your hard disk lean and mean

➤ Make Windows run faster

Your computer is like a car. You may be able to use it without ever cleaning it, tuning it up, or changing the oil, but it probably won't last as long or run as well. In this chapter, you'll learn some basic computer maintenance that will help keep your computer running trouble free and at peak performance.

If you don't feel comfortable with some of the advanced performance boosting tips covered later in this chapter, just skip them. Those tips aren't mandatory, but they will help you squeeze the maximum performance out of your PC.

Janitorial Tasks: Keeping Your Computer Clean

Computers are basically overpriced clean-air machines. Don't believe me? Then take a look around any office that has a computer in it. You'll see that all the shelves and desktops are virtually dust-free. But if you slide the computer out of the way, dust bunnies blow across the desk like tumbleweed. To prevent this dust from causing problems, you have to clean your equipment regularly:

➤ **Vacuum your work area.** With the hose part of a vacuum cleaner, vacuum the dust from around the system unit and the back of the monitor. Be sure to vacuum any slots or openings where dust gathers. Every year or two, take the cover off the system unit and vacuum inside with a plastic hose. Be careful not to whack the hose nozzle against any components.

➤ **Wipe the monitor.** Turn the monitor off, spray window cleaner on a paper towel (not on the monitor), and wipe any dirt or dust off the monitor. A used dryer sheet is also effective in cleaning monitors, giving the added feature of reducing static cling.

➤ **Decrumb the keyboard.** Turn the keyboard upside down and shake it lightly to remove any dust or debris. This prevents the keys from sticking. Another way to clean the keyboard is to vacuum it gently, or spray it with compressed air (you can purchase cans of compressed air from your local neighborhood computer store).

➤ **Clean the floppy disk drives.** You can buy a floppy drive cleaning kit at your neighborhood computer store. You squirt some goop on a special disk, insert it in the drive, and let it spin-wash your drive. I've never cleaned a floppy drive, and I've never had a problem. So, unless you stuck a slice of bread in your floppy drive thinking it was the toaster, don't worry about cleaning it. If the drive stops working, clean it; it's worth a try.

Accidental Spills

If you spill a drink on your keyboard, turn off the computer and use a paper towel to sop up as much liquid as you can. Flip the keyboard upside down, and let it dry out. You can use a blow dryer or fan to speed the process.

➤ **Clean the mouse.** A mouse picks up dirt and dust from the desktop. If the mouse gets too dirty, it may cause the mouse pointer to skip erratically across the screen. Flip the mouse over on its back, remove the ball cover, and remove the ball. Wipe the ball with a paper towel dipped in window cleaner. Inside the mouse are some rollers. Gently pick any dust balls out of the rollers (a toothpick works well). Make sure the mouse ball is dry before you reassemble the mouse.

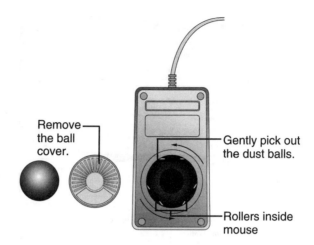

Remove the ball cover.

Gently pick out the dust balls.

Rollers inside mouse

A mouse comes apart easily for cleaning.

Flying Toasters and Other Screen Savers

In case you haven't heard, there's a nasty rumor going around that if you keep the same picture on your screen for a couple of hours, the image is going to burn itself into the screen. There's some truth to this, assuming you have an older monitor and you crank the brightness way up. If you're afraid that your monitor is going to get fried, you can use a screen saver.

A screen saver automatically blanks your screen or displays moving images after a set amount of idle time. For example, you can set up a screen saver to start if you haven't used your keyboard or mouse for 15 minutes. When that time is up, the screen saver starts to display pictures (usually moving pictures) such as Captain Kirk, Homer Simpson, or winged toasters that make their way across your screen.

If you must have a screen saver, Windows comes with a couple free ones. To pick a screen saver, open the **Main** group window, double-click on the **Control Panel** icon, and then double-click on the **Desktop** icon. Open the **Screen Saver Name** drop-down list and click on the screen saver you want to use. You can click on the **Test** button to see the selected screen saver in action. Click on the **OK** button when you're done.

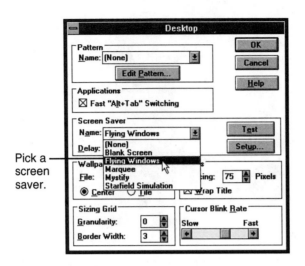

Pick a
screen
saver.

Windows comes with free screen savers.

Optimizing Your Hard Disk

As you install programs and save files, your hard disk becomes cluttered. Each time your computer needs a file, the disk drive has to rummage through all this garbage to find what it needs. After some time, this can slow down your drive and make your computer seem sluggish. To prevent this from happening to your computer, perform the following monthly maintenance:

File Fragmentation
A natural process in which parts of a file are saved to different areas of a disk. As you delete and save files to a disk, they become more and more fragmented. To read a fragmented file from disk, the drive's read-write head must skip around to the various storage locations. This takes time and places additional strain on the drive.

Perform a backup. In addition to protecting your files on a daily basis, a backup can help you recover files if they are damaged during other disk maintenance and disk fix operations. See Chapter 28, "Backing Up Your Work," for instructions on backing up your files.

Delete obsolete programs and old files. If you no longer use a program, delete it and its directories. Do the same for any document files you created and no longer need. To get rid of Windows files that you don't use, open the Main program group window and double-click on the **Windows Setup** icon. Then, open the **Options** menu and select **Add/Remove Windows Components**. Use the screen that appears to remove specific Windows files.

Run CheckDisk or ScanDisk. If you have DOS 6.2 or later, change to the drive you want to clean up, type

scandisk, and press **Enter**. Follow the on-screen instructions. If you have an earlier version of DOS, type **chkdsk /f** and press **Enter**. Both programs locate lost pieces of files and let you remove them from the disk, uncluttering the disk and making it run faster.

Run a defragmenting program. DOS 6.0 and later come with Defrag, a program that tidies up your disk, placing the pieces of each file next to each other. This makes your disk run more efficiently. To run Defrag, type **defrag** at the DOS prompt, and press **Enter**.

Speeding Up Windows

On DOS, a 386 16MHz computer with 2 megabytes of RAM flies. On Windows, it barely chugs along. The trouble is that the Windows easy-to-use interface takes a lot of computing power just to show its pretty face. However, there are a few steps you can take to speed up Windows.

Editing Your System Files

Whenever Windows starts, it reads two files into memory: WIN.INI and SYSTEM.INI. You can edit the command lines in this file to make Windows run faster and give Windows less to read. Be careful, though; if you delete an important command by mistake, you may not be able to start Windows, or you may have problems with your Windows applications. Copy the files from the WINDOWS directory to a floppy disk before editing them.

To edit these files (and AUTOEXEC.BAT and CONFIG.SYS), use the Windows System Editor. To create an icon for the editor, first open the program group window in which you want the icon to appear. Open the Program Manager's **File** menu, select **New**, click on **Program Item,** and then click on **OK**. Type **SysEdit** in the Description text box. Tab to the Command Line text box, and type **c:\windows\system\sysedit**. Click on the **OK** button. To run the System Editor, double-click on its icon.

Once you have the System Editor running, try the following changes:

➤ **Delete blank lines.** Windows reads every line in WIN.INI and SYSTEM.INI. By deleting blank lines, you give Windows less to read on startup.

Easy Memory Optimization

If you have DOS version 6.2 or later, you have a program that can edit your AUTOEXEC.BAT and CONFIG.SYS files for you to optimize memory for both DOS and Windows. Exit Windows, and then enter **memmaker** at the DOS prompt. Follow the on-screen instructions.

➤ **Tell Windows where the temporary swap file is.** Whenever Windows starts, it has to determine which drive to use for its temporary swap file. You can save Windows some time by specifying the location in the SYSTEM.INI file. Under the section labeled [386Enh], type the line **PagingFile=c:\win386.swp** where c is the letter of the fastest drive with the most free space. Save SYSTEM.INI and restart Windows.

➤ **Make sure Smart Drive is loading.** *Smart Drive* is a disk-caching program that stores often-used data in memory so Windows can access the information more quickly (rather than having to read it from disk). Check your CONFIG.SYS and AUTOEXEC.BAT files to make sure a SMARTDRV command is in one of those files. If it's not, add the command C:\DOS\SMARTDRV.EXE to your AUTOEXEC.BAT file. Then, exit Windows and reboot your computer. See "Making an Application Run from Any Directory" in Chapter 13 for details on how to edit your AUTOEXEC.BAT file.

Removing Useless Fonts

Whenever you install fonts, the font names are added to WIN.INI, which loads the fonts whenever you start Windows. If you don't use some of these fonts, you should remove them.

There's one exception. Do *not* remove the font called **MS Sans Serif**. Windows uses this font (which is easy to read) to display text in its windows, menus, and dialog boxes. If you remove this font, you may not be able to read all the on-screen text.

To remove a font, here's what you do:

1. Open the **Main** group window.

2. Double-click on the **Control Panel** icon.

3. Double-click on the **Fonts** icon. The **Fonts** dialog box appears, showing a list of installed fonts.

4. Select each font you want to remove:

   Single font: Click on it.

   Group of neighboring fonts: Click on the first one in the group, and then hold down the **Shift** key while clicking on the last font in the group.

   Group of non-neighboring fonts: Hold down the **Ctrl** key while clicking on each font you want to remove.

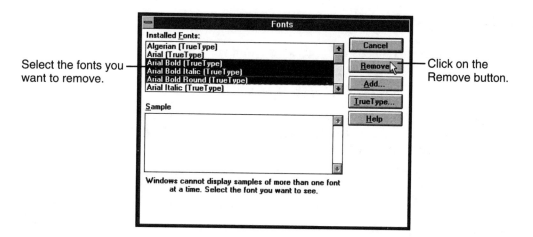

Select the fonts you want to remove.

Click on the Remove button.

Removing useless fonts.

5. Click on the **Remove** button. The **Remove Font** dialog box appears.

6. (Optional) If you want the font files removed from disk, click on the **Delete Font File From Disk** option. If you leave this option off, the font is removed from the font lists and does not load at startup, but the file is left on disk. You can then reinstall the font easily.

7. Click on **Yes** to remove this font and go on to the next one, or click on **Yes to All** to remove all selected fonts without asking for your okay. You are returned to the **Fonts** dialog box.

8. Click on the **Close** button.

Uninstalling Windows Applications

If you break out in hives whenever you consider deleting any Windows files, get an uninstaller program for Windows. Such programs lead you through the process of deleting all the application's files and icons and removing any references to them from your Windows .INI files. Two of the more popular uninstaller programs are Uninstaller and Remove It.

Other Windows Speed Tricks

If Windows still seems sluggish to you, try the following fixes:

➤ To start Windows, type **win :** and press **Enter**. The colon tells Windows not to display the Windows advertising screen at startup.

➤ Create a permanent swap file, instead of a temporary file. Check out the end of Chapter 12, "Installing New Applications," to learn how to use virtual memory in Windows and change the swap file size and type.

➤ Run fewer applications. Each application consumes memory. By exiting any applications you are not currently using, you give more system resources to the application you are using. To find out which applications are running, press **Ctrl+Esc**.

➤ Use solid window colors and wallpaper. If you used the Control Panel Desktop to change the window colors or display a fancy wallpaper design, go back in and change the design to something a bit more plain. Your screen won't look as pretty, but Windows will run faster.

The Least You Need to Know

As you can see, you can do a lot to keep your computer cleaned and tuned. However, if you like to do as little as necessary to keep your computer in shape, make sure you do the following regularly:

➤ Vacuum your work area monthly.

➤ Wipe your monitor with a damp cloth whenever it appears dusty.

➤ Extract fur balls from your mouse when the pointer starts to skip around the screen.

➤ Run ChkDsk or ScanDisk monthly.

➤ Run Defrag every month or two.

➤ If you have DOS 6.2 or later, run MemMaker at least once to optimize your computer's memory.

Chapter 27

Preparing an Emergency Disk

By the End of This Chapter, You'll Be Able To:

➤ Make a floppy disk that can boot your computer

➤ Copy essential programs to the floppy disk

➤ Recover files from a damaged disk

➤ Get your hard drive up and running after a crash

Although a computer's hard disk is fairly reliable, catastrophes can occur that render it inoperable. One day, you'll try to boot your computer, and you'll get a message that the computer can't find drive C or that one of your startup files is corrupted. When this happens, it helps to have an emergency disk on hand: a floppy disk that you can use to boot your computer and restore your system to normal.

Making a System Disk

You can't use just any disk to boot your computer. The disk needs to be formatted for drive A and has to have these three essential files: IO.SYS, MSDOS.SYS, and COMMAND.COM. You can add these files while formatting a disk in DOS or Windows. Remember to format the disk in drive A; your computer can't boot from drive B.

➤ In DOS, add the /S switch to the FORMAT command. For example, type **format a: /s** and press **Enter**.

➤ In Windows File Manager, open the **Disk** menu and select **Format Disk**. After selecting the disk size and capacity, click on the **Make System Disk** option and then click on the **OK** button. (Refer to Chapter 20, "Formatting and Copying Floppy Disks," for details about formatting a disk.)

In either case, the computer formats the disk and copies the files required to make the disk bootable.

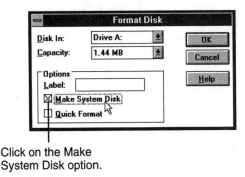

Click on the Make
System Disk option.

Creating a system disk in Windows File Manager.

Copying Startup Files to the Recovery Disk

The system disk you just created will boot your computer, but it will not enter important startup commands for your mouse or CD-ROM drive. Those commands are stored in the AUTOEXEC.BAT and CONFIG.SYS files, which DOS runs automatically whenever you

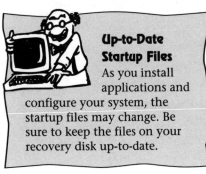

Up-to-Date Startup Files

As you install applications and configure your system, the startup files may change. Be sure to keep the files on your recovery disk up-to-date.

start your computer. If you want your recovery disk to enter those commands, you need to copy CONFIG.SYS and AUTOEXEC.BAT to it. These files are stored in the root directory of drive C. Flip back to Chapter 22, "Copying, Moving, and Deleting Files," for details on how to copy files.

While you're at it, change to the WINDOWS directory and copy SYSTEM.INI and WIN.INI to your recovery disk. If you ever edit these files and then encounter problems, you can use these backup files to recover.

Adding Data Recovery Files

In addition to helping you jump start your computer, a good emergency disk should have programs that help you recover any damaged or deleted files from your hard disk. If you have a recent version of DOS, you have most of the programs you need. Simply copy the following files from the DOS directory to your recovery disk: UNDELETE.EXE, CHKDSK.EXE, and SCANDISK.EXE.

When you're done copying those files, write-protect your recovery disk. This prevents it from getting accidentally formatted or damaged during the recovery process, and it prevents it from being infected by a computer virus, which is a rogue program designed specifically to destroy files and turn your system upside-down. (For more information about computer viruses, see Chapter 29, "Protecting Against Computer Intruders.")

Recovering with Utilities

If your computer crashed before you had a chance to create a recovery disk, you may still be able to recover. You can either create a recovery disk using a friend's computer or you can purchase a utility program, such as *The Norton Utilities* or *PC Tools*. Don't install the utility program, because that could make the problem worse. Use the utility program's floppy disks to recover your data.

Performing CPR with the Recovery Disk

If you turn on your computer one day and get an error message telling you that you don't have a system disk in a drive or that some of your files are corrupted, you may need to use the emergency disk to boot your computer. But first, try the following:

➤ Check the floppy disk drives to make sure you didn't leave a floppy disk in drive A. Remove the disk, and press any key to continue the boot operation.

➤ Make sure your monitor is connected and turned on. I know, this sounds obvious—but when your computer apparently won't start, it's easy to overlook the obvious.

➤ Turn the system unit off, wait two minutes, and then turn it back on. Sometimes, a glitch in the system will prevent the computer from booting properly. A second attempt may be all it needs.

➤ If you have DOS 6, and you get the error message after you see the **Starting MS-DOS...** message, try rebooting. When you see **Starting MS-DOS...**, press and release the **F8** key. This allows you to step through the startup commands and find out which one is causing problems.

If none of the previous solutions works, use the emergency disk to boot your computer:

1. Insert the emergency disk in drive A and close the drive door (if there is one).

2. Press **Ctrl+Alt+Del**. This reboots the computer from the disk in drive A.

Once your computer is up and running, you can change drives and directories and bring up lists of files to determine if your data has been damaged. In addition, you can use the data recovery programs on the emergency disk to repair your disk and recover your data:

➤ **Running ScanDisk.** If you have DOS 6.2 or later, you have a program called ScanDisk that gives you more tools for fixing problem disks. To run ScanDisk, change to drive A, type **scandisk c:**, and press **Enter**. ScanDisk checks the specified drive (C in this case) and fixes any problems. Follow the on-screen instructions to proceed.

➤ **Checking a disk.** If you don't have ScanDisk, use Check Disk to correct the problem. Change to drive A, type **chkdsk c: /f**, and press **Enter**. If a message appears saying that Check Disk found file fragments, type **Y** to save the fragments or **N** to delete them.

➤ **Undeleting files.** If you caused a problem by accidentally deleting some files, you may be able to recover the files by using the DOS Undelete program. Change to drive A. Then, type **undelete** *c:\dirname* (where *c* is the drive letter and *dirname* is the path to the directory that contains the accidentally deleted files). Press **Enter**, and then follow the on-screen instructions to continue.

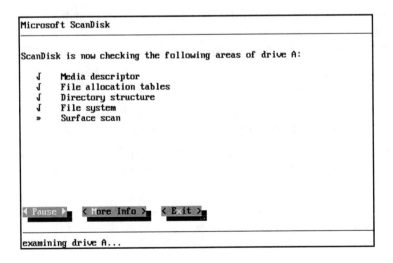

ScanDisk can uncover and fix most disk problems.

The Least You Need to Know

A recovery disk is like a Get Out of Jail Free card. It can help you jump start your computer and recover damaged disks and deleted files. To create and use a recovery disk, here's what you do:

➤ Get a blank disk for drive A.

➤ Format the recovery disk with the DOS **format /s** command, or format the disk in Windows and click on the **Make System Disk** option.

➤ Copy AUTOEXEC.BAT, CONFIG.SYS, WIN.INI, and SYSTEM.INI to the recovery disk.

➤ Copy UNDELETE.EXE, CHKDSK.EXE, and SCANDISK.EXE from the DOS directory to the recovery disk.

➤ Write-protect the recovery disk.

➤ To boot your computer, insert the recovery disk in drive A, close the drive door, and then turn on the computer.

Chapter 28

Backing Up Your Work

By the End of This Chapter, You'll Be Able To:

➤ Stick the entire contents of your hard drive on floppy disks

➤ Make backup copies of only the data files you created

➤ Pick a backup plan that works for you

➤ Recover files from your backups

➤ Tell your spouse why you need a tape backup drive

Recently, my boss lost everything on his hard drive (poor guy). Some computer glitch wiped out the entire drive and everything on it. He had no backups; backing up took too much time, too many floppy disks. Now he has to face the painful task of reformatting his hard drive, reinstalling all his applications, and rebuilding all the spreadsheets and other documents he had taken so much time to create.

Had he backed up (at least his data files), he would have had a much easier time of it. He could simply reformat his hard drive, reinstall his backup program, and restore all his files from floppy disks (or a backup tape) to his hard drive. The process would have taken hours rather than days.

Backup Programs and What They Do

DOS 6.22 Is a Real Bargain If you have pre-6.0 version of DOS, upgrade to DOS 6.22. It comes with several utilities that make the upgrade well worth the price, including MemMaker (for memory optimization), ScanDisk (for repairing disk and file problems), Undelete (for recovering accidentally deleted files), and Defrag (for optimizing your hard disk).

Theoretically, you can back up your files by copying them from your hard drive to floppy disks. You can also trim your fingernails with a meat cleaver, although that's not the best tool for the job. To back up files, you should use a special backup program. Backup programs perform two important tasks: they compress the backup copies so the copies take up less space, and they place the backups on a series of disks, so you don't have to divvy up the files yourself.

If you have DOS 6.0 or later, you already have a good backup program: Microsoft Backup, which I cover in this chapter. However, you can purchase better backup programs such as CP Backup (which comes with PC Tools) and FastBack Plus. These backup programs are faster and provide better file compression (so you use fewer floppy disks), but they work much the same way as Microsoft Backup.

Backup Strategies You Can Live With

Backups are worthless if you don't have a backup strategy—a plan that ensures the backup copies are up-to-date. Like most strategies, backup strategies vary depending on how you work and how you organize your files. Following is a list of common strategies that may help you develop your own plan:

➤ **My backup strategy** consists of backing up my entire hard disk every month. I then back up the data files (the files I create and edit) daily. I keep all my data files in several subdirectories under a DATA directory. That way, I can back up all my data files simply by backing up the DATA directory.

➤ **The "I feel lucky today"** strategy consists of backing up when you feel like it. People who follow this strategy rarely back up and are at a high risk of losing data.

➤ **The standard strategy** is to back up all your files monthly and back up only those files that have changed daily. To do this, you perform a full backup monthly. On a daily basis, you perform an *incremental backup*, which backs up only those files that have changed since the last backup.

➤ **The "everything every other week"** strategy consists of backing up all your files every two weeks. The trouble with this (and similar strategies) is that it results in old backup copies. If you restore your files from old backups, you're going to get old files.

➤ The "**I'm special, I have a tape backup**" strategy is for rich people who have a tape backup drive. Say, for example, your computer at work has a tape backup drive. You *schedule* a full backup every week and an incremental backup at the end of the day. As you're driving home from work, your backup program backs up all your files for you. Most fancy backup programs have a built-in scheduler. Microsoft Backup does not have this feature.

Full and Incremental Backups

Whenever a backup program copies a file, it turns the file's *archive attribute* off, indicating that the file has been backed up. If you edit the file, DOS turns the archive attribute on, indicating that the newly edited file has not been backed up. If you then perform an incremental backup, the backup program knows that it must back up this changed file. When you perform a full backup, the backup program copies all the files, no matter what the archive attribute is set to. The backup program then turns off the archive attribute for all those files.

Setting Up Your Backup Program

Before you start using your backup program, you have to set it up and tell it the type of equipment you're using (for example, a 3.5" disk or a tape backup). The backup program then tests the equipment for you and performs a sample backup to make sure everything is working right. To start and set up Microsoft Backup, perform the following steps (other backup programs use a similar procedure):

1. Perform one of the following steps to start Microsoft Backup:

    DOS To run Microsoft Backup for DOS, display the C:> prompt, type **msbackup**, and then press **Enter**.

    Windows If you installed MS Backup for Windows, run **Windows**, open the **Microsoft Tools** program group, and then double-click on the **Backup** icon.

    A dialog box appears, indicating that you have not set up the backup program to run on your computer.

2. Read the dialog box, and select **Start Configuration**. Microsoft Backup tests your mouse and video driver and displays the Video and Mouse Configuration dialog box.

3. To change a setting, click on the button for the setting you want to change. Select a setting from the dialog box that appears, and then select **OK**.

4. To accept the Video and Mouse Configuration settings, select the **OK** button. The Floppy Drive Change Line Test dialog box appears.

5. Remove any disks from your floppy disk drives, and select the **Start Test** button. You will hear your floppy drives grind, as Microsoft Backup tests your system to determine the type of drives you can use for backups. The Backup Devices dialog box appears.

6. If the drive types displayed are correct, select the **OK** button. Otherwise, click on a drive button and select the correct drive; or select **Auto Config** and then select **Start Test** to have Microsoft Backup determine the drive type during the backup test.

7. Select the **OK** button to start the backup test. Microsoft Backup performs some diagnostic tests on your hard disk drive and displays the Floppy Disk Compatibility Test dialog box. This test will perform a test backup on your system to make sure the backup is reliable.

8. Select **Start Test**. Microsoft Backup automatically works through several dialog boxes to select a set of files to back up. A dialog box appears telling you that the program is now pausing so you can select a drive to back up to.

9. Select **Continue**. The Backup To dialog box appears.

10. Select the drive and disk type to which you want to back up the test files, and then select the **OK** button. A dialog box appears, instructing you to insert a floppy disk into the specified drive.

11. Insert a floppy disk into the specified drive, close the drive door (if necessary), and then select **Continue**. Backup starts backing up the test files to the floppy disk. Backup displays a prompt when it needs the next disk. (If you get a message telling you that the disk contains data, change disks and select **Retry**, or select **Overwrite** to replace any data on the disk with the backup test files.)

12. When Backup instructs you to insert the next floppy disk, remove the first disk from the floppy drive, insert the second disk, and press **Enter**. When Backup is done backing up the test files, it displays the Backup Complete dialog box.

13. Click on the **OK** button to continue. Backup works through a series of dialog boxes to select the compare operation. This operation will compare the backed up files on the floppy disks to the original files on the hard disk. You are instructed to insert the first backup floppy into the floppy drive.

14. Remove any disks from the floppy drive. Insert the first floppy disk into the specified drive, close the drive door (if necessary), then press **Enter** to continue. Backup starts comparing the backed up files to the originals. Backup displays a prompt when it needs the next disk.

15. Remove the first disk from the floppy drive, insert the second disk, then press **Enter**. When Backup is done comparing the test files, it displays the Compare Complete dialog box.

16. Click on the **OK** button. The Compatibility Test dialog box appears, showing whether the backup test was successful.

17. Click on the **OK** button. The Configure dialog box appears, allowing you to enter any changes to the configuration settings.

18. Change any of the configuration settings, as desired, and select the **Save** button to save your settings.

Backup Test Failure?
If your computer can't pass the test at any speed, make sure all memory-resident programs are unloaded from memory, and then retest your computer:

1. Start Microsoft Backup as explained earlier to display the Backup menu.

2. Select **Configure**.

3. Select **Compatibility Test**.

4. Select **Start Test**.

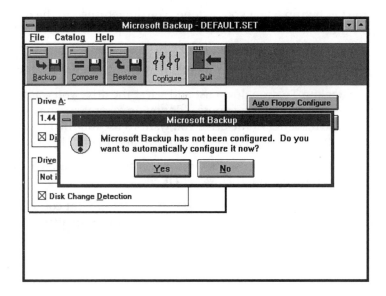

Microsoft Backup can configure itself.

Backing Up Your Files

The hard part's over. Once you've set up Microsoft Backup, you simply select the files you want to back up, pick the drive you want to back up to, and select a backup type (full or incremental). Microsoft Backup does the rest, leading you through the entire process. Here's what you do:

1. Start Microsoft Backup as explained earlier.

2. Click on the **Backup** button. The Microsoft Backup program window appears.

3. Open the **Backup From** list and right-click on the drive that contains the files you want to back up. Right-click one or more times to pick **All Files** or **no files**.

   Display **All Files** if you want to back up all files and directories on the disk or most of the files and directories.

   Turn off **All Files** if you want to back up a select group of files (say two or three directories).

4. (Optional) Choose the **Select Files** button to include or exclude files or directories. The Select Backup Files window appears.

5. To include or exclude a directory or file, highlight it and then press the **Spacebar**, or right-click on the file. A box appears next to an item that will be backed up.

6. Select the **OK** button when you're done. You are returned to the original Microsoft Backup window.

7. Open the **Backup Type** drop-down list and click on **Full** (to back up all the files or **Incremental** (to back up only those files that changed since the last backup).

8. Open the **Backup To** drop-down list and select the drive you want to use for storing your backup copies. You can choose a floppy drive, or you can select **MS-DOS Path** and then type the letter of the drive you want to use followed by a colon. (MS-DOS Path is useful for backing up to a tape drive or another hard drive.)

9. To use less disk space, click on the **Options** button, make sure you select the **Compress Backup Data** option, then select **OK**.

10. If you're backing up to floppy disks, look in the lower right corner of the window to find out how many disks you need (they need not be formatted).

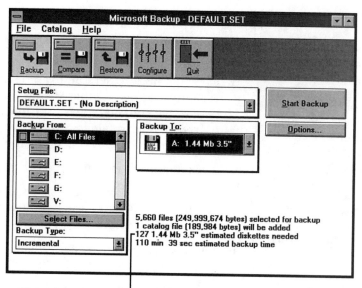

Check here to see the approximate number of disks you'll need.

Microsoft Backup estimates the required number of disks.

11. Select the **Start Backup** button. Microsoft Backup prompts you to insert the first disk of the backup set into a floppy drive.

12. Follow the on-screen instructions, ejecting and inserting disks when directed.

When the backup operation is complete, put the disks in order and store them in a safe location. If a directory or file ever gets accidentally destroyed, you'll need the backup disks to restore them.

Restoring Files from Backup Copies

If your hard disk crashes or you accidentally delete a directory or file, you may need your backup files to restore the originals. However, you should first try to restore the files by undeleting them, as explained in Chapter 22, "Copying, Moving, and Deleting Files." Undeleting gives you the most recent versions of the files. If undeleting does not work, take the following steps to restore the files from backups:

Cryptic Catalog Names

If you have several backup catalogs, you probably have no idea which catalog is for which backup set. Insert the last disk of the backup set into the floppy drive and enter the Retrieve command: in DOS, click on the **Catalog** button and then on the **Retrieve** button; in Windows, open the **Catalog** menu and select **Retrieve**. This gives you the name of the backup catalog.

1. Start Microsoft Backup as explained earlier.

2. Click on the **Restore** button. The Restore screen appears.

3. Open the **Backup Set Catalog** drop-down list. For each backup you perform, Microsoft Backup creates a *catalog* that contains a list of the files and directories it backed up. This catalog is stored on your hard disk and on the last floppy disk of the backup set.

4. Click on the desired catalog.

5. Select **Restore From**. This displays a list that allows you to select the drive and type of disk on which the backup files are stored.

6. Select the type of disks that contain the backup files you want to restore.

7. Insert the first disk of the backup set into the selected floppy drive.

8. To restore only certain files, double-click on the **Select Files** button, select the files you want to restore, and click on **OK**.

9. Select **Start Restore**. Microsoft Backup starts restoring the files from the floppy disk to the hard disk. If Restore finds a file on the hard disk whose name matches one of the backup files, you'll see an Alert box that offers the following options:

   Overwrite replaces the hard disk file with the backup file.

   Do Not Restore skips this file and proceeds to the next file in the backup.

   Cancel Restore quits the Restore program and returns you to the Microsoft Backup opening screen.

10. If the Warning box appears, enter your selection.

11. Follow the on-screen prompts, and swap disks when told to do so.

The Least You Need to Know

To avoid losing your data and your mind, you should back up your program and data files regularly:

➤ You should have a complete backup of all the files on your hard disk.

➤ Each day you should back up any files that have changed during the day.

➤ To run Microsoft Backup for DOS, type **msbackup** at the DOS prompt and press **Enter**.

➤ To run Microsoft Backup for Windows, open the **Microsoft Tools** group window and double-click on the **Backup** icon.

➤ To back up files, pick the drive you want to back up from, the drive you want to back up to, and the backup type.

➤ Click on the **Restore** button to recover backed up files.

Chapter 29

Protecting Against Computer Intruders

By the End of This Chapter, You'll Be Able To:

➤ Make file names invisible

➤ Password-protect a file using an encryption program

➤ Prevent other people from changing your files

➤ Use Microsoft Anti-Virus to hunt out computer viruses and kill them

➤ Set up your computer so you have to enter a password to use Windows

If you think somebody is out to destroy the files on your hard drive or is snooping around for classified information, you're probably just paranoid. However, snoops and vandals do live in the computer world just as anywhere else, so you may have to be a bit careful at times, especially if you have important confidential information. In this chapter, you'll learn some ways to protect your system and prevent your data from becoming damaged or leaked.

Protecting Your Files from Prying Eyes

Most people have at least a few documents that they don't want other people poking around in: a diary, plans for an invention, or maybe some juicy graphics downloaded from the Internet. To prevent people from opening files and viewing their contents, you should protect the files with a data encryption program. Such a program scrambles the file's contents, and then unscrambles the contents only when you enter the correct password. Most utility programs such as PC Tools and The Norton Utilities come with an encryption program.

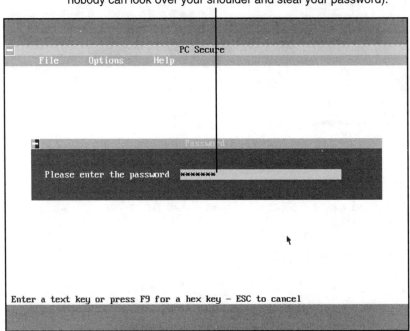

Type a password (what you type appears as asterisks, so nobody can look over your shoulder and steal your password).

Pick the files you want to protect, and then enter a password.

Without an encryption program, you can't do much to protect your files. The only option you have is to hide the files and prevent their names from appearing in a DOS directory listing. To hide files, you turn on each file's *Hidden* attribute. (An *attribute* is a switch that tells DOS how to deal with the file.)

You can hide files using Windows File Manager or the DOS ATTRIB command. In File Manager, select the files you want to hide. Open the **File** menu and select **Properties**. Click on **Hidden** and then click on the **OK** button. Now the files won't show up in a directory listing if you use the DOS DIR command. Follow the same steps to turn the Hidden attribute off.

To hide files using the DOS ATTRIB command, change to the drive and directory that contain the file you want to hide. At the DOS prompt, type **attrib +h** *filename.ext*

264

(where *filename.ext* is the name of the file you want to hide) and press **Enter**. To turn the Hidden attribute off, perform the same steps, but type **-h** rather than **+h**.

Write-Protecting Files and Disks

If you don't mind having people view your files as long as they don't change anything, you can lock the files (or the floppy disk that the files are on). You already learned (in Chapter 12) how to write-protect floppy disks. To write-protect individual files on floppy or hard disks, you have to turn the file's *Read Only* attribute on:

➤ In Windows' File Manager, select the files you want to write-protect. Open the **File** menu and select **Properties**. Click on **Read Only** and then click on the **OK** button. Perform the same steps to turn the Read Only attribute off.

➤ In DOS, change to the drive and directory that contain the file you want to write-protect. Type **attrib +r** *filename.ext* (where *filename.ext* is the name of the file you want to protect) and press **Enter**. To turn the Read Only attribute off, perform the same steps, but type **-r** rather than **+r**.

Hidden No More

Hiding files does little good, because most file management utilities can display the names of hidden files. For example, in Windows File Manager, you can display hidden files as follows: open the **View** menu, select **By File Type**, click on **Show Hidden/System Files**, and then click on **OK**. The hidden files reappear. Hiding files only works with people who know very little about computers.

Password Protection in Windows

Windows provides a cheap (though not very secure) way to prevent unauthorized use of your computer. You simply assign a password to the Windows screen saver. To add a password, here's what you do:

1. Open the **Main** group window, double-click on the **Control Panel** icon, and double-click on the **Desktop** icon.

2. Open the **Screen Saver Name** drop-down list and click on the screen saver you want to use.

3. Click on the **Setup** button, and make sure there is an X in the **Password Protected** check box.

4. Click on the **Set Password** button.

5. Type your password in the **New Password** text box.

Forget Your Password? If you forget your password, start Windows and turn off the screen saver password protection before the screen saver kicks in. You can also remove the password by deleting it from the CONTROL.INI file.

6. Press the **Tab** key and type the same password in the **Retype New Password** text box.

7. Click on the **OK** button, and then click on the **OK** button in the Setup dialog box.

8. For maximum protection, crank the Screen Saver Delay time down to one minute. (This way, the password protection kicks in before the unauthorized user has time to do much damage.)

9. Click on the **OK** button.

Protecting Against Viruses

A *virus* is a program specially designed to destroy files and lock up computer systems. A virus can enter your system through its modem, through network lines, or from an infected floppy disk. The virus then spreads to infect your hard disk and any floppy disks you happen to use after contracting the virus. The virus infects files and then works in the background to destroy files on disk, sometimes wiping out an entire disk. Fortunately, there are some preventions and cures for viruses.

An Ounce of Prevention...

Computer viruses are much less common than most people think. However, you should take the following precautions just to remain on the safe side:

➤ **Avoid unknown bulletin board systems.** A bulletin board system (BBS) lets you connect to it with a modem and copy files. Most BBSs check files for viruses before allowing them to be placed on the system. Before copying (downloading) files from a BBS, make sure the BBS has a good reputation.

➤ **Write-protect program disks.** Before you install a commercial program, write-protect the disks you purchased. If your hard disk is infected with an undetected virus, the write-protection will at least protect the program disks. You can then use the disks to reinstall the program after you destroy the virus.

➤ **Back up your data files separately.** Although viruses can wipe out data files, they rarely hide in them.

➤ **Check floppy disks and downloaded files before running them.** Use your anti-virus program to check any floppy disks you get from outside sources and any program files you download from an information service or BBS. You'll learn how to do this in the following section.

Trolling for Viruses

One of the best ways to reduce or eliminate the damage a virus can cause is to identify the virus early and remove it. To do this, you need to use an anti-virus program on a regular basis. Anti-virus programs scan your files for the following two indications of virus activity:

➤ **Signatures of known viruses.** Most virus programs contain data that is unique to that virus. Anti-Virus checks for this unique data and identifies the virus.

➤ **Changes in executable program files.** When a virus program infects a program file, the virus usually changes the file in some way. Anti-Virus keeps track of file sizes and other information and lets you know if any program file such as CONFIG.SYS has been changed recently. You are then given the option of updating Anti-Virus' records, skipping over the file, or removing the virus.

If you have DOS 6.0 or later, it comes with an anti-virus program called Microsoft Anti-Virus, which you can run from Windows or from the DOS prompt:

1. Start Microsoft Anti-Virus by performing one of the following steps:

   At the DOS prompt, type **msav** and press **Enter**.

   In Windows, open the Microsoft Tools program group window and then double-click on the **Anti-Virus** icon.

2. Select the drive you want to check:

   In the DOS version, click on the **Select new drive** button and then click on the letter of the drive you want to scan (drive letters appear at the top of the screen).

   In the Windows version, simply click on the letter of the drive you want to scan.

3. Choose **Detect** (to scan for viruses without getting rid of them) or **Detect & Clean** (to scan for and remove any viruses). The Scanning Memory for Viruses dialog box appears as Anti-Virus scans your computer's memory for viruses. Anti-Virus then scans all the files on the selected drive. If Anti-Virus detects a known virus, the Virus Found dialog box appears, identifying the virus.

4. If Anti-Virus finds a virus, choose one of the following options: **Clean** (to remove the virus from the infected file), **Continue** (to continue scanning without removing the virus), **Stop** (to stop scanning), or **Delete** (to delete the infected file).

The Update Option
Choose **Update** only if you know that you have done something to change a file. For example, if you edited your CONFIG.SYS file, the reason it has changed is because you changed it. Likewise, if you installed a new version of a program, all the program files have changed because they are new.

267

5. If Anti-Virus detects a suspicious change in a program file, it displays the Verify Error dialog box. Choose one of the following options: **Update** (to update the Anti-Virus records, so it won't notify you of this same problem next time), **Delete** (to delete the infected file), **Continue** (to skip this file and continue scanning for viruses), or **Stop** (to stop scanning for viruses).

6. When Anti-Virus is done scanning the files on the current drive, it displays the Viruses Detected and Cleaned dialog box, showing the number of files checked, infected, and cleaned. Select **OK** to continue.

Anti-Virus has found a file that's been changed.

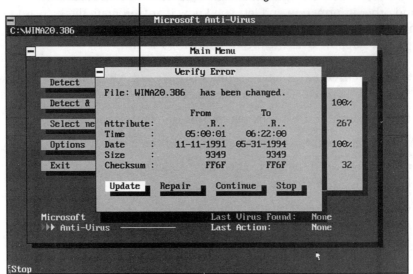

Anti-Virus lets you know of any changes in a file that look suspicious.

Although scanning for viruses ensures that your system is not currently infected, scanning does not prevent viruses from attacking your system in the future. To keep a lookout for viruses, consider setting up Anti-Virus to run whenever you start your computer.

To have Anti-Virus run each time you start your computer, add the following command line to your AUTOEXEC.BAT file (see Chapters 13 and 26 for details on how to edit this file):

c:\dos\msav /p

Using an Anti-Virus Shield

In addition to running Anti-Virus at startup, you can run a special memory-resident program called VSafe that acts as a virus watchdog. Once you've run VSafe, it stays in your computer's memory and keeps an eye out for any suspicious activity. If VSafe notices anything funny going on (such as unauthorized file activity), VSafe displays a warning, indicating that a virus may be at work.

To run VSafe, type **vsafe** at the DOS prompt and press **Enter**. To have VSafe loaded automatically whenever you boot your computer, add the following command to your AUTOEXEC.BAT file:

> **c:\dos\vsafe**

To remove VSafe from memory, type **vsafe /u** and press **Enter**.

Don't Run VSafe with Windows
If you plan on running Microsoft Windows, don't run VSafe. VSafe doesn't like some of the things Windows does.

The Least You Need to Know

The only way to completely protect your data and program files is to lock your computer in a vault and not use any files that aren't already on it. But that technique is far too impractical, so take the following precautions:

➤ If you have confidential files, buy an encryption program and use it to password-protect your files.

➤ You can turn on a file's Hidden attribute in DOS or Windows to prevent the file from showing up in a directory list, but this method isn't foolproof.

➤ Using write-protected program disks is the best way to prevent the files from getting damaged or infected by viruses.

➤ If you have Windows, you can password-protect it by adding a password to the screen saver.

➤ If you have MS-DOS 6.0 or later, you have an anti-virus program you can use to check for viruses on your disks.

Chapter 30

If Something Goes Wrong

By the End of This Chapter, You'll Be Able To:

➤ Figure out what to do in a crisis (and what not to do)

➤ Sniff out the cause of a problem

➤ Make sense out of at least five DOS error messages

➤ Bring your mouse pointer out of hiding

➤ Get your keyboard back to normal when it flips out

Computers are fickle. You might use your computer all week without a problem. Then, on Friday, you try to run a program you've been using all week, and the following message appears on-screen:

Bad command or filename

Or you try to print a file, and the file won't print. The printer is on, it has paper in it, and everything else seems to be okay. But, no matter what you do, the printer won't print the file.

What should you do? In this chapter, you will learn how to react in a crisis and how to solve your own computer woes. Although I can't cover every problem, I will cover many common ones to give you a taste of the types of things that can go wrong.

Troubleshooting Tactics: Solving Your Own Problems

With a little patience, you can solve most of your own problems. You just have to know how to go about it—what to do and what not to do. The overall approach is twofold: you need to trace the problem to its cause, and you need to avoid making the problem worse than it already is.

When you run into a problem that doesn't have an obvious solution, the best course of action is inaction; that is, don't do anything. If you're fidgety to do something, take a walk or wash the dishes until you're no longer in a panic. Then come back and try some of the following tactics.

Look for Clues

The answer to most problems is probably staring you in the face. So, the first thing you should do is look at the monitor for any messages that indicate a problem. Although on-screen messages are usually very general, they provide a starting point. If you don't see anything on-screen, start asking yourself some questions.

Is everything plugged in and turned on? If a part of your computer is dead—no lights, no sound, no action—it probably isn't connected or isn't turned on. Turn everything off and check the connections. Don't assume that just because something looks connected that it is; wiggle the plugs.

Check the Obvious
Many problems have quick solutions. Maybe the printer's not turned on, or a cable's loose or disconnected, or maybe you are looking for a file in the wrong directory. Sometimes, you need to look away from a problem in order to see it.

When did the problem start? Think back to what you did before the problem arose. Did you install a new software program? Did you enter a command? Did the computer freeze up? Knowing when the problem started can often reveal the cause.

Is the problem limited to one program? If you have the same problem in every program, the problem is probably caused by your computer. If the problem occurs in only one program, it is probably caused by the program.

When did you have the file last? If you lost a file, it probably did not get sucked into a black hole. It is probably somewhere on your disk—in a strange directory. Try to think back to when you had the file last and to what directory you saved it.

It's Probably Not the Computer

Most novice computer users (and some experienced users) automatically assume that whenever a problem arises, the computer is on the blink. Although the computer itself can be the cause of some major problems, it is rarely the cause of minor, everyday problems. The problem is usually in the software: DOS, Windows, or one of your applications.

My Computer Won't Boot

A computer is a lot like a car; the most frustrating thing that can happen is that you can't even get the engine to turn over. To solve the problem, consider these questions:

Is the computer on? Are the lights on the computer lit? If so, the computer is plugged in and is on; make sure the power switch on the system unit is turned on.

Is the screen completely blank? Even though the screen is completely blank, the computer may have booted; you just can't see it. If you heard the computer beep and you saw the drive lights go on and off, the computer probably booted fine. Make sure the monitor is turned on and the brightness controls are turned up.

Is there a disk in drive A? If you see a message on-screen that says **Non-system disk or disk error**, you probably left a floppy disk in drive A. Remove the disk and press any key to boot from the hard disk.

Can you boot from a floppy disk? If you still can't get your computer to boot from the hard disk, try booting from a bootable floppy disk. Insert the bootable floppy disk in drive A, close the drive door, and press **Ctrl+Alt+Del**. If you can boot from a floppy, the problem is on your hard disk. You'll need some expert help to get out of this mess.

Common DOS Messages in Plain English

As you work in DOS, you may come across some error messages and warnings and wonder what they mean. The following sections translate the DOS messages you're most likely to encounter.

All files in directory will be deleted
Are you sure (Y/N)?

You probably entered the **delete *.*** command at the DOS prompt. This tells DOS to delete all the files on the current drive or directory. If you meant to do this, press **Y**. If not, press **N**.

Bad command or file name

You see this message most often when you have a typo in the command you entered. Check to make sure the command is typed correctly. If the command is typed correctly, maybe DOS cannot find the command's program file. For example, you may have to be in the DOS directory to use the DOS FORMAT command. In such a case, you must change to the directory that contains the program file before you can run the file.

File cannot be copied onto itself

You see this message if you try to copy a file into the same directory that already contains the file. To create a copy of a file in the same directory, you have to give the copy a different name.

File not found

You see this message when you try to copy, delete, rename, or perform some other operation on a file that does not exist or on a file that is in a different location from where you think it is. If you get this message, make sure you typed the file name correctly. If the file name is okay, change to the drive and directory where you think the file is stored and use the **DIR** command to view a list of files. See if the file is where you think it is.

Insufficient disk space

DOS displays this error message when you try to copy more files to a disk than the disk can hold. If you get this error message, you may need to copy the files to more than one disk.

Non-system disk or disk error
Replace and press any key when ready

You may get this error message when you boot your computer. If your system files are on a hard drive, this message usually means you left a disk in drive A. Remove the disk and press any key to continue.

If you normally boot from a floppy disk, you may have forgotten to insert the DOS startup disk in drive A. Insert the DOS startup disk, close the drive door, and press any key.

Not ready reading drive A
Abort, Retry, Fail?

You will usually get this message for one of these reasons:

➤ You forgot to put a disk in drive A. Insert a disk, close the drive door, and press **R** for Retry.

➤ You forgot to close the drive door. Close the drive door and press **R** for Retry.

➤ The disk in drive A is not formatted. If a brand-new, never-been-formatted disk is in drive A, DOS will not be able to read the disk. Insert a formatted disk into drive A, close the drive door, and press **R**.

➤ If you changed to drive A by mistake, press **F** for Fail or **A** for Abort. This tells DOS to stop looking to drive A. A message appears telling you that drive A is no longer valid. Type **c:** and press **Enter** to return to drive C.

➤ You have a double-density drive and put a high-density disk in the drive.

My Screen Is Flickering

If your screen is flickering or turning odd colors, the plug that connects the monitor to the system unit has probably come loose. Turn everything off and check the connection. If the plug has screws that secure it to the system unit, tighten the screws.

I Can't Get the Program to Run

You bought a new program, installed it, and entered the command to run the program. The following message appears on-screen: **Bad command or file name**. What's wrong?

Are you in the drive and directory where the program's files are stored? Some programs install themselves and set up your system so you can run the program from any drive or directory. With other programs, you must change to the drive and directory that contains the program's files in order to run the program.

Did you type the correct command? The command must be typed exactly as specified in the documentation. If you mistype the command, the program won't run. If you don't have the documentation, refer to Chapter 15, "Surviving Without Documentation," to figure out what to do.

Did you install the program correctly? Installing some programs consists of merely copying the program's files to a directory on your hard disk. With other programs, you must run an installation program. If the program requires you to run an installation program, and you did not, the program probably won't run.

Is it a Windows program? You cannot run a Windows program from the DOS prompt. Run Windows first, and then try running the program. (See Chapter 8, "Ditching DOS: Running Microsoft Windows.") Or try typing **win** followed by the command required to run the program, and then press **Enter**. For example, to run Excel, type **win excel** and press **Enter**.

I Have a Mouse, but I Can't Find the Pointer On-Screen

Once you get your mouse working, you will probably never have to mess with it again. The hard part is getting the mouse to work in the first place. If you connected a mouse to your computer and you don't see the mouse pointer on-screen, there are a few possibilities you should investigate:

Am I in a program that uses a mouse? Some programs don't *support* a mouse, so you won't see the mouse pointer in these programs. For example, you won't see a mouse pointer at the DOS prompt, but you should see one in the DOS Shell. Run a program that you know uses a mouse to see if it works there.

Is the mouse pointer hidden? Mouse pointers like to hide in the corners or edges of your screen. Roll the mouse on your desktop to see if you can bring the pointer into view.

When you connected the mouse, did you install a mouse program? Connecting a mouse to your computer is not enough. You must install a program (called a *mouse driver*) that tells the computer how to use the mouse. Follow the instructions that came with the mouse to figure out how to install the program.

Record Your Changes

It's a good idea to always write down changes you make to your system. It takes a little extra time, but it enables you to retrace your steps later.

When you installed the mouse program, did you specify a COM port? When you install a mouse program, the program may ask you if the mouse is connected to COM1, COM2, or COM3, the serial ports on your computer. Give the wrong answer, and your computer won't be able to find your mouse. Run the installation or setup program again and select a different COM port. Reboot after each change, and write down every change you make.

My Mouse Pointer Is Jumpy

If your mouse pointer jumps around the screen rather than moving smoothly, your mouse may have fur balls. To find out what these fur balls are and how to get rid of them, check out Chapter 26, "Keeping Your Computer in Tip-Top Shape."

I Can't Get My Modem to Work

You're not the only one. Every day, someone down the hall from me has the same problem. Usually, the problem occurs in Windows. Some evil wizard apparently enters the computer and messes things up. Whatever the problem, the following questions may help you resolve it.

➤ **Is the modem plugged in and turned on?** If you have an external modem, it must be plugged into a power source, to the system unit, and to a phone line, and it must be turned on.

➤ **Is the phone working?** You can check a phone jack by plugging a regular phone into the jack. Lift the phone off the hook and listen for a dial tone. If you don't hear a dial tone, the jack is dead, and your modem won't be able to dial out.

➤ **Am I dialing the wrong number?** Silly question, but it's a common cause. If you hear an angry voice coming out of the modem, you probably woke somebody up. Hopefully, they don't have Caller ID. Also, if you normally have to dial a number before dialing out (say 9), type the number, a comma, and then the phone number.

➤ **Do I have pulse or tone service?** Pick up your phone and dial a few numbers. If you hear clicks, you have pulse (or rotary) service, even if you have a phone with buttons. If you hear beeps, you have tone service. If your telecommunications program is set for tone service, and you have rotary service, it won't be able to dial out. Try resetting your telecommunications program for rotary service; it's usually as easy as checking an option box.

➤ **Does my program know where the modem is?** Most computers have two COM ports. Usually, a mouse is connected to COM1, and COM2 is left open for another device, often a modem. Your communications program or online service program allows you to specify the COM port being used by your modem. Try changing the COM port setting.

➤ **Are my communications settings correct?** If your communications program can find your modem, dial a number, and establish a connection, but can do nothing else, your communications settings are probably incorrect. If your baud setting is 9,600 bps or higher, try changing it to 2,400. If the modem works with one program but not with another, write down the communications settings from the program that works, and then use those same settings for the program that doesn't work.

The Computer Won't Read My Floppy Disk

Don't feel bad, it happens to everyone. You stick a floppy disk in the disk drive, close the drive door, change to the drive, and you get an error message saying basically that the disk is no good. DOS can't read it or write to it or even see that it's there. What happened? That depends.

277

Fixing Bad Disks

If a disk is bad, you may be able to salvage it using the DOS ScanDisk, as explained in Chapter 26, "Keeping Your Computer in Tip-Top Shape." If a drive is bad, you'll have to take it to a computer mechanic and get it fixed. Usually the problem is that the drive is not spinning at the right speed or that the arm that reads and writes data to the disk is not aligned properly on the disk.

➤ **Is the disk inserted properly?** Even the most experienced computer user occasionally inserts a disk upside-down or sideways into the disk drive. Check to make sure the disk is in the right slot the right way.

➤ **Is the disk drive door closed?** If the drive has a door, it must be closed. Otherwise, you'll get an error message saying that DOS can't read or write to the disk.

➤ **Is the disk write-protected?** If the disk is write-protected, you won't be able to save a file to the disk.

➤ **Is the disk full?** If you try to save a file to a disk, and you get an **Insufficient disk space** message, the disk has insufficient free space to hold any more data. Use a different disk.

➤ **Is the disk formatted?** If you buy new, unformatted disks, you must format the disks before you can use them.

➤ **Did you format the disk to the proper density?** If you format a high-density disk as a low-density disk, or vice versa, you will probably run into problems when you try to use the disk.

➤ **Is the disk bad?** Although it's rare, disks do go bad. Some disks even come bad from the manufacturer. If you get a **Sector not found** or **Data error** message, the disk may be bad. Then again, the drive might need a tune-up. Try some other disks. If you're having problems with all disks, the problem is in the drive. If you are having trouble with only one disk, it's the disk.

My Keyboard Is Schizophrenic

Some fancy keyboards allow you to *remap* the keys. For example, you can make the F1 key on the left side of the keyboard act like the Enter key, or you can make it perform a series of keystrokes. Advanced users like to remap keys to customize the keyboard and make it a time-saver.

However, if you accidentally press the remap key and then continue typing, you may remap your entire keyboard without knowing it. You'll know it when you press the K key and get a Z or you press the Spacebar and delete a paragraph. You can usually unmap the keyboard. If you have an AnyKey keyboard (a brand of keyboard packaged with Gateway computers), you can return a key to normal by pressing the Remap key and then pressing the key you want to return to normal twice.

My Keys Stick

If you have an old keyboard or if you spilled something on the keyboard, the keys may start to stick. Take the keyboard to a computer service store and have it cleaned. Or buy a new keyboard; they're cheap. If your keyboard is completely dead, or if your computer displays the message **Keyboard not found** when you boot your computer, do a quick inspection to make sure the keyboard is plugged in and the cord is in good shape.

My Printer Won't Print

Printers are a pain. They're a pain to set up and a pain to use. And even if you get the printer to finally work with one program, there is no guarantee that it will work with the next one. So if you're running into printer problems, you will probably have to do more fiddling than Nero. To solve most printer problems, see Chapter 19, "Printing Your Creations."

When in Doubt, Get the Heck Out

If no fix works, try rebooting your computer by pressing **Ctrl+Alt+Del**. If that doesn't work, turn everything off and leave it off for three minutes. (This lets the computer clear its head.) Turn on your monitor, then turn on your printer, and then turn on the system unit. If this doesn't fix it, call for help.

Before You Call Tech Support

Many hardware and software companies offer technical support for their products. Usually you have to call long-distance, and you may be charged for advice. To save yourself some money and save the tech support person some headaches, take the following steps before placing your call:

➤ Try everything in this chapter.

➤ Write down a detailed description of the problem, explaining what went wrong and what you were doing at the time.

➤ Write down the name, version number, and license (or registration) number of the program you are having trouble with.

➤ Write down any information about your computer, including the computer brand, chip type and speed, and monitor type.

➤ Turn your printer on, change to the C:\ directory, type **print config.sys**, and press **Enter**. Type **print autoexec.bat** and press **Enter**. Keep the pages handy when you call tech support.

➤ Make sure your computer is turned on. A good tech support person can talk you through most problems if you're sitting at the keyboard.

➤ Now you can call.

The Least You Need to Know

If you don't remember all the specifics given in this chapter, don't worry. Chances are, your specific problem isn't covered. The important thing to remember is how to trace a problem back to its cause. Here are some reminders:

➤ Don't panic.

➤ Look all over the screen for any clues.

➤ Ask yourself when the problem started. Did you install a new program?

➤ Isolate the problem. Does it happen in all programs or just this one? Does it happen all the time?

➤ If you suspect a hardware problem, turn everything off and check the connections. Wiggle the plugs; a loose connection can be as bad or worse than no connection.

➤ As a last resort, turn your computer off, wait three minutes, and then turn everything back on.

Upgrading a PC: How to Spend Even More Money

By the End of This Section, You'll Be Able To:

➤ Get more memory for your computer without adding RAM chips

➤ Install a joystick on your computer

➤ Install a multimedia upgrade kit (or at least understand what's involved)

➤ Name five ways to give your computer more storage space

➤ Add a video accelerator to speed up your computer

If you have a couple thousand bucks sitting in a money market account, this chapter will help you spend it. You'll learn how to install a multimedia upgrade kit to the tune of seven hundred bucks, add memory for seventy bucks per megabyte, add a hard drive for about three hundred bucks, slap on a fax modem for a couple hundred, and add a joystick for about seventy bucks. I'll give you a couple pointers on how to *save* money, too.

Upgrade or Buy New?

Like a house, a computer can be a money pit. One month, you decide you need a new hard disk. The next month, you just gotta have a CD-ROM drive and a sound card. And you always need more memory. By the time you're done, you're a thousand bucks poorer and you have a deskful of fancy new equipment yoked to your incredibly slow 386SX.

To prevent this from happening to you, make a list of all the upgrades you'll need to make your current computer what you want it to be. Add up the costs for the items, and then compare the total cost to what it would cost for a brand-spankin' new computer that has everything you want. Chances are, there won't be much difference.

Putting Off the Upgrade As Long As Possible

If you're having a hard time parting with your old PC, you may be able to string it out for a year or so. That way, prices for more powerful computers will drop, making them more affordable. Here are some money-saving things you might try to wring more power out of your old PC:

More disk space   If your hard disk is getting full, copy the files you don't use to floppy disks, and then delete them from your hard disk. You'll be surprised at how much a little housekeeping can help. If you're still strapped for space, you can use DOS 6.2 or a special disk space doubler program to *compress* the files on your disk so they take up less room. Your computer will run a bit more slowly, but you'll end up with twice as much disk space.

More memory   Most computers have one megabyte of memory, but 384 kilobytes of that is reserved. DOS 5.0 and later can help you free up the reserved memory and make it available to your programs. (DOS 6 and later come with a program called MemMaker that does everything for you.) If you have at least two megabytes of RAM and you have Windows, you can run Windows in enhanced mode and can use your hard disk as *virtual memory*. Although this "disk memory" is slower than real RAM, it does allow you to run more complex programs in Windows. (Refer to your Windows documentation or the Help system for details.)

Faster computer   If your computer seems overly sluggish, your hard disk may be in disarray. As the computer saves files to the hard disk, the files get fragmented, and the drive has to look all over for the parts of each file. To get help, go to the DOS prompt, type **chkdsk /f** and press **Enter**. Follow the on-screen instructions. You can also purchase a program (PC Tools or The Norton Utilities) that can help defragment the disk. (A disk that is too full can also slow your computer, another reason for good housekeeping.)

RAM disk   If you have extra RAM (not likely), you can set part of the RAM aside to use as a disk. Because RAM is faster than disk storage, if you store the file on your RAM disk, your program can work with it more quickly. The only hitch is that you eventually need to save the file that's on your RAM disk to a real disk, or else you'll lose it when you quit the program. Refer to your DOS or Windows manual for details.

Adding sounds   I know, all your friends' computers make nifty sounds, but yours doesn't. Instead of adding a sound board, you may be able to get by with a free program for Windows that allows your dinky computer speaker to make similar sounds. You can get the program from an online service or local user group.

Faxing through a service   If you send only one or two faxes a month, you might not need a fax modem. You can send a fax through most online services. It may cost a couple bucks per fax, and it's not as convenient, but it may suit your needs.

Pictures sans scanner   If you don't want to shell out big bucks for a scanner, you can leave space on your printouts and then paste a picture in the space. Xerox the sheet on some high-quality paper, and nobody will ever know the difference.

If these cheap fixes don't quite do it, you may have no choice but to buy a bag of RAM chips, a new hard disk, or some other hardware. If that's the case, read on.

Cramming In the RAM

Four years ago, I bought a computer with two megs of RAM. I was convinced that Windows would never catch on, and two megs was plenty for the work I had in mind. Boy, was I wrong. Once I fired up Windows 3.1, I realized how wrong I was. I couldn't even get it to run in enhanced mode so I could set up some virtual memory. I had to slap four more megs of memory into my computer to satisfy it.

If you're facing the same predicament, you're probably wondering what it takes to install more memory. The answer is, "It depends." On most computers you can insert memory chips in the motherboard. You turn off your computer, unplug it, take the cover off, and use little tweezer-like things called chip handlers to plug the chips in. Some computers (like mine) require a memory board. The board contains the RAM chips. You insert the board into one of the expansion slots inside the system unit.

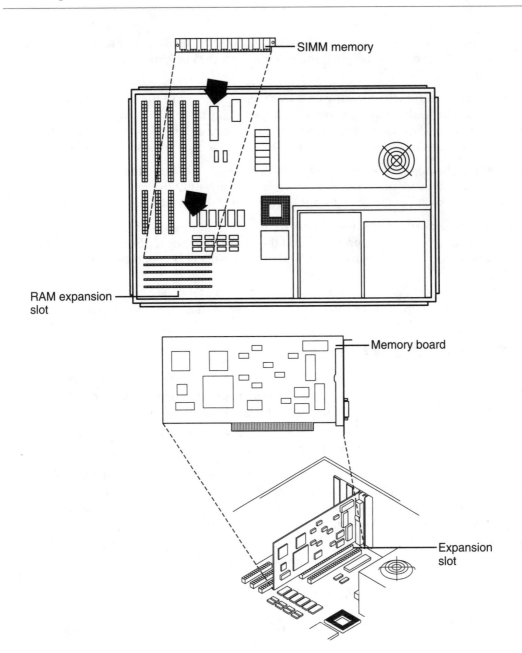

You can plug RAM chips into the motherboard or add a memory board.

But installing the chips isn't the hard part. The hard part is deciding which chips to buy. Chips differ in respect to three things: type, capacity, and speed. The *chip type* can be

284

DIP (Dual In-line Package), SIP (Single In-line Package), or the more popular SIMM (Single In-line Memory Module). A SIMM is basically a small card that has a bunch (three or nine) of DIPs plugged into it. *Capacity* refers to how many kilobytes or megabytes the chip can store. Common capacities are 256K, 512K, and 1M. (Refer to your computer manual to determine which capacity your computer accepts.) *Speed* is measured in nanoseconds (ns), and ranges from 50ns to 120ns. Don't mix chips of different speeds. If you're not sure what type of chips you need, ask at your local computer store or look in a catalog. Most stores have a chart that shows the types of RAM chips used in most of the popular computer brands.

Out of Disk Space?

Today's programs consume gobs of disk space. For example, a full installation of the latest version of Word for Windows requires about 20 megabytes. And the latest version of MathBlaster Plus grabs 10 megabytes. You can put off getting a bigger hard drive by running DOS 6.2's DoubleSpace utility, but even with that you'll eventually need more space. When that happens, you'll need to know what to look for in a hard drive.

The two biggest criteria for judging a hard drive are storage *capacity* and *speed*. Figure on spending a buck per megabyte; a 300 megabyte drive should cost about $300. Don't buy anything less than a 230 megabyte drive. Speed (access time) is measured in milliseconds (ms): 13ms is fast, 25ms is slow. (If speed is expressed as seek time, look for 10ms or faster.) Also, check out the drive's data transfer rate, measured in kilobytes per second. 700 kilobytes per second is fast. 500 kilobytes per second is slow. A faster drive might cost more, but it can speed up your entire system.

In addition to the drive itself, your computer may also need a controller card to plug the drive into. The controller card that your current hard drive is plugged into may have an open connection where you can plug in another hard drive. If you think you can use your existing controller card, check to see if the new disk drive is compatible with that card. If it's not, make sure the new drive comes with the card and cables you need to connect it. The most popular drives and controllers are IDE (Intelligent Drive Electronics), which are recommended for up to 1GB (gigabyte) of storage (over 1000 megabytes). SCSI (small computer system interface) are more expensive controllers. SCSI controller cards allow you to connect up to seven devices to your computer, including a CD-ROM drive, a hard drive, and a tape backup drive.

SCSI
Pronounced "scuzzy." Stands for small computer system interface. SCSI is a connection that allows high-speed information transfer between the computer and any external devices, such as a printer or hard drive. SCSI offers the additional advantage of allowing you to connect several devices to a single port, although you can use only one device at a time.

One last thing to look for in a new hard disk drive is a *cache* or *buffer*. The cache is built-in memory that stores often-used data electronically so the CPU can get it quickly. The cache size should be anywhere from 64K to 256K—the more the better.

Add a Hard Drive?

The easiest way to add another hard drive to your computer is to buy a hard drive expansion card (hard drive on a card) and plug it into one of your computer's expansion slots. These cards are slightly more expensive than a standard hard drive, but you don't have to mess with a drive controller and cable connections. These are especially good for laptop computers.

Do You Need Another Floppy Drive?

If your computer has a single 3.5" high-density floppy drive, you probably don't need another floppy drive. If someone hands you a 5.25" disk, just give the person a dirty look, and say, "What's this?!" Stand there until the person takes the disk and replaces it with a 3.5" disk. If you're the person with the 5.25" drive, you might want to install a 3.5" high-density drive.

A Dynamic Duo

If you have a thin, space-saving computer, you may have only two drive bays, but you want to install 3 drives: a 3.5" floppy, a 5.25" floppy, and a CD-ROM drive. In that case, you can purchase a dual floppy drive that accepts both the 3.5" and 5.25" disks and fits into a single drive bay. You can then use the other drive bay for your CD-ROM drive.

A floppy drive plugs into a controller card like a hard drive, as shown in the previous figure. Usually you have to do three things:

1. Pop the drive bay cover off the system unit.

2. Mount the floppy drive in the drive bay. (The floppy drive usually comes with mounting brackets.)

3. Connect the cable from the controller board to the back of the floppy drive.

I lied; there is a fourth step. Whenever you install a drive in your computer you must run your computer's setup program to specify the location and type of drive you installed. Otherwise, the computer may not recognize the drive and may not let you use it. Refer to the documentation that came with your computer. On many computers you run the Setup program by typing **setup** at the DOS prompt and pressing **Enter**.

Lightning-Fast Video

Because Windows likes to do somersaults with graphics, your entire system works up a sweat trying to keep up. Standard video cards just aren't up to the task. To help, you can get a video accelerator or Windows accelerator card. The card should handle 1024 by 768 resolution and 256 colors. It should have a 72Hz refresh rate and 1MB video RAM (VRAM). Watch out for cards that have a refresh rate of 70Hz or slower; the slower refresh rate causes the image to flicker.

Yank your old video card out, plug the video accelerator board into the now-open slot, and plug your monitor into the card. Most video accelerators also come with a disk that contains drivers, which tell the computer how to use the board. The process for installing these drivers varies depending on the manufacturer.

Game Cards and Joysticks

Before you run out and buy a joystick and game card, spin your system unit around and see if you have a game port on the back. Some computers have a built-in game port. If you have a sound card, it may have a game port as well. In either case, you can buy a joystick and connect it to this port and you won't need a game card. If you don't have a game port, you'll have to buy both a game card and a joystick. You might also have to install a joystick driver (a file that comes on disk and tells your computer what to do with the joystick).

Joining the Multimedia Madness

If you had the foresight (and money) to buy a multimedia PC, complete with sound board and CD-ROM drive, you can skip this section on multimedia. This section is for the less fortunate. First of all, let me define the minimum requirements for multimedia:

➤ 386 or better microprocessor and at least four megabytes of RAM.

➤ Microsoft Windows and Windows-compatible software.

➤ 100MB or larger hard drive (to store your Windows-compatible software).

➤ Super VGA monitor (to display all the pretty pictures and video clips).

➤ CD-ROM drive

287

➤ Sound card (make sure it can handle both digitized and synthesized sounds)

➤ Speakers and a microphone (the microphone is optional, but you'll probably want to record something)

Now that you know what you need, what next? You have two options: buy a multimedia upgrade kit, or buy the components separately. The easy option is to go with the kit. That way you know that the CD-ROM drive and sound card will work together, and you'll get all the cables and software you need. Most upgrade kits also include a small collection of CDs, so you get immediate gratification. Creative Labs, IBM, Sony, and Apple offer upgrade kits for under $700.

The second option (purchasing the components separately) is riskier. However, if you already have a sound card, it makes little sense to buy a complete kit. If you're buying the items separately, make sure all the items are compatible. Most sound cards and CD-ROM drives comply with MPC (Multimedia PC) standards, ensuring that they will work together—but ask the dealer or salesperson to be sure. Here's what to look for:

Sound card requirements Sound Blaster or AdLib compatible; stereo output; 16 bit record and play (MPC 2 standard); 44.1kHz maximum sampling rate; Wave or FM synthesizer; ports for a speaker, microphone, and joystick; SCSI port for a CD-ROM drive.

CD-ROM drive requirements 250ms access time; dual-speed drive of 150 Kbps to 300 Kbps; 64K on-drive cache; SCSI interface; MPC 2 compatible; output jack and volume control. If you have room, an internal CD-ROM is better.

Reaching Out with a Modem

Most users eventually add a modem to their computers to connect to an online service or to send and receive faxes. But I talked all about this in Chapter 23, so I won't beat it to death here. Just flip back to Chapter 23 for details on shopping for and installing a modem.

Adding a Scanner

Scanners enable you to copy text and graphics from paper and pull it into your PC. If you have a program that offers optical character recognition, you can have the program convert scanned text into text you can edit in a word-processing program. When shopping for a scanner, you have all sorts of decisions to make. Do you want a hand-held scanner, a flatbed scanner, or a 3-dimensional scanner? Do you need to scan in color? How much detail must the scanner pick up? Here's a list of things you should consider:

Scanner types   *Hand-held scanners* are the most popular and least expensive ($150 to $300). You drag the scanner across the page to scan in the image. For scanning whole pages or pages with text, a *flatbed scanner* is much better. You place the page on the scanner, and the machine does the work (like Xeroxing). A good flatbed scanner costs $600 and up. The most expensive scanners are *3-D document scanners*. These are essentially cameras that can "photograph" anything from a page to a basketball.

Color or grayscale   For printing in color or to capture color images for presentations, go color. If you're just going to print in black-and-white, go grayscale. Both types can handle different numbers of colors or shades of gray.

Resolution   Scanner resolution, like printer resolution, is measured in dots per inch (dpi). The higher the resolution, the sharper the image. However, at higher resolutions, the scanner requires more RAM and the scanned image file gets big. Your scanner should scan up to 400 dpi, but should have controls to scan at lower resolutions.

Twain compatible   Twain is a standard that enables various Windows programs to communicate with the scanner. For example, if you have CorelDRAW! (a popular drawing program), you can enter the Scan command in CorelDRAW! and then use your scanner to bring a picture into the screen. If a scanner is not Twain compatible, you have to leave CorelDRAW!, scan the image, save it as a file, and then import it into CorelDRAW!.

External controls   A scanner should have controls for adjusting brightness, contrast, color (or grayscale), and resolution.

Software included   The scanner should include software for scanning and manipulating the image. It should also contain OCR software for transforming scanned text into editable text. The software that comes with some scanners is primitive.

Installing a scanner is a lot like installing a joystick. You insert an expansion board into one of your system unit's open expansion slots, and then plug the scanner into the board. You also have to run software to tell your system where the scanner is located.

Slapping In an Expansion Board

Nine out of ten upgrades require you to "install" an expansion board. The process consists of plugging the expansion board into a slot inside your computer. The only hard part is keeping the board from breaking while you rock it into place.

Before you start, here are a few safety precautions to keep in mind. First, before you touch the expansion board, touch your computer case to discharge any static electricity (this static can fry the fragile components on the board). Second, touch the board by its edges; avoid touching any metal or solder. Finally, don't force the board into its slot; ease it in. Now, you're ready:

1. Read the instructions that came with the board.

2. Remove the system unit cover. There are usually screws on the back and/or sides. Don't touch anything inside the system unit.

3. Look for open expansion slots (more like slits) inside the system unit, near the back. Find the smallest slot that your board will plug into. (Leave larger slots for future upgrades.)

4. Behind the expansion slot is a metal bracket that covers the "hole." The port on the expansion board will poke through this hole. Remove the screw that holds the bracket in place, being careful not to drop the screw inside the system unit. (If you drop the screw, stick some tape on a pencil eraser and try to fish out the screw; don't use your fingers.)

5. Touch an unpainted part of your system unit's case to discharge any static electricity. Now, plant your feet firmly and don't move them. You don't want to generate more static.

6. Open the protective plastic bag that contains the expansion board, gently grab the board by its edges, and remove it from the bag.

7. Hold the board with the metal bracket facing the hole and the metal "feet" on the board pointing down.

8. Insert the metal feet on the board into the expansion slot, and gently rock the board back and forth until it seats itself firmly in the slot.

9. Tighten the old bracket's screw into the expansion card bracket to hold the board firmly in place. (Keep the old bracket in case you remove the board later.)

10. Replace the system unit cover, plug in the system unit, and boot your computer. (You may want to leave the screws off the system unit cover until you are sure everything is working.)

11. Run any software that came with the card. You may also have to run your computer's setup program.

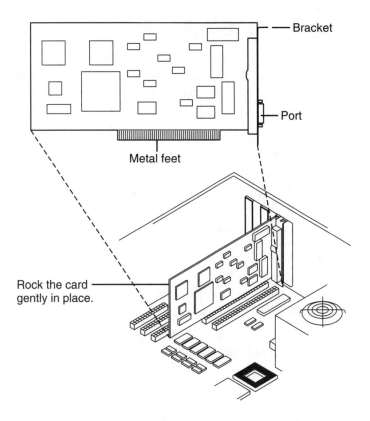

The expansion board slides into an expansion slot on the motherboard.

What Could Possibly Go Wrong?

The problem you are most likely to run into is that the expansion board has the same *address* as a board already in your computer. This causes a conflict that confuses your PC, so the new card won't function. Luckily, most boards have DIP switches that you can reset to a new address. DIP switches are small. Some are like little light switches, and others have jumpers that slide on and off pairs of pins. In either case, before you start, draw a sketch that shows the original settings of the switches. Then read the manual that came with the board to find some alternative configurations. Turn off the computer and discharge any static electricity before you start playing with the switches. Try one configuration at a time until you find one that works. This can be a maddening process.

291

The Least You Need To Know

If this chapter merely whets your appetite for upgrade information, you can purchase another book called *The Complete Idiot's Guide to Buying and Upgrading PCs* that contains scads of information about upgrading. If, however, the detail I provided was overwhelming, here's a boiled down version:

➤ If upgrading your current computer is going to cost almost as much as buying a new one, buy a new one.

➤ If your hard disk is running out of room, remove any files you don't use, and then run a disk doubler, such as DOS's DoubleSpace or Stacker.

➤ When shopping for RAM, make sure the RAM chips you get are the type, capacity, and speed that your computer can use.

➤ When shopping for a hard drive, don't settle for less than a 230MB, 13ms, IDE drive with a 64K cache or buffer.

➤ When shopping for a joystick, make sure your system unit has a game port, or you must purchase a game card, as well.

➤ Multimedia upgrade kits come with a CD-ROM drive and sound card that work together. These kits may also include CDs.

Savvy Shopper's Guide to Applications

Take a field trip to any of the big computer stores, and you'll see shelves dripping with the latest software—word processors, spreadsheets, databases, tax software, presentation programs, and everything else you can imagine. To sift through the programs and make an informed decision, use the following buyer's guide.

This guide includes the names of the most popular programs in each software category, an overall rating, a ballpark price, and a list of the hardware you need to run each application. The overall rating is based on several factors, including how easy the program is to learn and use, how many features it offers, and how well it stacks up against similar products in its price range. My top rating is four stars, three is okay, under three is okay if you get the program for free. I left any real lemons off the list, so the ratings don't usually dip below two and a half.

The Price Is Right

The prices shown in the table are prices I got at the local computer store. The manufacturer's list price is usually much higher, but no one sells the applications at those prices, so I'm not going to use them. They're too scary.

Software Product	$$$$$	Overall Rating	Hardware Requirements
Business Presentation Programs			
PowerPoint (Powerful, easy to use, lots of clip art)	$330	****	386 or higher processor EGA or VGA DOS 3.1 and Windows 3.1 2MB RAM 15MB hard disk space Microsoft mouse
Freelance Graphics (Easy to use)	$250	***$^1/_2$	286 or higher processor EGA or better DOS 3.1 and Windows 3.0 3MB RAM 9MB hard disk space Microsoft mouse
Harvard Graphics (DOS) (Best program if you don't have Windows)	$400	***$^1/_2$	286 or higher processor EGA or VGA DOS 3.0 640K RAM 4.5MB–12MB hard disk space Microsoft mouse
WordPerfect Presentations (Good for the price, some packages include a scanner)	$130	***	386 or higher processor EGA or VGA Windows 3.1 4MB RAM 9MB–22MB hard disk space Microsoft mouse
Databases			
Access (Contains Wizards that lead you through the process of creating a database)	$300	***$^1/_2$	386SX or higher processor EGA or better Windows 3.0 or higher 4MB–6MB RAM 8MB–14MB hard disk space Microsoft mouse

Software Product	$$$$$	Overall Rating	Hardware Requirements
Paradox for Windows (Powerful, but not the easiest to learn)	$140	****	386SX or higher processor EGA or VGA Windows 3.1 4MB–6MB RAM Hard disk
FileMaker Pro (Powerful and fairly easy to learn)	$120	***$1/_2$	286 or higher processor VGA Windows 3.0 or higher 3MB–4MB RAM Hard disk
FoxPro (DOS or Windows) $300 (Powerful and fast, excellent for creating your own database applications)	$300	***$1/_2$	8088 (DOS) or 386 (Windows) DOS 3.1 or Windows 3.1 (for the Windows version) 640K–3MB RAM Hard disk Microsoft mouse (for Windows)
Q&A (DOS or Windows) (Easy to learn and use, comes with a word processor, good for mail merges)	$160	***	DOS 2.0 640K RAM Hard disk Windows version requires Windows 3.1 and 2–4MB RAM

Desktop Publishing

PageMaker (Excellent for book-length publications)	$580	****	386 or higher processor VGA or better Windows 3.1 4MB RAM Hard disk Microsoft mouse

continues

continued

Software Product	$$$$$	Overall Rating	Hardware Requirements
FrameMaker (Excellent for manuals and hypertext documents)	$600	****	386 or higher processor VGA or better PostScript printer 8MB RAM 10–20MB hard disk space Microsoft mouse
QuarkXPress (Good for magazines and difficult page layouts)	$570	****	386 or higher processor VGA or better PostScript Printer with at least 2MB memory Windows 3.1 4MB RAM Hard disk Microsoft mouse
Microsoft Publisher (Excellent for creating greeting cards, brochures, and newsletters, but not for books)	$100	****	286 or higher processor VGA or better DOS 3.1 and Windows 3.1 4MB RAM 6–13MB hard disk space Microsoft mouse
Print Shop Deluxe (DOS or Windows) (Great for home and small-business use, but not good for long publications)	$50	***	286 or higher processor VGA DOS 3.0 and Windows 3.1 (for the Windows version) 2MB RAM (640K for the DOS version) Hard disk Microsoft mouse
Publish It! (Get this if you have an old PC that can't run anything else)	$45	*$^{1}/_{2}$	DOS 2.1 CGA or better 640K RAM Microsoft mouse

Software Product	$$$$$	Overall Rating	Hardware Requirements
Graphics			
CorelDRAW! (Great all-around graphics program, powerful and easy to use)	$400	****	386 or higher processor VGA or better Windows 3.1 4–8MB RAM Hard disk (CD-ROM version recommended) Microsoft mouse
Micrografx Designer (A bit complex for beginning users, but good for experienced graphics artists)	$460	****	386 or higher processor VGA or better Windows 3.1 4MB RAM Hard disk Microsoft mouse
Adobe Illustrator (Great for creating ads, technical illustrations, and brochures)	$550	****	386 or higher processor VGA or better PostScript printer DOS 3.3 and Windows 3.1 4MB RAM Hard disk Microsoft mouse
VISIO (Comes with predrawn images that you can combine to create illustrations. Good for business use)	$130	***	386SX or higher processor VGA or better Windows 3.1 4MB RAM 15MB hard disk space Microsoft mouse
PC Paintbrush (Good paint program, but does not offer the drawing capabilities of CorelDRAW!)	$40	***	EGA or better DOS 3.0 640K RAM Hard disk

continues

297

continued

Software Product	$$$$$	Overall Rating	Hardware Requirements
Windows Draw (Okay program for beginners)	$50	**$\frac{1}{2}$	286 or higher processor EGA or better Windows 3.0 2MB RAM Hard disk Microsoft mouse
Fax Software			
WinFax PRO (Best all-purpose fax program)	$100	****	286 or higher processor EGA or better Windows 3.0 2MB RAM 3MB hard disk space Class 1-, Class 2-, or CAS-compatible fax modem
DOSFax PRO (Best fax program for DOS)	$60	***	CGA or better Class 1- or Class 2-compatible fax modem
Eclipse FAX (Fairly inexpensive, yet powerful)	$70	***	286 or higher processor EGA or better Windows 3.0 or higher 2MB RAM 2MB hard disk space Class 1-, Class 2-, or CAS-compatible fax modem
Integrated Software			
Microsoft Office (Contains Microsoft Word for Windows, Excel, PowerPoint, and Microsoft Mail)	$600	****	386 or higher processor EGA or VGA DOS 3.1 and Windows 3.1 4–6MB RAM 25–62MB hard disk space Microsoft mouse

298

Software Product	$$$$$	Overall Rating	Hardware Requirements
Lotus SmartSuite (Contains Ami Pro, Lotus 1-2-3, Organizer, Freelance Graphics, and Approach)	$350	***1/2	386 or higher processor EGA or VGA Windows 3.0 or higher 4MB RAM 27MB hard disk space Microsoft mouse
ClarisWorks (Offers word processing, spreadsheet, database, drawing, and charting)	$130	***	386 or higher processor VGA or better DOS 3.1 and Windows 3.1 2MB RAM Hard disk Microsoft mouse
Microsoft Works (DOS or Windows) (Easy to use—this is a trimmed-down version of Microsoft Office)	$100	***1/2	386SX or higher processor VGA or better DOS 3.1 and Windows 3.1 2MB RAM 4–14MB hard disk space Microsoft mouse
Lotus Works (This is a trimmed-down version of Lotus SmartSuite)	$100	***1/2	286 or higher processor EGA or VGA DOS 3.0 or higher 640K RAM Hard disk Microsoft mouse

Money Management

Software Product	$$$$$	Overall Rating	Hardware Requirements
Peachtree Complete (Good accounting program for small or large businesses)	$120	****	386 or higher processor EGA or VGA DOS 3.1 and Windows 3.1 (for the Windows version) 640K RAM (for DOS) 2MB RAM (for Windows) Hard disk Microsoft mouse

continues

continued

Software Product	$$$$$	Overall Rating	Hardware Requirements
DacEasy (Not quite as easy to use as Peachtree Complete)	$100	***	DOS 3.1 640K RAM Hard disk Microsoft mouse
Quicken (DOS or Windows) (The best home-finance program)	$40	***$^1/_2$	286 or higher processor EGA or better DOS 3.1 and Windows 3.1 (for the Windows version) 640K RAM (for DOS) 2MB RAM (for Windows) Hard disk Microsoft mouse
Microsoft Money (Good for home finances)	$23	***	286 or higher processor EGA or VGA DOS 3.1 and Windows 3.1 2MB RAM Hard disk

Online Services

Software Product	$$$$$	Overall Rating	Hardware Requirements
PRODIGY (DOS or Windows) (Good family service, lots for kids)	$10 plus $15 monthly fee for unlimited access to basic basic features	***$^1/_2$	386 or higher processor VGA Windows 3.0 (for the Windows version) 640K RAM (DOS) 4MB RAM (for Windows) 3.5MB hard disk space Hayes-compatible modem
America Online (The service of choice for the hip generation)	$23 plus $10 monthly fee for 5 hours access	***$^1/_2$	386 or higher processor EGA or VGA Windows 3.0 for the Windows version) 640K RAM (DOS) 2MB RAM (Windows) 2MB hard disk space

Software Product	$$$$$	Overall Rating	Hardware Requirements
CompuServe (Good service for techies and business people)	$25 plus $9 monthly fee for unlimited access to basic features	***$1/2$	386 or higher processor EGA or VGA DOS 3.1 and Windows 3.1 2MB RAM 15MB hard disk space Microsoft mouse

Personal Information Managers

Software Product	$$$$$	Overall Rating	Hardware Requirements
Lotus Organizer (Great program for keeping track of schedules and addresses, easy to use)	$100	***	386 or higher processor VGA Windows 3.0 2MB RAM 4MB hard disk space Microsoft mouse
ACT! (DOS or Windows) (Excellent program for keeping track of contacts and accounts)	$270	****	286 (DOS) or 386 (Windows) EGA or VGA DOS 3.1 and Windows 3.1 (for the Windows version) 640K RAM (DOS) 4MB RAM (Windows) 3MB hard disk space Microsoft mouse (for Windows)
PackRat (Good general purpose organizer, very powerful and easy to customize)	$180	***$1/2$	386SX or higher processor VGA or better Windows 3.1 2–4MB RAM 8MB hard disk space Microsoft mouse

continues

301

continued

Software Product	$$$$$	Overall Rating	Hardware Requirements
Spreadsheets			
Lotus 1-2-3 (DOS or Windows) (One of the best DOS spreadsheets on the market)	$420 (DOS) $320 (Windows)	**** (DOS) ***$^1/_2$ (Windows)	286 or higher processor CGA (DOS) EGA or better (Windows) DOS 2.1 or DOS 3.3 and Windows 3.0 (for Windows) 640K RAM (DOS) 4MB RAM (Windows) 8MB hard disk space (Windows version) Microsoft mouse (Windows version)
Excel (This Windows spreadsheet is easy to use and powerful)	$300	****	386 or higher processor EGA or VGA DOS 3.1 and Windows 3.1 4MB RAM 8–22MB hard disk space Microsoft mouse
Quattro Pro (DOS or Windows) (Excel gets all the press, but this spreadsheet is as good or better, and is a lot more affordable)	$100	****	8088 (DOS) 386 or higher (Windows) CGA (DOS) VGA or better (Windows) DOS 2.1 (DOS) Windows 3.0 (Windows) 640K RAM (DOS) 4MB RAM (Windows) 12MB hard disk space (Windows)

Software Product	$$$$$	Overall Rating	Hardware Requirements
Telecommunications			
Crosstalk (Powerful, but may be more than a beginning user needs)	$120	***¹/₂	386SX or higher processor VGA or better Windows 3.1 2MB RAM 4.5MB hard disk space Modem
Smartcom (Affordable and easy to use)	$50	***	286 or higher processor EGA or better DOS 3.1 and Windows 3.0 2–4MB RAM Hard disk Hayes-compatible modem
PROCOMM PLUS (DOS or Windows) (Excellent for both DOS and Windows, works with a wide range of modems)	$100	****	8088 or 286 (for Windows) EGA or better (for Windows) Windows 3.0 (for Windows version) 192K free RAM or 2MB RAM (for Windows) Modem
Word Processors			
Microsoft Word (DOS or Windows) (The best in the Windows arena, but in DOS, WordPerfect is more flexible)	$300	*** (DOS) **** (Windows)	286 or higher processor EGA or better DOS 3.0 and Windows 3.1 (for Windows version) 640K RAM (DOS) 4MB RAM (Windows) 5–25MB hard disk space Microsoft mouse (Windows)

continues

303

continued

Software Product	$$$$$	Overall Rating	Hardware Requirements
WordPerfect (DOS or Windows) (If you're looking for a powerful DOS word processor, this is it. For Windows, look elsewhere)	$300	**** (DOS) *** (Windows)	286 or higher processor EGA or better DOS 3.0 and Windows 3.1 (for the Windows version) 640K RAM (DOS) 6MB RAM (Windows) 32MB hard disk space (Windows version) Microsoft mouse (Windows)
Ami Pro (Flexible and easy to use, a close second to Word for Windows)	$270	***$^1/_2$	386SX or higher processor EGA or VGA DOS 3.0 and Windows 3. 2MB RAM 11MB hard disk space Microsoft mouse
Q&A Write (Inexpensive and easy to use)	$30	**$^1/_2$	286 or higher processor EGA or VGA DOS 3.1 and Windows 3.1 2MB RAM 4MB hard disk space Microsoft mouse

Utility Programs

Software Product	$$$$$	Overall Rating	Hardware Requirements
The Norton Utilities (Best for data recovery)	$120	****	286 or higher processor 640K RAM 6MB hard disk space
PC Tools (DOS or Windows) (Offers data recovery and backup, virus protection, file management, database, word processor, and a lot more)	$100	****	286 (DOS) 386SX (Windows) EGA or better (Windows) DOS 3.3 (DOS) or Windows 3.1 (Windows) 640K RAM (DOS) 4MB RAM (Windows) 8MB hard disk space (Windows) Microsoft mouse (Windows)

Software Product	$$$$$	Overall Rating	Hardware Requirements
UnInstaller (Removes Windows applications)	$40	****	386SX or higher processor VGA or better Windows 3.1 2–4MB RAM Hard disk Microsoft mouse
The Norton Desktop (Transforms Windows into a Macintosh-like work area)	$120	***$1/_2$	386 or higher processor VGA or better DOS 3.3 and Windows 3.1 4MB RAM 15MB hard disk space Microsoft mouse
FastBack Plus (DOS or Windows) (Best backup program)	$100	****	8088 or 286 (Windows) EGA or better DOS 3.3 (DOS) Windows 3.1 (for Windows version) 640K RAM (DOS) 2MB RAM (Windows) 2.5MB hard disk space Microsoft mouse

Speak Like a Geek: The Complete Archive

The computer world is like a big exclusive club complete with its own language. If you want to be accepted into the Royal Order of Computer Geeks, you had better learn the lingo. The following glossary will help.

Keep in mind that you'll never achieve full geekhood by passively reading the terms and definitions. Try to say the term aloud and then use it in a sentence. When the other geeks hear you reciting computer terms to yourself, they will immediately accept you into their group.

access time The average time it takes a device (usually a disk drive) to find a random piece of data on a disk. Access time is measured in milliseconds (the lower the number, the faster the drive). Good access times are between 10 ms and 15 ms. (See also *transfer rate*.)

application Also known as *program*; a set of instructions that enable a computer to perform a specific task, such as word processing or data management.

ASCII file A file containing characters that any program on any computer can use. Sometimes called a *text file* or an *ASCII text file*. (ASCII is pronounced "ASK-key.")

AUTOEXEC.BAT A batch file that DOS reads whenever you boot or reboot your computer. This file contains a series of commands that DOS automatically reads and executes.

batch file Any file that contains a series of commands. You run the batch file just as you would run a program file (by entering its name at the DOS prompt). The most famous batch file is AUTOEXEC.BAT.

baud   A unit for measuring the speed of data transmission, which is usually used to describe the speed at which a modem transfers data, such as 2,400 baud. A more accurate measure of transmission speed is bps (bits per second).

BIOS (basic input-output system)   The start-up instructions for a computer. The BIOS tells the computer how to control traffic between the various elements that make up the computer, including disk drives, the printer, the ports, and the monitor.

boot   To start a computer with the operating system software (usually DOS) in place.

bulletin board system (BBS)   A BBS is a program that enables a computer to automatically answer the phone when other computers call. The BBS allows the calling computer to copy files to it (*upload* files) and copy files from it (*download* files). Although you can purchase a BBS program to set up your own BBS, most users work with BBSs set up by computer companies and professional associations.

bus   A superhighway that carries information electronically from one part of the computer to another. There are three such highways:

➤ A *data bus* carries data back and forth between memory and the microprocessor.

➤ An *address bus* carries information about the locations (addresses) of specific information.

➤ A *control bus* carries control signals to make sure traffic flows smoothly, without confusion.

byte   A group of eight bits that usually represents a character or a digit. For example, the byte 01000001 represents the letter A.

cache   Pronounced "cash," this is a part of memory that makes your computer run faster by holding the most recently accessed data from a disk. The next time the computer needs the data, the computer gets it from memory rather than from the disk, which would be slower. Sometimes called a *RAM cache*.

capacity   A measure of how much data a disk can store. For example, a 5.25", high-density floppy disk can be formatted to store 1.2MB; 1.2MB is the disk's *capacity*.

CD-ROM (Compact-Disc Read-Only Memory)   A storage technology that uses the same kind of discs you play in an audio CD player for mass storage of computer data. A single disc can store over 600MB of information. (Pronounced "see-dee-rahm.")

cell   The box formed by the intersection of a row (1,2,3...) and column (A,B,C...) in a spreadsheet. Each cell has an *address* (such as B12) that defines its column and row. A cell may contain text, a numeric value, or a formula.

click To move the mouse pointer over an object or icon and press and release the mouse button once without moving the mouse.

Clipboard A temporary storage area that holds text and graphics. The Cut and Copy commands put text or graphics on the Clipboard, replacing the Clipboard's previous contents. The Paste command copies Clipboard data to a document.

CMOS (Complementary Metal-Oxide Semiconductor) Pronounced "SEA-moss," CMOS is an electronic device (usually battery operated) that stores information about your computer.

COM port Short for COMmunications port. A receptacle, usually at the back of the computer, into which you can plug a serial device such as a modem, mouse, or serial printer. If your computer has more than one COM port, the ports are numbered COM1, COM2, and so on.

command An order that tells the computer what to do. In command-driven programs, you have to press a specific key or type the command to execute it. With menu-driven programs, you select the command from a menu.

computer Any machine that accepts input (from a user), processes the input, and produces output in some form.

CPU (central processing unit) See *microprocessor*.

crash Failure of a system or program. Usually, you realize that your system has crashed when the display or keyboard locks up. The term *crash* is also used to refer to a disk crash or head crash. A disk crash occurs when the read/write head in the disk drive falls on the disk. This would be like dropping a phonograph needle on a record. A disk crash can destroy any data stored where the read/write head falls on the disk.

cursor A horizontal line that appears below characters. A cursor acts like the tip of your pencil; anything you type appears at the cursor. (See also *insertion point*.)

data The facts and figures that you enter into the computer and that the computer stores and uses.

database A type of computer program used for storing, organizing, and retrieving information. Popular database programs include dBASE, Paradox, and Q&A.

density A measure of the amount of data that can be stored per square inch of storage area on a disk.

desktop publishing (DTP) A program that enables you to combine text and graphics on the same page and manipulate the text and graphics on-screen. You can use desktop publishing programs to create newsletters, brochures, flyers, résumés, and business cards.

dialog box   In many programs, you can enter a simple command to perform some task, such as saving a file. However, you may need to enter additional information before the program can perform the task. In such cases, the program may display a dialog box, which allows you to carry on a "conversation" with the program.

directory   Because large hard disks can store thousands of files, you often need to group related files in separate directories on the disk. Think of your disk as a filing cabinet and think of each directory as a drawer in the cabinet. By keeping files in separate directories, it is easier to locate and work with related files.

disk   A round, flat, magnetic storage medium. See *floppy disk* and *hard disk*.

disk drive   A device that writes data to a magnetic disk and reads data from the disk. Think of a disk drive as being like a cassette recorder/player. Just as the cassette player can record sounds on a magnetic cassette tape and play back those sounds, a disk drive can record data on a magnetic disk and play back that data.

DOS (disk operating system)   DOS, which rhymes with "boss," is an essential program that provides the necessary instructions for the computer's parts (keyboard, disk drive, central processing unit, display screen, printer, and so on) to function as a unit.

DOS prompt   An on-screen prompt that indicates DOS is ready to accept a command. It looks something like C> or C:\.

download   To copy files from another computer to your computer, usually through a modem. See also *upload*.

e-mail   Short for *electronic mail*, e-mail is a system that enables people to send and receive messages from computer to computer. E-mail is usually available on networks and online information services.

EMS (Expanded Memory Specification)   See *expanded memory*.

environment   An *environment* is an electronic setting in which you perform tasks on your computer. Microsoft Windows, for example, displays a graphical environment that lets you enter commands by selecting pictures rather than by typing commands. This makes it much easier to use your computer (assuming you know what the pictures stand for).

executable file   A program file that can run the program. Executable files end in .BAT, .COM, or .EXE.

expanded memory   A special way for IBM computers to use memory beyond 640 kilobytes. With expanded memory, additional memory is added to the computer in the form of memory chips or a memory board. To access this additional memory, an expanded memory manager reserves 64 of the standard 640 kilobytes as a swap area. The 64 kilobytes represent four *pages,* each page consisting of 16 kilobytes. Pages of data are swapped into and out of this 64 kilobyte region from expanded memory at a high speed. Not all programs can use expanded memory. See also *extended memory.*

expansion slot   An opening on the motherboard (inside the system unit) that allows you to add devices to the system unit.

extended memory   Extended memory is the same sort of memory that makes up the one megabyte of base memory that most PCs have. Extended memory is directly available to the processor in your computer, unlike expanded memory in which data must be swapped into and out of the base memory. See also *expanded memory.*

extension   In DOS, each file you create has a unique name. The name consists of two parts: a file name and an extension, separated by a dot. The file name (to the left of the dot) can be up to eight characters. The extension (which is optional and is to the right of the dot) can be up to three characters.

field   In a database record, a field contains a single piece of information (for example, a telephone number, a ZIP code, or a person's last name).

file   A collection of information stored as a single unit on a floppy or hard disk. Files always have a file name to identify them.

file allocation table (FAT)   A map on every disk that tells the operating system where the files on the disk are stored. It's sort of like a classroom seating chart.

fixed disk drive   A disk drive that has a nonremovable disk, as opposed to floppy drives, in which you can insert and remove disks.

floppy disk   A wafer encased in plastic that stores magnetic data (the facts and figures you enter and save). Floppy disks are the disks you insert in your computer's floppy disk drive (located on the front of the computer).

font   Any set of characters of the same *typeface* (design) and *type size* (measured in points). For example, Times Roman 12-point is a font: Times Roman is the typeface, and 12-point is the size. (There are 72 points in an inch.)

format (disk)   Formatting creates a map on the disk that tells the operating system how the disk is structured. The operating system uses this map to keep track of where files are stored.

format (document)   To establish the physical layout of a document, including page size, margins, running heads, line spacing, text alignment, graphics placement, and so on.

function keys   The 10 or 12 F keys on the left side of the keyboard, or 12 F keys at the top of the keyboard (on some keyboards there are both). F keys are numbered F1, F2, F3, and so on and are used to enter specified commands in a program.

geek   A person who eats, sleeps, and drinks computers. Geeks are usually very eager to help new users with their computer emergencies.

graphical user interface (GUI, pronounced "GOO-ey")   A type of program interface that uses graphical elements such as icons to represent commands, files, and (in some cases) other programs. The most famous GUI is Microsoft Windows.

hard disk   A disk drive that comes complete with a nonremovable disk. It acts as a giant floppy disk drive and usually sits inside your computer.

Hayes-compatible   Used to describe a modem that uses the Hayes command set for communicating with other modems over the phone lines. Hayes-compatible modems usually are preferred over other modems because most modems and telecommunications software is designed to be Hayes-compatible.

icon   A graphic image on-screen that represents another object, such as a file on a disk.

initialize   To reset a computer or program to some starting values. When used to describe floppy or hard disks, the term means the same as format.

insertion point   A blinking vertical line used in some word processors to indicate the place where any characters you type will be inserted. An insertion point is the equivalent of a *cursor*.

integrated program   A program that combines the features of several programs such as a word processor, spreadsheet, database, and communications program. The names of integrated programs usually end with the word *Works*.

interface   A link between two objects, such as a computer and a modem. The link between a computer and a person is called a *user interface* and refers to the way a person communicates with the computer.

keyboard   The main input device for most computers.

kilobyte (K)   A unit for measuring the amount of data. A kilobyte is equivalent to 1,024 bytes.

load   To read data or program instructions from disk and place them in the computer's memory, where the computer can use the data or instructions. You usually load a program before you use it or load a file before you edit it.

macro   A recorded set of instructions for a frequently used or complex task. Macros resemble small programs and can be activated by pressing a specified key combination.

megabyte   A standard unit used to measure the storage capacity of a disk and the amount of computer memory. A megabyte is 1,048,576 bytes (1,000 kilobytes). This is roughly equivalent to 500 pages of double-spaced text. Megabyte is commonly abbreviated as M, MB, or Mbyte.

memory   An electronic storage area inside the computer, used to temporarily store data or program instructions when the computer is using them. The computer's memory is erased when the power to the computer is turned off.

menu   A list of commands or instructions displayed on-screen. Menus organize commands and make a program easier to use.

microprocessor   Sometimes called the central processing unit (CPU) or processor, this chip is the computer's brain; it does all the calculations for the computer.

modem   An acronym for MOdulator/DEModulator. A modem is a piece of hardware that enables a computer to send and receive data through an ordinary telephone line.

monitor   A television-like screen on which the computer displays information.

mouse   A hand-held device that you move across the desktop to move an indicator, called a mouse pointer, across the screen. Used instead of the keyboard to select and move items (such as text or graphics), execute commands, and perform other tasks.

MS-DOS (Microsoft Disk Operating System)   See *DOS.*

multitasking   The capability to run two programs at the same time. Some programs, such as the DOS Shell, enable you to switch between two or more programs (task-switching), but do not allow a program to perform operations in the background (multitasking).

online   Connected, turned on, and ready to accept information. Used most often in reference to a printer or modem.

parallel port   A connector used to plug a device, usually a printer, into the computer. Transferring data through a parallel port is much faster than transferring data through a serial port, but parallel cables can carry data reliably only 15 or 20 feet.

partition   A hard disk drive can be divided (or *partitioned*) into one or more drives, which DOS refers to as drive C, drive D, drive E, and so on. (Don't be fooled; it's still one disk drive.) The actual hard disk drive is called the *physical* drive; each partition is called a *logical* drive.

path   The route that the computer travels from the root directory to any subdirectories when locating a file.

peripheral   The system unit is the central part of the computer. Any devices attached to the system unit are considered *peripheral* (as in "peripheral vision"). Peripheral devices include the monitor, printer, keyboard, mouse, modem, and joystick. Some manufacturers consider the keyboard and monitor as parts of the computer, not as peripherals.

pixel   A dot of light that appears on the computer screen. A collection of pixels forms characters and images on the screen. Think of a pixel as a single peg in a Lite Brite toy.

ports   The receptacles at the back of the computer. They get their name from the ports where ships pick up and deliver cargo. In this case, the ports allow information to enter and leave the system unit.

POST (Power-On Self Test)   A series of internal checks the computer performs on itself whenever it is first turned on. If the test reveals that any component is not working properly, the computer displays an error message on-screen giving a general indication of which component is causing problems.

program   A group of instructions that tell the computer what to do. Typical programs are word processors, spreadsheets, databases, and games.

prompt   A computer's way of asking for more information. The computer basically looks at you and says, "Tell me something." In other words, the computer is *prompting* you or *prodding* you for information or for a command.

protocol   A group of communications settings that control the transfer of data between two computers via modem.

pull-down menu   A menu that appears at the top of the screen, listing various options. The menu is not visible until you select it from the menu bar. The menu then drops down, covering a small part of the screen.

random-access memory (RAM)   Where your computer stores data and programs temporarily. RAM is measured in kilobytes and megabytes. In general, the more RAM a computer has, the more powerful the programs it can run.

record   Used by databases to denote a unit of related information contained in one or more fields, such as an individual's name, address, and phone number.

ROM BIOS   See *BIOS*.

scanner   A device that converts images such as photographs or printed text into an electronic format that a computer can use. Many stores use a special type of scanner to read bar code labels into the cash register.

scroll   To move text up and down or right and left on a computer screen.

shell   A program that enables you to enter commands to the operating system by choosing them from a menu. Shell programs make it easier to use the operating system.

software   Any instructions that tell your computer (the hardware) what to do. There are two types of software: operating system software and application software. *Operating system software* (such as DOS) gets your computer up and running. *Application software* enables you to do something useful such as type a letter or chase lemmings.

spreadsheet   A program used for keeping schedules and calculating numeric results. Common spreadsheets include Lotus 1-2-3, Microsoft Excel, and Quattro Pro.

style   A collection of specifications for formatting text. A style may include information for the font, size, style, margins, and spacing. Applying a style to text automatically formats the text according to the style's specifications.

switch   A value you can add to a command to control the manner in which the command is carried out. For example, in DOS, you can use the /V switch with the COPY command to have DOS verify that the copied files are exact duplicates of the originals.

trackball   A device often used with laptop computers that works like an upside-down mouse. It requires less desk space for use than a mouse, because instead of moving it around the desk to move the pointer on-screen, you roll it in place to move the pointer. Some arcade video games use devices similar to trackballs.

transfer rate   A measure of how much information a device (usually a disk drive) can transfer from the disk to your computer's memory in a second. A good transfer rate is in the range of 500 to 600 kilobytes per second. The higher the number, the faster the drive. (See also *access time*.)

uninterruptible power supply (UPS)   A battery-powered device that protects against power spikes and power outages. If the power goes out, the UPS continues supplying power to the computer so you can continue working or safely turn off your computer without losing data.

upload   To send data to another computer, usually through a modem and a telephone line or through a network connection.

virus   A program that attaches itself to other files on a floppy or hard disk, duplicates itself without the user's knowledge, and may cause the computer to do strange and sometimes destructive things. The virus attacks the computer by erasing files from the hard disk or by formatting the disk.

widow/orphan   A *widow* is the last line of a paragraph that appears alone at the top of the next page. If the first line of the paragraph gets stranded at the bottom of a page, it is called an *orphan*. Just remember that an orphan is left behind.

wild card   Any character that takes the place of another character or a group of characters. Think of a wild-card character as a wild card in a game of poker. If the Joker is wild, you can use it in place of any card in the entire deck of cards. In DOS, you can use two wild-card characters: a question mark (?) and an asterisk (*). The question mark stands in for a single character; the asterisk stands in for a group of characters.

windows   A way of displaying information in different parts of the screen. Often used as a nickname for Microsoft Windows.

word processor   A program that lets you enter, edit, format, and print text.

word wrap A feature that automatically moves a word to the next line if the word won't fit at the end of the current line.

write-protect To prevent a computer from adding or modifying data stored on a disk.

Index

Z

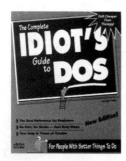

Okay, so you finished this book and now you can do all the basic stuff that gets you through the day. Congrats!

But what about those other cool features you never get to use? Welcome to the perfect follow-up to *The Complete Idiot's Guide!*

The Complete Idiot's Next Step!

The *Next Step* books begin where *The Complete Idiot's Guides* leave off. You learn how to use all those powerful features that make life easier. And it all comes in the same lighthearted, beginner-style format that the *Idiot's Guides* are famous for!

Plus, the *Next Step* books come with a free disk full of software to make your work even more impressive! Get full-powered results without all the work!

You too can do things like an expert—without actually being one!

Who Cares What *YOU* Think?

WE DO!

We're not complete idiots. We take our
readers' opinions very personally. After all,
you're the reason we publish these books!
Without you, we'd be pretty bored.

So please! Drop us a note or fax us a fax! We'd love to hear what you think about
this book or others. A real person—not a computer—reads every letter we get, and
makes sure your comments get relayed to the appropriate people.

Not sure what to say? Here's some stuff we'd like to know:

- Who are you (age, occupation, hobbies, etc.)?
- Which book did you buy and where did you get it?
- Why did you pick this book instead of another one?
- What do you like best about this book?
- What could we have done better?
- What's your overall opinion of the book?
- What other topics would you like to purchase a book on?

Mail, e-mail, or fax your brilliant opinions to:

Product Development Manager
Que New User Group
201 West 103rd Street
Indianapolis, IN 46290
FAX: (317) 581-4669

CompuServe: 75430,174
Internet: SFrantz@alpha.mcp.com